INDIA - AFRICA ENDURING PARTNERSHIP

INDIA-AFRICA ENDURING PARTNERSHIP

Emerging Areas of Cooperation

Prof. Dr. Aparajita Biswas

Foreword by Dr. Shashi Tharoor

GYAN

ISBN : 978-81-212-1209-0
₹ 950

First Published 2013

Published by

Gyan Publishing House
23, Main Ansari Road, Darya Ganj
New Delhi-110002
Phones : 23282060, 23261060
Fax : 011-23285914
E-mail: books@gyanbooks.com
Website: www.gyanbooks.com

Laser Typesetting : Rudra Computer Graphics, Delhi
Printed at : G. Print Process, Delhi

Cataloging in Publication Data—DK
Courtesy: D.K. Agencies (P) Ltd. <docinfo@dkagencies.com>

India-Africa enduring partnership : emerging areas of cooperation / Aparajita Biswas ; foreword by Shashi Tharoor.
p. cm.
Includes bibliographical references and index.

ISBN 9788121212090

1. India—Foreign relations—Africa—Congresses. 2. Africa—Foreign relations—India—Congresses. 3. India—Foreign economic relations—Africa—Congresses. 4. Africa—Foreign economic relations—India—Congresses. I. Biswas, Aparajita.

DDC 327.5406 23

Contents

Foreword

The India-Africa partnership has deep roots in history. Linked across the Indian Ocean, Indians have been neighbours and partners of East Africans for thousands of years. There was regular interaction between communities and traders, especially from the West Coast of Gujarat and parts of South India with Abyssinia, Somalia, Mombasa, Zanzibar and even as far south as Mozambique. These communities and groups played significant roles in the histories of both India and Africa; an Abyssinian warlord rose to political prominence in mediaeval India, and groups of African descent still populate parts of Western India. The advent of the Europeans and the era of colonial rule disturbed these interactions but could not disrupt them: indeed they added to them the painful experience of indentured labour, shipped from India to work on African plantations.

In many ways Indians and Africans trod a common path. As colonization came, our contacts acquired different dimensions, some of which remain with us. Both India and Africa shared the pain of subjugation and the joys of freedom and liberation. In the period of decolonization and the fight against apartheid, we stood shoulder-to-shoulder in the fight against apartheid and racial discrimination; India godfathered the entry of an increasing number of African countries into the international comity of nations. Satyagraha, non-violence and active opposition to injustice and discrimination were first devised by Mahatma Gandhi on the continent of Africa. The Mahatma always believed that so long as Africa was not free, India's own freedom would be incomplete. Our first Prime Minister, Jawaharlal Nehru, was also a firm believer and practitioner of the principle of Afro-

Asian solidarity and of support to the struggles of the people of Africa against discrimination and apartheid.

After India achieved independence, we embarked on a path of close cooperation with the newly independent nations of Africa who shared similar problems of under-development, poverty and disease. India's cooperation with Africa was based on the principle of South-South cooperation, on similarities of circumstances and experiences. India believes that Africa holds the key to its own development but it needs support, facilitation and durable partnerships. We have always been willing to share our development experience with Africa. In India we have sought to empower our people by investing in their capabilities and widening their development options, and we are happy to help apply that approach to Africa. Transfer of knowledge and human skills, going beyond government-to-government interactions and embracing civil society, will help strengthen our mutual capabilities. India is always open to sharing its strengths, its democratic model of development and its appropriate technologies, which many Africans found are low cost, resource efficient, adaptive and suitable to help identify local solutions to local problems.

There was also a continuous high level of interaction between the political leaderships of India and African nations, with scarcely a year going by without some African head of state or government visiting New Delhi. A startling number of African leaders, particularly but not exclusively from former British colonies, have studied in some Indian university, amongst the tens of thousands of African students who then returned home to contribute to the economic and social development of their respective countries. Indian officials visiting Africa have often been pleasantly surprised to discover that their interlocutors in high positions shared an alma mater with them.

Mahatma Gandhi also expressed the belief that "commerce between India and Africa will be of ideas and services, not of manufactured goods against raw materials after the fashion of the western exploiter." Here, though, the Mahatma cannot be credited with great prescience, since ideas and services play only a modest role in the growing Indian-African relationship, while manufactured goods and raw materials still dominate their trade links. Western-style colonial exploitation is, however, mercifully absent.

In the first few decades of our independence, Africa became the largest beneficiary of India's technical assistance and capacity building programmes. India extended over US $3 billion worth of concessional lines of credit to be used in those infrastructure and other development projects that were determined by African countries, a welcome change from the more top-down assistance extended by other donors, whether Western or Communist. These cooperation programmes laid the foundation of the political and economic partnership between India and Africa in the 20th century. It was against this background that India sought to re-engage in the 21st Century, by redrawing our framework of cooperation and devising new parameters for an enhanced and enlarged relationship commensurate with our new role in a changing world. The challenge of globalisation and the need to identify new opportunities for mutually beneficial cooperation led to a renewed vigour in the India-Africa relationship.

On the old foundations, a new architecture for structured engagement and cooperation for the 21st Century was designed and launched at the first India-Africa Forum Summit hosted by India in April 2008 in New Delhi. The Summit provided an occasion for the leaderships of India and Africa to come together to chart out the roadmap for a systematic engagement. As Prime Minister Manmohan Singh said in his address to the Summit, "Africa is our Mother Continent. The dynamics of geology may have led our lands to drift apart, but history, culture and the processes of post-colonial development have brought us together once again." The India-Africa Forum Summit adopted two historic documents, the Delhi Declaration and the India-Africa Framework for Cooperation - the first a political document covering bilateral, regional and international issues (such as common positions on UN reforms, climate change, WTO and international terrorism) and the second spelling out the agreed areas of cooperation, from human resources and institutional capacity building, to agricultural productivity and food security, and (perhaps inevitably) Information and Communications Technology. These were all areas in which African countries had great interest in what India had to offer.

The 2008 Summit received a commitment by the Government of India for upto $ 5.4 billion in new lines of credit in a five-year period — a quantum leap in governmental commitment to support the economic growth of Africa, which helped act as a stimulus package when the global financial crisis erupted shortly thereafter. Under this programme, India has committed about $ one billion every year, mainly in the form of soft loans at extremely low interest rates (around 0.75 per cent in most cases) that barely cover the costs of servicing the loans. The loans are "tied", in that 80 per cent has to be spent on purchasing Indian goods and services, though it is the African country itself that will decide on the choice of Indian supplier. The lines of credit lead to asset creation in Africa and help catalyze confidence in the Indian economic partnership.

The model of cooperation emerging from the first India Africa Forum Summit has governed India's approach since. The Delhi Declaration made clear that:

This partnership will be based on the fundamental principles of equality, mutual respect, and understanding between our peoples for our mutual benefit. It will also be guided by the following principles: respect for the independence, sovereignty, territorial integrity of states and commitment to deepen the process of African integration; collective action and cooperation for the common good of our states and peoples; dialogue among our civilisations to promote a culture of peace, tolerance and respect for religious, cultural, linguistic and racial diversities as well as gender equality with the view to strengthening the trust and understanding between our peoples; the positive development of intra-regional/sub-regional integration by complementing and building upon existing/sub-regional initiatives in Africa; recognition of diversity between and within regions, including different social and economic systems and levels of development; and further consolidation and development of plural democracy.

Beyond the diplomatic rhetoric, the strength of the Indian model of cooperation with Africa has lain in its non-prescriptive nature. India has made it clear throughout that it seeks mutual benefit through a consultative process. Indian diplomats do not instruct, impose or even demand certain approaches or projects in Africa, but offer to contribute to the achievement of Africa's development objectives as they have been set by our African partners. Besides the consultative process and the spirit of friendship, both of which are clearly linked to our desire to fulfill the developmental aspirations of African countries rather than to prescribe them ourselves, there is also the element of a sharing of knowledge and experience for which many African countries often want to relate to us. India's multi-cultural, multi-ethnic, multi-party pluralistic democracy has emerged as an attraction to many

African countries moving in the same direction. So are our Parliamentary institutions and procedures, and our manner of conducting free and fair elections. Our ability to work with the non-governmental sector and civil society in our quest for inclusive growth are also important lessons which many African countries have wanted to share with us. This sharing of experiences on political cooperation is, therefore, another aspect of our non-intrusive support to the development of democratic institutions in our partner countries.

Similarly, areas of human resource development and capacity building have been at the forefront of our partnership with Africa. Both India and Africa are blessed with young populations. At the first India-Africa Forum Summit, India announced a grant of US$ 500 million specifically to undertake projects in human resource development and capacity-building. It is only by investing in the creative energies of our youth that the potential of our partnership will be fulfilled. Tens of thousands of African students have received education and training in Indian institutions; at any time there are at least 10,000 to 15,000 African students studying in various parts of India. The over 15,000 African students at present in India, nearly 1000 of them on Government of India scholarships but a larger number on a self-financing basis, add to the experience of many African countries with Indian teachers and professors. Long-term scholarships for undergraduates, postgraduates and higher courses have been doubled and the number of slots under the Indian Technical and Economic Cooperation Programme (ITEC) has increased from 1100 to 1600 every year. This partnership in human resource development has been augmented by the tele-education component of the Indian Pan African e-Network project which is visionary in its appeal and impact. The role of ICT, science and technology, research and development, has contributed to the enhancement of our engagement with Africa in this important area of human resource development.

The 1600 training positions offered under India's technical co-operation programme to Africa have also become important avenues of capacity building. India is in the process of establishing 19 joint institutions on African soil jointly with the African Union Commission and the member states, including an India-Africa Institute of Information Technology, an India-Africa Institute of Foreign Trade, an India-Africa Institute of Educational Planning and Administration, an India-Africa Diamond Institute, ten Vocational Training Centres and five Human Settlement Institutes in Africa to contribute to capacity building. Such endeavours to invest in human capital and sustainable political systems have made human resource development a vital aspect of India's model of cooperation with Africa.

Technology has of course been a particularly valuable Indian calling-card. The Pan African E-network project that seeks to bridge the 'digital divide' between Africa and the rest of the world is one of the most far-reaching initiatives undertaken by India anywhere in the world. Already nearly 50 countries have joined this programme, which is intended to provide e-services (with priority for tele-education and tele-medicine services) and VVIP connectivity by satellite and fibre optic network amongst the Heads of State of all 53 countries. The Project would give major benefits to Africa in capacity building through skill and knowledge development of students, medical specialists and for medical consultation.

India has also offered to share with African nations its experience in using remote-sensing and satellite-imagery for weather-forecasting, natural resources management, land use and land-cover mapping and a variety of other applications.

What has not always worked as well as it might is the pace of implementation of many Indian projects in Africa. It is true that as a democratic country we have to have consultations and build consensus. Sometimes our overly strong bureaucracy takes too literally its obligation to act as a check and balance on decision-making. But if the Government is sometimes accused of being slow, once it takes a decision to go forward, progress is steady.

There is an undoubted need, however, for more careful management and audit of disbursements made through the Government's Lines of Credit for Africa. In 2009, several reports appeared of questionable transactions relating to the export of rice at subsidised prices to several African countries, but these were never fully investigated and the allegations have largely petered out. Given that these lines of credit amount to considerable sums of money - more than five billion dollars, or 25,000 crore rupees — there is a fundamental need for greater transparency in the allocation of funds, the choice of projects, the drawing up of the requirements for bidders and the selection of contractors. This should not be allowed to slow the process down, but it is essential that India's relations with Africa not be reduced in the eyes of some critics to an unsavoury boondoggle.

One way of compensating for the deficiencies of the governmental sector in this model of cooperation is India's increased reliance on its burgeoning private sector investment in Africa, which has acquired much greater visibility in the last few years. This has been more manifest ever since India liberalised its own economic system in 1991 and in the 21st Century, private Indian investment in Africa is giving the relationship a new vigour and impetus. Indian companies have made large investments in Africa running into several billion dollars in industry, agriculture, infrastructure and human resource development.

An illustrative example of an Indian private sector success story is Vedanta Resources' turn-around of Zambia's copper mining industry – which had been nationalised in the late 60s, driven into ruin, resold to the former owners, Anglo American PLC, the South African mining giant, which failed to revive them and were then essentially abandoned. Vedanta, an FTSE 100 Indian metals and mining group, came in 2004 to buy a majority shareholding in Konkola, the jewel in the crown of the Zambian mines, and other properties, and made them hugely profitable: its CEO, Anil Agarwal, likes to boast that he is "26 per cent of Zambia's GDP". Other examples, big and small, abound: Tata Steel's $1.5 billion joint venture in an iron project in Cote d'Ivoire, Apollo Tyres' manufacturing plants for rubber automobile tyres, and many ventures in the continent's fastest growing region, East Africa, which has the oldest historical links with India, and some of the largest communities of Indian origin.

Indian private investment is largely not government-led or government-subsidized but governed by the logic of commercial opportunities. And yet they are able to make a serious contribution to development. I never tired of telling my African interlocutors about the magnificent work being done by some Indian entrepreneurs who have introduced low cost irrigation pump sets in West Africa. These pump sets have made a significant impact in increasing the food production capacities of some African countries, particularly in Senegal. It is a good example of appropriate technological and investment intervention, something which serves the felt needs of African communities without requiring them to make huge investments. This can be a good example for others to emulate.

Indian investors are respected across Africa because they are reputed to be effective in the local environment, to ensure the highest employment generation, to not be reticent on transfer of technology and to be quite willing to live amongst Africans and employ African managers. Their entrepreneurship and business skills - attributes for which the Indian private sector has long been well known — have been buttressed by India's growing economic clout, which has added to the respect with which they are received. It helps, too, that they inevitably leave behind trained Africans well-equipped to use the newly-created assets.

The combined net flows from India to Africa emerging from governmental credits and private sector investment, therefore, form another part of our sustainable model of cooperation with Africa, which has in turn given a huge incentive to many Indian companies to seek opportunities in Africa. Cumulative Indian investments in Africa rose to $90 billion in 2010 and are likely to grow significantly in the years ahead. Indian investment in Africa is contributing to the fulfilment of domestic demand in African countries, intra-African trade and foreign exchange earnings through exports. The pharmaceutical sector is a good example. Indian pharmaceutical companies like Ranbaxy and Cipla are not just supplying low-cost generic drugs, particularly anti-retroviral drugs to combat AIDS, across the African continent; many also have production facilities in Africa. The Indian pharmaceutical industry has established such a significant reputation for providing Africans with urgently needed healthcare, at affordable prices, that Chinese knockoffs of Indian drugs have been found smuggled into several African countries, with fake Indian packaging. If imitation is the best form of flattery, counterfeiting is the ultimate confirmation of the indispensable role Indian pharma is playing in Africa.

Indian investment in agriculture and horticulture, on the other hand, contributes mainly to exports, with Indian firms increasingly attracted by the large tracts of fertile land available in many African countries, especially in regions blessed with abundant rainfall and sunshine. The idea that Africa could become a breadbasket for India, as Indian domestic demand outstrips the country's capacity to produce the food it needs, has begin to make Africa an important element in Indian thinking about long-term food security.

This has led, perhaps inevitably, to what Ethiopian Prime Minister Meles Zenawi described as "ill-informed and even ill-intentioned loose talk" about Indian farming companies conducting "land grabbing" in his country, charges that had indeed been aired in the Indian press. Ethiopia has three million hectares of unutilised land, Mr Zenawi explained, which it intended to lease out to foreign agricultural enterprises. An Indian investor, Krishna Karaturi, had already made a reputation for himself by growing roses in Ethiopia for export to Europe, and in 2011 he was awarded a lease of 300,000 hectares in the Gambela province to produce maize. "We want to develop our land to feed ourselves rather than admire the beauty of fallow fields while we starve," Mr. Zenawi declared, adding, "I want to reassure Indian companies that they are welcome here. We want them to come and farm what is virgin land." Similar offers from Mozambique, Liberia and other countries indicate a productive future for Indian investment in agriculture, horticulture and floriculture in Africa.

All these investment flows are matched by a multi-tiered cooperative partnership which involves, almost uniquely, a major engagement with Pan-African institutions, notably the African Union. While India has had successful bilateral partnerships with most African countries over decades, its willingness to inject multilateralism into its relations with Africa has been broadly seen as reflecting a more complete partnership and greater respect for Africa than other partners offer. A substantial amount of the funds committed for capacity building in Africa is being channelled through the AU in a Joint Action Plan involving shared decision-making on the allocation of resources. In West Africa, India has devised a regional initiative called the Team-9 framework for cooperation, which has brought in a regional focus for its development projects and concessional loans; African countries in the region have been clamouring to be included. This co-equal multilateralism is an important feature of India's new model of engagement with Africa.

India's trade with Africa has been growing rapidly. Two-way trade has risen from some $5.5 billion in 2001-02 to over 46 billion dollars in 2010-11, which represents an almost nine-fold increase in as many years. There is even talk of aiming for $70 billion by 2015. Even so, the true potential is much greater and the spread and the composition of the trade has to be substantially diversified. With a view to increasing trade flows between India and Africa, India has also extended a Duty Free Tariff Preferential Scheme for the 50 least developed countries, 34 of which are in Africa. This covers 94 per cent of India's total tariff lines and provides preferential market access on tariff lines for 92.5 per cent of the global exports of all LDCs.

India and Africa are also engaging closely on trade policy; there has been systematic coordination with African countries on the Doha Round of negotiations, especially on agriculture. India has been particularly close to South Africa in concerting positions on international issues of global interest, a process that has been accentuated with the establishment of IBSA, launched the India–Brazil–South Africa Dialogue Forum, a gathering of three large developing countries aiming to reify South-South co-operation. IBSA negotiated successfully together in the Doha Round and at other trade talks, and the three countries meet regularly, though insufficient progress has been made on concluding trilateral trade agreements among themselves. IBSA has set up its own cooperation fund, launching initial projects in Equatorial Guinea and Haiti, though the need for individual country branding of aid projects may still limit the possibilities for IBSA development projects. India also supported the inclusion of South Africa in the BRIC grouping, thus making that Goldman Sachs creation into "BRICS". But so far both BRICS and IBSA have been forums for meetings rather than incipient international organisations; no institutional structures have been created for either group.

In case most of this chapter seems to provide too economics-oriented an analysis, it is worth pointing out that India has also been extensively involved in peacekeeping efforts in Africa over the past six decades. At present, India has over 7000 peacekeepers serving in Africa, including a 5000 strong contingent in the Democratic Republic of Congo. The fourth batch of India's first full all-female formed police unit is currently deployed in Liberia. In addition to peacekeeping, this unit has been successful in reaching out to the most vulnerable sections of the society — women and children — and in inspiring women who have so often been victims of war to see themselves also as sources of succour and strength in this recently war-torn society. President Ellen Johnson Sirleaf, the first woman elected President on the Continent, told me when I met her that the Indian women police had inspired many young Liberian women to volunteer for their country's security service.

The presence of Indian-Africans adds an intriguing element to the relationship, especially when their numbers are a significant percentage of the population, as in Mauritius, disproportionately influential, as in South Africa or Nigeria, or visible and sometimes contentious, as in East Africa. I had the pleasure of visiting Mauritius in 2010 to participate in the Aapravasi Diwas - a historic date steeped in poignant memory, which marked the arrival of the first Indian labourers to that country. History is unforgiving to those who do not remember the forefathers and foremothers who sacrificed so much to convert a new, rocky, inhospitable land — in the face of both nature's fury and human cruelty, and through lives of unimaginable torment and drudgery — into a flourishing paradise. Commemorating the Indian connection reifies *le devoir de mémoire* ("the duty to remember") and of course unites the mother country with its diaspora. Similar stories can be told of the Indian presence in South Africa.

There are, on the whole, an estimated two million people of Indian origin living in Africa. Indian businessmen, teachers and even missionaries can be found in every African country. Though there have been no incidents of racial tension in recent years to mirror the dark days of 1972 when President Idi Amin threw ethnic Indians out of Uganda, the Indian diaspora has tended to remain distinct, engaging with but not integrating into the political and cultural environment of their host countries. There is all too little intellectual or cultural exchange between India and Africa either; journalists and academics from each are rarely to be found in the other. One point of cultural contact, amusingly enough, is the popular cinema of Bollywood. I have lost count of the number of African leaders I have met who spoke to me with nostalgia of growing up in small towns or villages in Africa, looking forward to the arrival of the latest Bollywood movie in the nearest town. This is an affinity India can, and should, build on.

A vibrant India and a resurgent Africa are thus witnessing an intensification of relations and growing convergence of interests in their common quest for sustainable economic growth and development. Our partnership encompasses priority sectors integral to the developmental goals of Africa in the 21st Century. The potential for growth and development in this relationship is considerable. There is a growing demand in Africa for developing infrastructure, new technologies, engineering services and manufacturing capabilities for local value addition. These offer excellent opportunities to Indian businesses in Africa, and to millions of young people in Africa who can be employed in the manufacturing and services sectors.

Some suggest that India and Africa have little in common. Nothing could be farther from the truth. We face emergent common challenges of food security, energy security, pandemics, terrorism and climate change. Africa and India also share a common societal commitment to pluralism, to inclusiveness across distinctions of region or religion, tribe or clan, language or class, and to the creation of a world that is fair to all its inhabitants. Our shared vision of the world should enable us to work together on the vital challenges facing our peoples, and for the world as a whole, whether in our bilateral relations or multilaterally. In my own experience, I have found that African leaders look at India not the way they look at the West or China - with admiration bordering on awe, and with gratitude admixed with resentment. Rather, they see India as a sort of kindred spirit - a country that has faced problems very similar to those confronted by most African countries, and which has managed in no small measure to overcome them through methods which strike African leaders as replicable in their own lands. From an African point of view, the successes of America and China may be intimidating; those of India seem accessible. The queue of African heads of state and government seeking to visit India is extraordinarily large, given India's limitations in accommodating more than a modest number of state visits every year.

Ironically for a country focused on capacity building in Africa, India suffers from its own capacity limitations in the continent, with far too few Embassies in crucial countries, and the existing ones far too thinly staffed. At a time when I was spearheading a major thrust into improving relations with Liberia — newly emerging from civil war but overflowing with minerals (notably iron ore) and large tracts of lush agricultural land, to name just two assets - India relied there entirely on an intrepid businessman who served as our Honorary Consul-General, while our official diplomacy covered the country through an Embassy situated in French-speaking Cote d'Ivoire. Indian companies and citizens need the reassurance of a supportive Embassy presence if they are to be encouraged to work in a new country. There is also a case to be made for India's embassies in Africa to be staffed by a larger number of young and energetic diplomats anxious to establish their reputations, rather than by those promoted from the ranks or at the tail end of their careers, who might tend to regard an African posting as a punishment and who are disinclined to develop much interest in the local language or culture.

On frequent visits to Africa in pursuance of the many consultative mechanisms that have been established with New Delhi, Indian officials have made it clear that India envisions an Africa that is self-reliant, economically vibrant and at peace with itself and the world. In saying this they could look to a familiar source of inspiration. While highlighting the vitality of African continent, the first Prime Minister of India, Jawaharlal Nehru, had said, "Of one thing there can be no doubt, and that is the vitality of the people of Africa. Therefore, with the vitality of her people and the great resources available in this great continent, there can be no doubt that the future holds a great promise for the people of Africa."

It is this promise that our Partnership with Africa seeks to fulfil. It has become fashionable these days to ask openly what we expect of each other. This perhaps overlooks the fact that India and Africa have been close to each other over so many centuries that our relationship is not one of immediate give-and-take but has been that of a family where each one provides the best advice, the best support and the best sharing of experience, so that when we walk the same path, we learn from each other and not make the same mistakes. India will offer its fullest cooperation to harness the great potential of the African people for the cause of Africa's progress and development. As I stated when addressing the United Nations General Assembly in 2009 on the New Partnership for Africa's Development: "The objective of our partnership is to cooperate with all the countries of Africa, within the limits of our capacities and capabilities, in their efforts towards achieving economic vibrancy, peace, stability and self-reliance. Towards this end, it is our intention to become a close partner in Africa's resurgence."

In the process, a global debate has arisen as to whether India and China – the other Asian power that has made major inroads into Africa in recent years – are engaged in a new "scramble for Africa", reminiscent of the one amongst European powers in the 19th Century. Africa's mineral wealth and energy resources are undoubtedly of interest to both countries, but the notion of a competition for Africa, let alone a scramble, is considerably exaggerated. While it is true that each country has sought advantages for itself across the continent, they have also co-operated with each other; India and China are jointly exploring and developing a Sudanese oilfield, for instance. And when China decided to set up an Embassy in Liberia, it was

India's Honorary Consul-General, a long-standing presence in Monrovia, who facilitated the Chinese Ambassador's efforts to establish his Embassy.

African leaders are mildly insulted by Western attempts to describe their relations with either country in language borrowed from the colonial era. In any case, the core competences of each country are actually complementary rather than competitive, with China's huge edge in the sale of manufactured goods, in the construction of large infrastructure projects and in the gift of everything, from buildings to vehicles, to African elites, versus India's somewhat more modest focus on capacity building, education and training and of course its strengths in information technology. The Chinese have been known to move into certain nations and practically buy up their governments; democratic India has neither the capacity nor the inclination to try anything remotely like that. On the other hand, Indians are active in sectors like agriculture and floriculture from which the Chinese are virtually absent.

There is a broader strategic dimension as well to the alleged rivalry in Africa – India's reported discomfort with the growing Chinese presence on the African rim of the Indian Ocean and its corresponding desire, if London's Royal Institute of International Affairs at Chatham House is right, to strengthen its countervailing presence there. There is no doubt that the security of the Indian Ocean sea lanes is an area of major concern for India, as it is for China. But analysts such as those at Chatham House seem to overlook the fact that both China and India have compatible interests in this area, since both depend heavily on the Indian Ocean for the movement of goods, especially vital energy supplies, through those waters. India has discretely provided security to certain East African nations through offshore naval patrols when requested to do so, and the Indian navy regularly calls at a number of African ports. But there is no credible reason to believe that any policy-maker in New Delhi would lose any sleep if Chinese ships were to drop by as well.

One interesting area of difference between the two countries' roles in Africa is that the Chinese inroads have prompted something of an African backlash, with Zambia, in 2011, electing a President who had campaigned on an openly anti-Chinese platform. India, by contrast, is seen as low-key and assimilative, willing to leave behind more than it takes out of Africa. The management styles of Indians and Chinese are a study in contrast; Indians handle their African employees better, with greater communication, trust and respect, as well as willingness to train, so that even non-Indian companies often hire Indian managers for their African operations. There is no doubt that in strictly dollar terms, China is way ahead of India in Africa, and the gap is likely to widen. But India's own strengths and successes in Africa suggest that there is more than enough room for both to flourish in the Oldest Continent.

So what is the future for India's presence in Africa? The second India-Africa Forum Summit in Addis Ababa in 2011 confirmed that India's development assistance programme, its long record of political engagement, and the effectiveness of its private sector enterprises, have contributed effectively to strengthening its role in Africa. As Africa continues to grow steadily - the continent has even been described, by the OECD's Javier Santiso, as "the new frontier of emerging markets" - the opportunities for an older emerging market, one which President Obama declared has "emerged", remain considerable.

Energy is moving increasingly to the forefront of India's strategic objectives in Africa. With some 70 per cent of India's oil supply imported, mainly from the Middle East, the need to diversify the country's sources of supply is self-evident. According to International Energy Agency (IEA) estimates, India's current growth patterns will require an annual increase of some 3.6 per cent in its energy consumption. This will oblige India to import 90 per cent of the petroleum it needs to meet its energy requirements, making Africa a key geographical focus for the Indian government's oil and gas exploration and production company, the Oil and National Gas Corporation (ONGC) and its foreign arm, ONGC Videsh. Nigeria already supplies about 15 per cent of the Indian market, ranking as the India's second largest supplier, and it has sold shares in oil exploration ventures to ONGC Videsh. The Indian public sector giant has also made substantial investments in the hydrocarbon sector in other African countries, notably Libya, Sudan (mainly in the new Republic of South Sudan) and off the coast of Cote d'Ivoire. The Indian private sector is not absent from the energy field either; Reliance Industries is active in such countries as Angola and Nigeria, and continues to explore farther afield. Despite such ventures, India has been unable to shake off the widespread perception that it lacks the hard-nosed strategic drive for energy resources displayed by its Asian neighbour, China, on the African continent. While the two countries' oil corporations have co-operated in Sudan, they have made competing bids elsewhere in Africa, and China has always prevailed. (Indians would respond, of course, that there is enough for both countries' needs in Africa).

Another key area for future progress is telecommunications, with Indian companies investing heavily in Africa, notably Bharti Airtel, whose acquisition of Zain has given it a presence in 15 African countries. Despite the failure of Bharti's negotiations in 2009 to acquire a controlling share in South Africa's Mobile Telephone Networks, the largest mobile phone-operator in Africa, it remains interested in expansion across the continent. Providing a low-cost telecom model to a growing African population where mobile telephony has already vastly outstripped fixed-line communications is a "natural" for Indian telecommunications firms, which have already demonstrated the effectiveness of their model at home.

Mineral resources will also be essential to the growing Indian economy. Africa's enormous natural resources, including iron ore, copper and coltran, and its rich agricultural lands, many of which have been lying fallow because of civil conflict, neglect or simple economic mismanagement, are of obvious interest to India. India will undoubtedly add to its burgeoning presence in these areas, though it will have to be particularly attentive to ensure that extraction does not slip over into exploitation.

African opinion has also largely been welcoming of the Indian presence, while understandably stressing that care must be taken to avoid exploitation. A prominent online journal from Uganda, for instance, *New Vision*, wrote not long ago that Africa had a lot to gain from deeper links with India: "there are lessons to learn from its strengths in agriculture, technology, financing and land tenure systems, and its development path offers a highly relevant example for Africa." My former United Nations colleague KY Amaoko, then the Executive Director of the Economic Commission for Africa, declared in 2008 that: "There is much we could learn from India on improving the African business environment for private sector investment, public-private partnership as well as strengthening capital markets. India has been especially successful at developing its small- and medium-scale enterprises, an area where we lag behind terribly in Africa." He added a point not made often enough, that Indian democracy could serve as a model for the continent: "India is the world's largest democracy and has a proud record of regular elections. Many African countries have recently reverted from one party or military to multiparty systems of governments. On our continent, we are grappling more severely with strengthening the rule of law and the divisions of power between the legislative, executive and judiciary arms of governance, as well relations between citizens and state institutions. We can learn from India."

Africa is visibly moving from being a relatively modest priority in India's foreign policy — far less significant in commercial or political terms than the Middle East or Southeast Asia - to a significant area of focus. New Delhi has rightly eschewed any temptation to concentrate its attention principally on the major powers even as it develops a global role as a major player on the 21st Century stage. But as India cultivates this globe-striding presence, Africa has emerged as a vital area for its own "rebranding" - a continent where it has begun effectively positioning itself as a visionary benefactor, a source of investment, a partner in development efforts, a donor in humanitarian need, and a guide on the new information highway that will lead the developing world into the knowledge economy of the 21st Century.

Yours Sincerely,

Shashi Tharoor

Preface

This book is based on the proceedings of an international conference organized by the Centre for African Studies, University of Mumbai, and Policy Research Institute of African Studies Association of India (PRIASA). [It is a landmark in the development of the African Studies Association of India, since the setting up of PRIASA.] While PRIASA was created for a number of inter-related reasons, the central mission is to initiate a social science policy-oriented dialogue in the true spirit of partnership among academics, policy makers, business people and NGOs. The collective aim is to enhance India-Africa relations in the changing global dynamics of contemporary international relations.

The international conference was held to meet three broad objectives: First, to bring together national and international Africanists, researchers, policy makers, industrialists, senior officials from public and corporate sectors, and consultants working in this field, to share their views and provoke critical debate on India-Africa Relations as they stood in 2011. Secondly, it sought to stimulate academic and policy debate on ways to build policy relevant knowledge and conceptual understanding on issues of India-Africa Relations and, thirdly, to promote African Studies in India.

One of the recommendations of the conference was the creation of a 'knowledge base' on India-Africa Relations involving policy aspects, and the successes and failures of these policies. India's policy of capacity building in Africa featured prominently throughout the presentations and discussions at the conference. The authors identified the need for energy security of India, new investment destinations of India's multinationals in Africa, India's defence cooperation in Africa, and presence of Indian diaspora as a strategic asset in Africa as the main drivers of India's Africa relations in the backdrop of India's re-engagement with the African countries.

Thus, the book is a culmination of ideas of Africanists in India and abroad who are working on changing perspectives of India-Africa relations, particularly in the backdrop of a major shift in India's foreign policy since the post-reform era of the 1990s. The end of the Cold War and subsequent introduction of economic reforms in India brought new challenges in India's foreign policy discourse. Some Indian foreign policy analysts referred to the foreign policy shift as being a pragmatic move, arguing that India's traditional foreign policy was no longer relevant to the post-Cold War world. These analysts also lauded the push for an unabashed consideration of India's national interests rather than global justice or ethics. Moreover, the collapse of the Soviet Union had created the space for India to rearrange its relations with the West and, particularly, USA. Since then, India has also become active in its extended neighbourhood in South Asia, South-East Asia, Africa, Central Asia and the Middle East, on a completely different framework. There are two main reasons for this. On the one hand, India wants to achieve a more secure supply of resources (especially oil and gas) for its industrial production, rather than relying on global markets. On the other hand, its growing clout in international affairs has led to its search for fruitful economic engagements everywhere. This foreign policy framework emphasises national interests, economic relations and energy diplomacy, rather than the impulse of Third World solidarity.

This is reflected in Raja Mohan observation on India's new foreign policy strategy:

"The Cold War and India's insular economic policies in the first four decades had undermined India's standing to the East and West of its neighbourhood and prevented New Delhi from ensuring its much vaunted importance in the Indian Ocean littoral. But India's new economic and foreign policies have given India a real opportunity to realize the vision of Lord Curzon, the British Viceroy at the turn of the 20th century of Indian leadership in the region stretching from Aden to Malacca. After decades of neglecting economic and political regionalism, India is now an active participant in various regional organisations from the East Asia Summit to the African Union."

At the multilateral level, to promote relations with developing countries, India has joined many regional groupings such as India-Brazil-South Africa (IBSA), BRICS, Asia-Pacific Economic

Cooperation (APEC) and the Bay of Bengal Initiative for Multi Sectoral Technical and Economic Cooperation (BIMSTEC), as a more direct way of promoting South-South co-operation, besides establishing stronger political and economic relations.

India-Africa relations too have experienced qualitative transformation after the Cold War. On this, an elaborate debate has been initiated by Prof. Rajen Harshe in his article "India and Africa in the post-Cold War World: An Overview" wherein he offers *an overview of Indo-African ties in the post-Cold War world in the context of the accelerated pace of globalisation and economic reforms.* According to him, initially, India's constant support to anti-colonial and anti-racist struggles had placed Indo-African ties on a sound footing. In those early days, although India was much poorer, it tried to help African countries economically through infrastructural projects, building of railroads, setting up small scale industries, joint ventures in textiles, etc. In the next several decades, India provided technical and medical expertise, educational scholarships and various other forms of aid, under the Indian Technical and Economic Co-operation programme. However, in recent years, political changes in African countries, characterised by the introduction of democratic rule, end of racist minority regimes in Southern Africa, and the rise of India as a major regional power have together enabled India to engage African countries in furthering development co-operation.

At the India-Africa Forum Summit, New Delhi, hosted by India in April 2008, two major agreements were adopted. These were the Delhi Declaration and the Africa-India Framework for Co-operation. Both agreements offer a direction to Indo-African relations in the coming years, and provide a framework for the establishment of a long-term and stable partnership of a new type, based on equality and mutual benefit, as well as a blueprint for India-Africa co-operation in political, economic, social development and other fields, in the future. The 2008 Summit also marked the culmination of India's renewed focus on Africa. It was inspired largely by India's desire to change the world's perception of it - from being a recipient to being a donor - in order to boost its global political status. The second India-Africa Forum Summit, held in Addis Ababa, Ethiopia, in May 2011, was intended to build on the momentum of growth. The Summit's theme was 'Enhancing Partnership: Shared Vision'. It affirmed the critical importance of South-South co-operation as an instrument to effectively supplement existing international efforts that would lead to tangible benefits for developing countries.

The Framework for co-operation, mentioned earlier, lists several areas (and sub-areas) for co-operation such as economic co-operation, political co-operation, science, technology and research, social development, tourism, infrastructure, energy and environment. It lists a number of focus areas therein, such as agriculture, trade, regional integration, peace and security, ICT and culture. These areas highlight India's attractiveness as an alternative development partner for African countries.

Between the first India-Africa Forum Summit of 2008 and present times, India's trade and investment in Africa have increased significantly. The push by India's private sector is helping the Indian government define a distinctive strategic vision in Africa. Traditionally, Indian investments in Africa have been small to medium scale in size. Lately, however, Indian MNCs are showing growing interest in African countries.

Most of the FDIs in African countries from India are in the oil and gas sector, since India has increasingly looked to Africa as a means to diversify its energy sources, and reduce its dependence on the Middle East, which presently accounts for two-thirds of its oil imports. A large proportion of Indian FDIs have gone into infrastructure, engineering, chemicals, services, banking and finance, and IT and telecommunication sectors of African countries. Indian pharmaceutical companies were also able to make major inroads into Africa. Moreover, Indian firms have made impressive contributions to agricultural extension in Senegal and commercial farming in Ethiopia.

Under the circumstances, the growing Indian economy and India's international profile have enabled it to proactively involve itself in peacekeeping operations in Africa. Currently, it has 3000 troops in Sudan, 3500 troops in Democratic Republic of Congo and over 1000 troops on the Ethiopia-Eritrea border. The presence of an Indian diaspora in the African continent added another important cornerstone to India-Africa relations. Africa has around two million Indian diasporas spread across several countries of Africa-Anglophone, Francophone, and Lusophone. They served as an additional source of strength to enable closer Indo-African cooperation.

In the case of development assistance, India has gradually changed from a recipient of aid and assistance to a giver of aid. The India Development Initiative (IDI) dedicates a $1.5 billion soft credit fund over a period of five years through the Exim Bank, for supporting development projects, mainly in Africa.

However, it is not just India but several other Asian countries who have had impactful engagements in African countries in recent years. Scholars on the subject emphasise that Asian engagements in Africa differ fundamentally from that of Western countries, particularly with regard to aims, objectives and political discourse, besides the instruments and modalities of engagement in recent times. The continent which was categorised by the World Bank and Western scholars as 'doomed' and 'marginal' with economies in 'free fall', now boasts of a significant growth rate. This can be attributed to increasing investment of Asian countries in Africa.

In this book, scholars have identified strategic determinants and drivers of India's re-engagement with Africa in its post-reform period. They have tried to answer important questions... *What are the forces that are pushing India into Africa? What are the emerging sectors of cooperation?* These scholars have also examined the question of whether India-Africa relations help in breathing new life into South-South cooperation, in the background of a complex world order.

In the prologue, I have included two papers. In the first, Dr. Denis Venter surveys key drivers of contemporary India-Africa Relations in his paper, *'Some Trends in India-Africa Relations: Towards a Lasting Partnership'*. According to him, India-Africa relations have intensified across the spectrum of political, diplomatic, cultural, and defence, but have essentially been economically motivated. He analyses the specifics of India's policy on Africa with regard to energy security, trade and investment, economic relations and defence co-operation. In the second, titled *'India and Africa: What Partnership for Research and Development?'*, Dr. Carlos Cardoso has raised an important question on co-operation in social science research and also discussed the matter of whether India and African countries have convergent interests in social science research and, if so, what are these interests, and what platforms and mechanisms can be envisaged to make this co-operation possible and fruitful?

On *Issues of Indian Diaspora* in the Section 2, Prof. Makumi Mwagiru's paper, *'India-Africa Relations: Perspectives, Perceptions and Prospects'* examines India-Africa relations from a very contemporary perspective revolving around issues of a geo-economic nature, such as the search for natural resources or quest for bigger business opportunities. The author argues that the proper perspective from which to examine these relations should be a historical one. As a professor of the Institute of Diplomatic Studies, Nairobi, Kenya, he examines India-Africa relations through the Kenyan lens. There is a large Indian diaspora in this region, with the Indian community of settlers becoming East African in nature and spirit. This reality, according to him, has changed the very perspective of relations between the two countries. Prof. Mwagiru argued that as the Indians have settled in the region through the ages, India is perceived as 'one of us' because of these entrenched communities. According to him, India-Kenya relations should be based on equality and mutual respect between each other.

Prof. Ajay Dubey's presented his paper *'Diaspora as a Heritage Resource between Indo-African Relations'* in this section. He proposed a framework for the analysis of the Indian diaspora as a heritage of resources, noting that they are not only key drivers in development efforts but also help in strengthening bilateral relations between host and home nations. This potential of the diaspora has gained growing international recognition, both in political and academic/research circles, as well as among diaspora members themselves.

On the Non-Traditional security issues in Section 2, Prof. Aparajita Biswas's paper *'India's Energy Security and its Relations with Oil-rich African Countries'* unfolded a debate on the widening concept of security where energy has come to be increasingly securitized and energy flashpoints projected as the focus of international politics. She has discussed the Government of India's strategy to diversify energy imports and the role of India's public and private oil companies in African oilfields. She argues that one of the reasons for the Government of India's proactive policy towards African countries is to acquire oil, since the African continent holds ten per cent of the world's oil reserves.

In this section, Dr. Alex Vines' paper *'Asian Oil Investments in Africa: Lessons from Angola and Nigeria'* looked at Asian oil investments in Sub-Saharan Africa and focused on the lessons learnt from Angola and Nigeria. He argued that although in recent years India has been purchasing more oil from Angola, and although Nigeria accounted for some 12 per cent of India's oil imports in 2010 and remains one of India's key African partners, it could not make any significant inroads towards oil equity gains in these two countries.

On India-Africa security issues in Section 3, Prof. Musambayi Katumanga in his paper *'Horizontal Africa and Future Securities in India'* put forth an interesting proposition for scholarly analysis. He explained how Mahan and Mackinder's naval and continental logic transformed Africa into a bridgehead for the securitisation of the British colonial rule. Mahan's concept of "sea power" was based on the idea that the most powerful navy will control the globe; it was most famously presented in his book, published in 1890, titled *'The Influence of Sea Power Upon History, 1660-1783'*. The concept had an enormous influence in shaping the strategic thought of navies across the world, especially those of USA, Germany, Japan and Britain. This paper sets out three core tasks: Firstly, to recapitulate on the Curzonian Africa-Raj security coupling; secondly, it imagines a similar construction anchored on dual security which enhances energy and trade driven horizontal infrastructure in the East and Horn of Africa. Thirdly, it elucidates on how co-operation in the realisation of the foregoing tasks will likely underpin security-based economic inter-dependence critical for stability in Africa.

Dr. Utham Kumar's paper *'Indian Navy's African Odyssey'* in this section argued that India's programme for training of defense personnel, supply and requisition of weapons and related equipment to and from African countries, initiating naval exercises with African powers as part of South-South cooperation, establishing naval facilities at strategic points and extending development related assistance through its naval arm have been some of the highlights of the Indian Navy's functioning. While there have been consistent relations in the naval dimension, much more needs to be accomplished. New challenges that have global ramifications, such as the rampant piracy attacks off the Somali coast; threat of maritime terrorism, and danger to the security of energy sea lanes strengthen the case for deeper naval contact with this vast continent.

Dr. Nivedita Ray, in her paper *'India-Africa Expanding Ties: Strategic Interests and Concerns'*, discussed the strategic significance of India and African countries for each other and common interests which have contributed to this invigorated partnership in the true spirit of South-South co-operation. However, in her paper she raised very pertinent questions despite these commonalities of interests. While seizing opportunities in Africa, is India mindful and sensitive to Africa's concerns? Would India's current involvement in Africa, which is more private sector-led, work in the interests of less privileged citizens, workers and consumers in Africa? As India emerges as a key player in shaping the multilateral polity and global economy, would it be able to strike a balance between the South-South co-ordination promoted by its policy-makers and its economic commercial interests?

In Section 4, India-Africa Relations: Expanding Ties, five papers have been included.

Dr. Saji S in his paper, *'India's Involvement in Africa since 1990's: Emerging State Business Relationship'*, while throwing light on the involvement of Indian companies - both private and public - in African states in general, has analysed the impact of such involvement in addressing India's concerns and the needs of African countries. The paper essentially argues that Indian public and private entities have to balance the needs of Africa while searching for market and natural resources such as oil, in order to have sustainable ties with African states and their communities. In his paper on *'India Africa Trade: A Statistical Review'*, Dr. Manendra Sahu has reviewed the growth of trade in some key sectors, highlighting sectors that worked as engines of growth in the overall trade. He has identified sectors like refined petroleum products and pharmaceuticals as contributing a much higher percentage to the growth of trade.

Dr. Vidhan Pathak presented his paper *'India Relations with Francophone Africa'*. It focuses on the shift and changes in India's Francophone Africa policy, and underlines the priorities of India's foreign policy in the region. According to him, there has been a significant change in India's Francophone Africa policy since 1990's when it stopped seeing these countries in terms of the old Third World agenda of decolonisation and non-alignment. The recent Indian efforts were aimed at plugging a huge gap in India's strategy of intensifying political and economic contact with these countries. The Team-9 initiative is an important point of reference in India's relations with Francophone African countries.

Dr. Jamal Moosa in his paper *'India Engaging with Africa for Development'*, raised some pertinent questions in this section, including the critical one of the kind of response of the African continent to the rest of the world's desire to engage with Africa by adopting different approaches. In other words, how is Africa engaging with the rest of the world? Are they continuing the old pattern of interaction? Similarly, are they following the same pattern of engagement with different regions or are there crucial differences? More importantly, what do they expect in return?

Dr. Usov in his paper '*Indian Investments in African Agriculture and the Question of "Land Grabbing"*' argued forcefully against huge Indian investments in agricultural land in Africa for commercial use. It may be noted here that the Indian government has allowed Indian private companies to acquire land in Africa and specifically in East African countries. According to a media report, approx. 70 Indian companies have collectively invested in land valued at US$2.3 billion, in Ethiopia, Kenya, Madagascar, Senegal and Mozambique. In Ethiopia, Indian private investment touched $4.5 billion in 2011, dominated mostly by floriculture and agriculture.

Dr. Suresh Kumar's paper '*Agro-Industry as an Emerging Sector: Mutual Interests of India and Africa*' sought to explain how the private regional agricultural sector in Africa, which is capable of adding maximum value to and raising the competitiveness of agricultural commodities, is not expanding because of a lack of proper policies and environmental environment. He has argued that India's experience of agro-industry can strengthen agricultural commodity chains across the borders and meet the needs of both the African population and global markets.

The various articles in this book have offered detailed analyses on the various determinants and drivers of India's new intimacy with the African countries. *It lays emphasis on emerging sectors which need the urgent attention of India's policy makers. India's policy of capacity building in Africa has featured prominently throughout the presentations and discussions at the conference. Moreover, India's ITEC programme, need for human resource development in Africa, and exchange of experiences were identified as key determinants in progress of India-Africa relations.*

In organising the conference, I have received significant financial support from the Ministry of External Affairs, Government of India, Indian Council of Social Science Research, New Delhi and India-Africa Chamber of Commerce, Mumbai. The inaugural address by Mr. Rajinder Bhagat, Joint Secretary (West Africa), Ministry of External Affairs, Govt. of India, was the curtain-raiser. Mr. Bhagat spoke on India-Africa partnership in development, expansion and co-operation in existing and emerging areas, which has helped lay the foundation for the analysis of India's policy perspectives in the emerging areas of co-operation with African countries.

I wish to thank the World Trade Centre, Mumbai, for their support in providing the facilities for the second day's conference which was attended by prominent industrialists like Vijay Kalantri, top officials from pharmaceutical houses and the Exim Bank, all of whom have a presence in Africa. I am immensely grateful to Mrs. Gennet Zewide, Ambassador of Ethiopia to India, for her immense support to the conference.

The aim of the Policy Research Institute of African Studies Association of India (PRIASA) are to organise seminars and conferences at regular intervals, with the association of the Centres and departments of African Studies all over India, on key themes of India-Africa relations, in various Asian and African countries. The objective is to promote African Studies in India. The first of such conferences was on India-East Africa Relations, and was held in Nairobi, Kenya in February 2012 in association with Nairobi University, Kenya. The second conference will be held in Durban, South Africa, on the theme of Africa-India Relations, between 26th and 27th September, 2012, in association with University of KwaZulu, Natal, Durban. The third conference will be held in Mumbai in association with Institute of African Studies, Academy of Science, Moscow in November, 2012.

We hope that, over the next several years, PRIASA conferences and seminars will be held at different locations in India, besides China and Korea in Asia, and Sudan, Uganda and Senegal, among other African countries. PRIASA also hopes to publish at least one book summarising main research findings, at the end of each conference. I wish to conclude by emphasising that PRIASA is always on the lookout to expand its regional and international linkages, and is eager to discuss and take forward research training or consultancy proposals. In this regard, it has received excellent support from the University of Mumbai and Jawaharlal Nehru University. This is besides the Ford Foundation, Ministry of External Affairs, Government of India, and the Norwegian Institute of International Affairs all of whom have been generous in their support. Finally, I wish to thank my research students, Ms. Prajakta Bagwe, Ms. Veda Vaidyanathan and Mr. Lalkholian Guite, for providing valuable research assistance.

Aparajita Biswas

References

1. C. Raja Mohan, "India and the Balance of Power", *Foreign Affairs*, July-August, 2006. Also see India's New Foreign Policy Strategy, Draft paper presented at a Seminar in Beijing by China Reform Forum and the Carnegie Endowment for International Peace, Beijing, May 26, 2006. http://carnegieendowment.org/files/mohan.pdf
2. Rajen Harshe, "Indo-African Ties in the Post Cold War World: An Overview", *International Studies*, International Studies Vol. 47 No. 2 and 4, 2012, pp. 347-361.
3. See "Dr. Manmohan Singh's Statement" in First India-Africa Summit, *http://intellibriefs.blogspot.com/2008/04/first-india-africa-summit-dr-manmohan.html (may*, 2011)
4. G.O.I., Ministry of Commerce, "Focus Africa Program: a Program for Enhancing India's Trade with the African Region", http://www.pdexcil.org/news/53N0204/focus1.htm

AFRICA - Acronyms

AMISOM	African Union Mission in Somalia
ANPIA	Angolan National Private Investment Agency
APISA	Asian Political and International Studies Association
APRM	African Peer Review Mechanism
APSA	African Peace and Security Architecture
ARMSCOR	Armaments Corporation of South Africa Ltd.
ARV	Anti-Retroviral
ASAIndia	African Studies Association of India
ASCM	Anti-ship Cruise Missiles
ASO	Anywaa Survival Organisation
ASSOCHAM	Associated Chambers of Commerce
AU	African Union
AWACS	Airborne Warning and Control Systems Aircrafts
BHEL	Bharat Heavy Electricals Limited
bn	billion
BOAD	Banque Ouest Africaine de Développement
CAADP	Comprehensive African Agricultural Development Programme
CBD	Convention on Biological Diversity
CCB	China Construction Bank
CFS	Committee on Food Security
CIF	China International Fund
CII	Confederation of Indian Industries
CISSC	Centre for International Scientific Studies and Collaboration
CLACSO	Latin American Council of Social Sciences
CNOOC	China National Offshore Oil Corp
CNPC	China's National Petroleum Corporation

COMESA	Common Market of Eastern and Southern Africa
CPA	Comprehensive Peace Agreement
CSIH	China Sonangol International Holding
CSO	Civil Society Organisation
CSR	Corporate Social Responsibility
DAC	Development Assistance Committee
DFLs	Disease Free Laying eggs
DRC	Democratic Republic of Congo
E&P	Exploration and Production
ECOWAS	Economic Community of West African States
EEZ	Exclusive Economic Zone
EFA	Education for All
EIA	Energy Information Administration
EU	European Union
Exim bank	Export-Import Bank
FDI	Foreign Direct Investment
FTI	Fast Track Initiative
GAIL	Gas Authority of India Limited
GDP	Gross Domestic Product
GOI	Government of India
GOPIO	Global Organisation of People of Indian Origin
GRN	*Gabinete de Reconstrução Nacional*
GSPC	Gujarat State Petroleum Corporation
HLPE	High Level Panel of Experts on Food Security and Nutrition
IBSA	India-Brazil-South Africa
ICCR	Indian Council of Cultural Relations
ICT	Information and Communications Technology
ICWA	Indian Council of World Affairs
IDSA	Institute of Defence Studies and Analyses
IO	Indian Ocean
IOC	Indian Oil Corporation
IOC	International Oil Company
IONS	Indian Ocean Naval Symposium
IOR-ARC	Indian Ocean Rim Association for Regional Cooperation
IPU	Investment Publicity Unit
ITEC	Indian Technical and Economic Cooperation
ITI	Indian Telecom Industries

JBC	Joint Business Council
LDC	Less/ Least-developed Country
LOC	Line of Credit
m	million
MDG	Millennium Development Goals
MEA	Ministry of External Affairs
mmt	million metric tonnes
MONUC	UN Mission of the Democratic Republic of Congo
MoU	Memorandum of Understanding
NAM	Non-Aligned Movement
NEP	New Economic Policy
NEPAD	New Partnership for Africa's Development
NOC	National Oil Company
NRI	Non-resident Indian
NTPC	National Thermal Power Corporation
OEML	ONGC Mittal Energy Limited
ONGC	Oil and National Gas Company
OVL	ONGC Videsh Ltd
PIO	Person / People of Indian Origin
PRC	People's Republic of China
PSC	Peace and Security Council
RECs	Regional Economic Communities
RENAMO	*Resistance Nacional Macambicano*
RITES	Rail India Technical and Economic Services
RPF	Rwandan Patriotic Front
RTC	Recommended Transit Corridor
SADC	Southern African Development Community
SANDF	South African National Defence Force
SCAAP	Special Commonwealth Assistance for Africa Programme
SIGINT	Signal Intelligence
Sinopec	China Petroleum and Chemical Corporation
SLOC	Sea Lines of Communication
SME	Small and Medium Sized Enterprise
SPV	Special Purpose Vehicle
SSI	Sonangol Sinopec International
tcf	trillion cubic feet
TCIL	Telecommunications Consultants India Ltd.
tcm	trillion cubic metres

TEAM-9	Techno Economic Approach for Africa India Movement
UN	United Nations
UNAMIR	UN Assistance Mission in Rwanda
UNAMSIL	UN Mission in Sierra Leone
UNAVEM I	UN Verification Mission in Angola I
UNCCD	UN Convention to Combat Desertification
UNCTAD	UN Conference on Trade and Development
UNFCCC	UN Framework Conference on Climate Change
UNIPEC	United Petroleum and Chemicals
UNITA	*Uniao Nacacional para Independencia Total de Angola*
UNITAF	Unified Task Force
UNMEE	UN Mission of Ethiopia–Eritrea
UNMIL	UN Mission of Liberia
UNMIS	UN Mission of Sudan
UNOSOM	UN Operation in Somalia
UNSC	UN Security Council
UNTAG	UN Transitional Assistance Group
US	United States
WADB	West African Development Bank
WSSR	World Social Science Report
WTO	World Trade Organisation

List of Contributors

1. **Dr. Denis Venter**, Former Director of Africa Institute of South Africa, Pretoria, South Africa.
2. **Dr. Carlos Cordoso**, Head, Research Programme, CODESRIA, Senegal. Council for the Development of Social Science Research in Africa, Darkar, Senegal.
3. **Prof. Ajay Dubey**, Chairperson, Centre for African Studies, Jawaharlal Nehru University, New Delhi, India. Secretary General, Policy Research Institute of African Studies Association of India.
4. **Prof. Makumi Mwagiru**, Director, Institute of Diplomacy and International Studies, University of Nairobi, Kenya.
5. **Prof. Aparajita Biswas**, Director Centre for African Studies, University of Mumbai, India.
6. **Dr. Alex Vines,** Director, Area Studies and International Law; and Head, Africa Programme Chatham House, London, UK.
7. **Dr. M. Katumanga**, Associate Professor, Department of Political Science and Public Administration, University of Nairobi, Kenya.
8. **Dr. S. Utham Kumar**, Senior Lecturer, Department of Defense and Strategic Studies, University of Madras, India.
9. **Dr. Nivedita Ray**, Research Fellow, Indian Council of World Affairs (ICWA), JNU.
10. **Dr. Shaji S.**, Lecturer, University of Hyderabad, India.
11. **Dr. Manendra Sahu**, Senior Lecturer, Centre for African Studies, University of Mumbai, India.
12. **Dr. Jamal Moosa**, Associate Professor, Academy of Third World Studies, Jamia Millia Islamia, New Delhi.

13. **Dr. Vyacheslav Usov**, Research Fellow, Institute for African Studies, Russian Academy of Sciences, Moscow, Russia.
14. **Dr. Suresh Kumar**, Associate Professor, Department of African Studies, University of Delhi, India.
15. **Dr. Vidhan Pathak**, Assistant Professor, University of Mumbai, India.

PROLOGUE

1

Some Trends in India-Africa Relations: Towards a Lasting Partnership?

Denis Venter

India has a reasonably successful policy towards the African continent, one that reflects a balance between Indian values and interests; it takes into account the diversity of Africa, as well as the policies of other key players such as the United States (US), the European Union (EU), China (the People's Republic of China, PRC), and Japan. New Delhi has never locked itself into a specific foreign policy or national security framework for too long. India's approach, while often reactive, may suit the country's interests best, given the knack for improvisation, however late in the day it sometimes occurs. However, there is a need for New Delhi to coordinate its efforts in Africa, as the pursuit of its policies is characterised by rather irregular bursts of activity.

Introduction

Evolved over time, India's policy towards Africa owes a lot to—Mahatma Gandhi, who became a beacon of hope for the continent; Prime Minister Jawaharlal Nehru, who left an indelible imprint on India-Africa relations; and Prime Ministers Indira Gandhi and Rajiv Gandhi, who contributed immensely to India's friendship with African countries. In international forums, India played a leading role in assisting and expediting Africa's decolonisation process. At the root of Nehru's belief was that India's independence would be incomplete without African countries attaining their freedom. As a visionary, he also foresaw and strengthened Afro-Asian unity that led to the birth of the Non-Aligned Movement (NAM) at the 1955 Bandung Conference.[1]

Towards the end of Nehru's tenure as prime minister, India's Africa relations dipped to a low, and by the mid-1960s it was forced to make a serious reassessment of its Africa policy and to take new initiatives. India and Africa have a common colonial past, and in the post-colonial period from the 1960s to1980s India continued to support liberation struggles in Africa, working closely with African countries not just at the United Nations (UN) but also in other multilateral forums such as NAM and the Commonwealth. Political relations have since been marked by mutual understanding and support, even more so as India did not attempt to impose any developmental model on African countries and left them to make their own choices. India clearly indicated, rather, that it would be privileged to be a development partner with African countries; and later, when parts of Africa were torn by conflict and restoring and maintaining peace became a priority, India willingly cooperated in UN peace-keeping missions in Congo, Somalia, Liberia, Burundi, and Sudan, amongst others.[2]

The best exposition of India's Africa policy, one anchored in Afro-optimism, was articulated by Prime Minister Manmohan Singh in his opening and concluding statements at the first India-Africa Forum summit held in New Delhi in April 2008. In an effort to strengthen relations, the focus was on furthering broader cooperation in areas such as the environment, education, energy and mining, as well as developing common viewpoints on regional and international issues, including the fight against terrorism, climate change, and World Trade Organisation (WTO) negotiations. Since then, India's engagement with Africa has clearly become multilayered, focused at three levels: first, at the pan-African level through growing ties with the African Union (AU); second, at the African regional level through the Regional Economic Communities (RECs) – e.g. the Economic Community of West African States (ECOWAS), the Southern African Development Community (SADC), and the Common Market for Eastern and Southern Africa (COMESA); and third, with all African countries through the establishment of bilateral economic relations.[3]

India also wants to expand its global influence through an involvement in wider regional economic cooperation. It is one of the lead countries in the Indian Ocean Rim Association for Regional Cooperation (IOR-ARC), an organisation of eighteen member states aiming to overcome the impediments to trade and investment within this vast region. The country is also a member of the India-Brazil-South Africa (IBSA) Dialogue Forum, a grouping of three important powers of the developing world promoting South-South co-operation.[4] Both India and Africa agreed they deserve permanent representation on the UN Security Council (UNSC) and would support each other in this endeavour. They had earlier joined forces, working together for UN reform, and they are now ready to push an agenda to make the UN more representative and democratic. For India, it would eliminate a disadvantage it always had vis-à-vis China, and provide a political spine to the body of its Africa policy.[5]

However, until very recently, India has lacked the resources and infrastructure to compete directly with other major players in Africa. India does not regard Africa simply as a supplier of natural resources; and this difference in conduct, this 'soft-power' approach, has clearly put it apart from most other countries.[6] New Delhi can build on this 'soft-power' approach by also showcasing its democracy, without seeking to export it, as well as its admirable struggle for human rights. Many years ago, Mahatma Gandhi observed that the interaction between India and Africa 'will be of ideas and services, not of manufactured goods [as] against raw materials'; and in 2008, Jairam Ramesh, at the time Indian minister of commerce, noted: '... [the] first principle of India's involvement in Africa is .... to add value'.[7] Consequently, at the first India-Africa Forum Summit the tone was one of creating a wider partnership, not confined to the business sector only.[8]

Deliberations at the forum resulted in the 'Delhi Declaration' and the 'India-Africa Framework for Cooperation', providing for collaboration in human resources development, science and technology, economic and industrial growth (including the development of small and medium-sized enterprises) and the minerals sector, and the boosting of African exports to world markets), health services, information and communications technology (ICT), security matters (including food security), and judicial reform. India undertook to grant preferential market access to exports from thirty-four least-developed countries (LDCs) in Africa and to raise its lines of credit to the continent to

US$5.4 bn. Also, by increasing its aid package to Africa to US$500 mn by 2012, New Delhi recognised that development has been a pressing need, giving African students access to higher education institutions in India, mainly under the auspices of the Indian Council of Cultural Relations (ICCR), and offering technical cooperation and training in terms of the Indian Technical and Economic Cooperation (ITEC) and related programmes.[9] 'These have been innovative, though modest, instruments — but their effectiveness lies in identifying Africa's felt needs and India's suitable response to these needs.'[10] Moreover, they reflect the priority New Delhi attaches to human-resource development and capacity-building.[11]

Energy Security, Trade and Investment, Economic Relations and Defence Cooperation

Although India has always approached Africa with no preconceived ideas and a particularly strong business focus, a new phenomenon in the Indo-African relationship is 'the notion of building a "partnership", which is mainly motivated by the importance of energy security'.[12] India is the fourth largest consumer and the fifth largest importer of oil in the world. While this can create new opportunities for Africa, the critical question remains whether and how Africa can benefit from this new interest and competition, which is not only between India and China but also between them and Western countries. Will Indian investments go beyond those in crude oil, and what kind of policy space will be created in Africa as a result of these new investments? Matters of energy security have made oil an issue of global power politics and this has put Africa back into the spotlight of business activities.[13]

India is largely dependent on oil imports and by 2020 this dependency is forecast to increase to 90 per cent; therefore, it is increasingly looking at African oil-producing countries like Nigeria, Angola, Sudan, and Libya.[14] Indeed, more than 50 per cent of India's oil imports come from Africa, while Nigeria alone provides a share of around ten per cent.[15] As a result, Indian companies have become very active in the upstream component of the oil sector and are busy exploring a number of new oil sources, not only in Nigeria but also in Madagascar, Ghana, and Uganda. India's efforts at building a sustainable partnership with Africa in the oil sector are based on five growth areas: increasing oil purchases; investing more in upstream oil production; fostering new exploration; making Indian skills and technology available to African partners; and developing a holistic approach to the entire energy sector, including access to India's downstream expertise.[16]

Given that oil supply is vulnerable to interruptions due to conflict or piracy, the human security dimension is of huge concern.[17] Although ONGC Videsh Ltd (OVL) invested in the oil industry in Sudan and developed a pipeline from Khartoum to Port Sudan at a cost of US$1 bn, there was always opposition to India's presence in Sudan both at home and in the international community, primarily because of human rights abuses in southern Sudan and, some allege, genocide in Darfur. But debate in New Delhi centred more on the safety of India's investments in Sudan, rather than alleged human rights violations.[18] ONGC Videsh not only produces Sudanese oil, but has invested some US$2 bn in eight other African countries, including Angola, Gabon, and Côte d'Ivoire.[19] Coal is also of strategic importance as it is India's main source of energy: currently, 53 per cent of the country's energy needs are met by domestic coal reserves. India is, however, seeking to diversify its supplies and there are high-quality coal deposits in Mozambique. Besides the involvement of Coal India Ltd, the Indian government has offered US$500 mn for energy and agricultural infrastructure projects, including institutions to support capacity-building in the coal industry.[20] However, political instability in some oil-producing countries and constant pressure from the global community to cut down on carbon emissions is forcing India to look closer at renewable energy technologies.[21]

Especially in recent years, India's Africa policy has emphasised the expansion and diversification of trade, investment, and economic relations.[22] Bilateral trade between India and Africa has grown rapidly from US$967 mn per year in the mid-1960s to more than US$40 bn by the late 2000s, and is projected to increase to US$70 bn by 2015. Nigeria, South Africa and Tanzania, in particular, feature prominently as India's major export destinations and import partners. India's exports to Africa are comprised of a wide variety of products, including cotton fabrics, iron and steel products, industrial machinery, mechanical appliances, power-station boilers, and nuclear reactors, while importing crude oil, rough diamonds, precious and semi-precious stones, copper and other mineral ores, coffee, coconut, edible fruits and nuts from Africa. Uranium is gaining importance as New Delhi pursues its ambitious civil nuclear power programme, and this is signalled by moves to establish tighter links with countries like Namibia.[23] Moreover, investment abroad is increasingly becoming an instrument of global integration. This is the context in which to see the impact of India's US$29 bn investment into Africa, most of which has gone into the hydrocarbon sector. Clearly, a rapidly industrialising India's quest for resources as a means of energy self-sufficiency has been an important reason for investing in Africa. In terms of manufacturing, India's investment has gone into apparel, small industry, pharmaceuticals, mining, agriculture and agro-processing, irrigation, power generation, road construction, and general infrastructure; and in the growing services sector, Indian investment has gone primarily into health care, information technology, e-education, and telecommunications.[24]

Indian businesses have found Africa to be familiar territory as it is similar to other emerging markets and also relatively easy to compete in, despite numerous bureaucratic hurdles. Sourcing raw materials for Indian companies has put pressure on price levels because of competition from China and this, in turn, has benefited African countries. Also, many Indian companies have gone into the extraction industry and this has provided employment to many Africans. In fact, the growing footprint in Africa of leading members of 'India Incorporated' (Tata, Mahindra, Essar, NIIT, and Bharti Airtel), of public-sector undertakings (ONGC Videsh, RITES, Ircon, and NSIC), of the banking industry (the State Bank of India, the Bank of Baroda, the Bank of India, and ICICI), of the pharmaceutical sector (Ranbaxy, Zydus, TCS, and Infosys), and the contribution by prominent national business chambers to wide-ranging business promotion has given content to India's economic presence on the continent. The Tata Group, India's leading investor in Africa, now has a presence in eleven African countries; in South Africa, apart from its investment in ferrochrome, Tata is also the ninth largest vehicle manufacturer.[25] But clearly, Indian investments in Africa face challenges such as low governance standards, inadequate local labour capacity, and security issues.[26]

Although energy security is a major concern for India (only food security is more important), it is seen to be linked to economic growth which, in turn, is linked to poverty reduction.[27] Over the years, Indian industrial technology has concentrated on products that are adaptable, appropriate and affordable. As a result, Africa has emerged (or has re-emerged) as a vast potential market for Indian entrepreneurs;[28] and, consequently, India-Africa business links, especially in the areas of energy resources, precious metals and uranium, have boomed. Nigeria remains the largest consumer in Africa of Indian manufactured goods and pharmaceuticals; but despite this strong relationship, East Africa as a region has been the largest consumer of Indian imported goods since the mid-1990s, followed by West Africa and North Africa.[29] So, although Indian private-sector companies in Nigeria have had some impact, the Indian government seems to be content to merely ride on the coat-tails of their initiatives.[30] Clearly, there is a major disconnect in the link between critical constituencies in Nigeria and India. The human potential, people-to-people relations, is an area that India has not adequately exploited.[31] Thus, the Nigerian relationship with India has fallen short of expectations and its vast potential has failed to be realised.[32]

Another significant aspect of India's Africa policy has been to cultivate good relations with the Indian diaspora in view of their role as a bridge between their host countries in Africa and India, although this does not necessarily always translate into an advantage.[33] Many have argued that cultural and economic linkages through the historical presence of South Asian communities in Africa give India a head start.[34] Having gained such an advantage, India should not allow itself to play second fiddle to China as a vigorously engaging ally of Africa.[35] Nevertheless, a fractious history of local race relations influenced the impressions of many Kenyan leaders of India; they unjustifiably believed that 'exploitative Kenyan Asians' misused their economic linkages to India. This was increasingly inaccurate as Nehru dissociated himself from People of Indian Origin (PIOs) in Africa, unfortunately creating a sense of abandonment amongst them. Over the years, race relations improved, yet the place of 'Asians' remains uncertain and relations with various 'African' groups are often uneasy. India's early post-colonial South Asian foreign policy introversion, domestic economic insularity before 1991, and dissociation from the diaspora led to relatively weak linkages to East Africa; and Kenya's own foreign policy reservations compounded this distancing. However, such dynamics have been changing, especially since the mid-2000s;[36] now, the three focus areas of India's foreign policy are to ensure a peaceful periphery, sustain relations with major world powers, and tackle issues affecting food security, accessibility to water and energy sources, and protection of the environment.[37]

India's current engagement with Kenya is primarily characterised by resurgent private-sector, market-seeking investments. Indian companies are exploring opportunities largely without the assistance of diaspora linkages and Indian government networks. Perhaps, the most well-known Indian investments in Kenya relate to telecommunications and oil-refining (the Essar Group), and horticulture (Karuturi Networks). Large deal-making in Kenya is often conducted in opaque and elite government-to-government arenas; the 'monetisation of Kenya's post-colonial politics' and the intertwining of political and business elites are, therefore, important for the more unscrupulous investor. However, India's initiatives are more private-sector-driven, companies are responsible to shareholders, and there is pressure for transparency from domestic civil society, rendering access to controversial avenues of economic advantage more and more problematic. Kenya is often viewed as a 'gateway' for investment into, and technological and private-sector linkages with, the wider East African region, thanks to its littoral position on the Indian Ocean, relatively well-developed infrastructure, and several multilateral institutions headquartered in Nairobi. In this sense, Kenya should remain a hub for Indian investment into Africa.[38]

Trade between India and South Africa has been growing at a rate of some 30 per cent annually. South Africa now accounts for more than two-thirds of Africa's exports to India, and bilateral trade has trebled from US$2.5 bn in 2004 to US$7.5 bn in 2009 and is projected to increase to some US$10 bn by 2012.[39] South Africa is also a strategic partner for India in terms of South-South relations, but relations have somehow not prospered because of capacity deficiencies, especially on the South African side where there has been no forward momentum on a lot of good ideas, and a lack of clarity over the country's position with regard to permanent seats on, and veto powers in, the UN Security Council. South Africa's position on nuclear non-proliferation is another point of contention, as well as the trade in arms with countries that are not particularly friendly towards India, and the issue of uncompetitive practices in the South African pharmaceutical and telecommunications industries. The biggest challenge for South Africa is to choose between what can be a stifling African consensus and solidarity, and a more robust leadership role requiring it to sometimes be prepared to stand apart from the Africa group when it comes to vitally important international issues. This hesitancy to lead politically, despite recognition of African sensitivities towards South Africa's role within Africa, has caused many frustrations for New Delhi. Consequently, Indo-South African relations have experienced many highs and lows. Moreover, India and South Africa are competitors within Africa, and in this sense their relations differ from those between India and other African countries. For relations to be mutually productive, therefore, a careful balance needs to be struck between being potential commercial and trade competitors in the African context, being democracies at the centre of South-South relations and, on international governance issues, being key drivers towards a fairer global order.[40]

Africa has moved up on India's political agenda and its goal of gaining a permanent seat on the UN Security Council has given impetus to the development of a new aid programme.[41] As a result, India is emerging as a non-Development Assistance Committee (DAC) donor, and Africa has started to benefit. India's economic (as distinct from its trading) links are no longer restricted to its traditional Indian Ocean and Commonwealth partners, and since 2003 it has extended credits worth some US$2 bn to various African countries.[42] As a post-colonial donor, New Delhi generally avoid the terminology of 'donor-recipient' and rather cast its interaction with partners in terms of reciprocity, mutual opportunity and benefit, South-South solidarity, and empathy. Indeed, India is in an ideal position to offer advice to other developing countries as it has only recently experienced similar developmental and growth challenges.[43] So, although India's engagement with Africa is about trade and economic links, the search for markets, it is also about global influence, the need for friends and allies to support its global ambitions. Development cooperation is important, therefore, and India is providing appropriate technology and capacity-building assistance in the ICT sector, in the provision of health care, and in the development of educational systems. However, there must be technological transfer to provide mutual benefit to the India-Africa relationship.[44] India wants to build a long-term partnership with Africa, rather than focusing on short-term business objectives and economic gains from the extractive sector. Consequently, the potential for economic partnership is strong and includes important sectors such as agriculture, agro-business, and the pharmaceutical industry. Moreover, India is looking for a wider partnership with Africa, promoting democratisation and the role of civil society organisations (CSOs), training and research for capacity-building, and skills transfers.[45]

Since as early as the 1960s, India has provided military training to a number of African countries, primarily from Anglophone Africa. Most African countries lack military training institutions, and officers are often sent abroad either to the military colleges of former colonial powers or friendly countries like India.[46] An important element in India's Africa policy, therefore, relates to defence cooperation with select countries such as Nigeria, Zambia, Lesotho, and Botswana in order to assist their armed forces through training programmes and exposure to the best practices and professionalism of the Indian military.[47] Moreover, India has moved to protect its own interests, particularly in the African Indian Ocean rim countries by strengthening defence ties with Mozambique, Madagascar, and the Seychelles. As early as 1977, India signed a cooperation agreement with Mauritius, providing air force and naval assistance and training. More recently, in 2003, an agreement was reached with the Seychelles to patrol its vast territorial waters and, generally, fostering naval cooperation through joint exercises and routine visits. India has also set up a radar surveillance station in Madagascar with high-tech digital communications systems to monitor shipping movements, partly in response to Somali piracy and to China's 'string of pearls' strategy of establishing sea lines of communication reaching from Hong Kong through the Straits of Malacca to Port Sudan on the Red Sea. India is heavily dependent for oil and other imports, as well as exports, on the safety and security of particular sea-route 'choke points', including the Strait of Bab el Mandeb (at the entrance from the Gulf of Aden to the Red Sea) and the shipping lanes of the Mozambique Channel (commanding the sea route northwards from South Africa to Tanzania, and on to India). Monitoring the waters off Africa's east coast protects the security of India's energy supplies from right across the Indian Ocean and beyond.[48]

India's updated 2009 maritime doctrine, therefore, incorporates new constabulary operations for the navy, with a heavy emphasis on anti-piracy and counterterrorism measures. It is estimated that US$50 bn worth of Indian imports and US$60 bn of exports pass through the Gulf of Aden alone. The Indian Navy has been particularly aggressive in combating piracy in the Arabian Sea, off the Horn of Africa and along the East African seaboard, and to protect both Indian and foreign vessels as 85 per cent of the country's foreign trade is carried in foreign-owned vessels. Thus, India intends to demonstrate its ability to project naval force beyond its own territorial waters and into the vast reaches of the Indian Ocean. Consequently, increasing cooperation has been fostered with South Africa, Tanzania and Mozambique, all countries on the Indian Ocean littoral. But, unfortunately, so far this cooperation has been of a rather haphazard and ad hoc nature, and needs to be put on a much sounder footing. Nevertheless, as a vigorous supporter of UN Security Council reform, India's 7,000-strong contribution to various UN peace-keeping missions in Africa is intended to further strengthen its case.[49]

Towards a Lasting Partnership in India-Africa Relations

The activity of the Indian private sector in Africa has gained considerable momentum, and its profile is set to increase further. In this unfolding scenario, Indian companies should follow a trajectory different from that of European and Chinese firms: they would do well to adhere to the basic canons of corporate social responsibility (CSR) and to a partnership-oriented business culture; and they must assist Africa through value-addition, employment creation, and skills development. African countries expect them to introduce new technologies and substantial investment in socio-economic development which, in turn, will generate attractive business opportunities.[50] In this context, India's engagement in Africa needs to be matched by sustainable new doctrines and capabilities, as current diplomatic representation is rather thinly spread. India's commercial footprint in Africa has been private sector-led, so business and industry are likely to remain the key drivers of India's renewed diplomatic efforts. India has missions in twenty-five of the forty-seven sub-Saharan African countries, plans to reopen its embassy in the Democratic Republic of Congo (DRC) and its high commission in Malawi, and add other missions in Niger and Gabon. But it is in South Africa, Eastern Africa and the western Indian Ocean region that there is the most comprehensive Indian diplomatic presence, because of geographical proximity and quite sizeable Indian diaspora communities in several of these countries.[51]

Three years ago, the Indian government designated Africa as 'an emerging priority' in foreign policy; now, in 2011 and beyond, Africa should be treated as one of India's key priorities. Sustained attention to Africa at the political level is essential. In 2010, India's Vice President and External Affairs Minister paid official visits to Zambia, Malawi, Botswana, Mauritius and Mozambique; and New Delhi hosted high-ranking leaders from Seychelles, South Africa, Botswana, and Malawi. This momentum should be maintained; even more so in the wake of the second India-Africa Forum summit of May 2011, as close personal relationships at the summit level are deemed very important in Africa's political culture.[52] The multidimensional relationship between India and Africa, operating at the continental, regional and bilateral levels, will ensure that even when New Delhi succeeds in achieving some of its short-term objectives (the restructuring of an institution of global governance such as the UN Security Council), its longer-term ambition to play a role as a major global economic power will lead to an ever-growing engagement with Africa.[53] Clearly, India's ability to engage with Africa will be defined by the opportunities and risks that New Delhi faces in the global system.[54]

There are ways in which India might further constructively engage with Africa within the rhetoric of a broader South-South partnership, using its own particular strengths: for example, with skills transfer in the ICT sector, in which it is justifiably regarded as a world leader.[55] But India will have to strike a balance between its role as South-South 'co-ordinator', promoted by its policy-makers, and the economic self-interest of its business sector.[56] Ahead of the second India-Africa Forum summit, Indian Prime Minister Manmohan Singh described the India-Africa partnership as 'a living embodiment of South-South cooperation'. This partnership, resting on the three pillars of capacity-building and skills transfer, trade relations, and infrastructural development, is based on 'equality, mutual trust, and a consultative and transparent approach', and is designed 'to respond to the needs and priorities of Africa, and for India to learn from Africa's rich experience'. He noted:[57]

> ... [today] both Africa and India are on the move. Africa is emerging as a new growth pole, while India is on a path of sustained and rapid economic development. Relations between India and Africa are marked by strong people-to-people interaction and a deep sense of solidarity and goodwill.
>
> ... [both] Africa and India have the advantage of a youthful population, commitment to democracy, pluralism, and [a] spirit of entrepreneurship. These are compelling factors for

a strong and purposeful partnership between India and Africa that responds to the realities of the ... [twenty-first] century.

Thus, in 2011 the Indian government seems to be reinvigorated with a renewed determination and sense of urgency to strengthen economic and trade links with Africa. Bilateral trade figures reflect this growing relationship, projected to increase from the current US$39 bn to some US$50 bn by early 2012 and to reach around US$70 bn by 2015.[58]

In the lead-up to the second India-Africa Forum summit there was much speculation, some of it unnecessary, about how New Delhi would play catch-up with Beijing in Africa. Prime Minister Singh has managed to answer many of the questions that were raised and, just as importantly, neatly sidestep others about the purported rivalry between the two Asian giants. Nevertheless, the numbers emanating from the discussions in Addis Ababa, Ethiopia, make for impressive reading: a US$5 bn line of credit for three years for development projects, and US$300 m for an Ethiopia-Djibouti railway line. Other initiatives must be understood in the context of a key phrase, repeatedly used at the summit – 'capacity-building'. This has been New Delhi's thrust since the first summit in 2008 when it offered just more than US$5 bn for regional integration through infrastructure development. In terms of trade, however, it is not even in the same league as Beijing; China-Africa trade in 2010 was US$126.9 bn, while India-Africa trade was barely US$40 bn. But by focusing on leveraging Indian experience in institution-building and economic growth, there is a chance to enhance African capabilities, both material and human, in a way that is economically advantageous for India. Also, engaging Africa is not a zero-sum game; by emphasising a model that builds on historical links and plays to some of India's strengths, Singh has effectively shifted the conversation.[59] The outcomes of the second India-Africa Forum summit, therefore, promises to further deepen India's engagement with Africa. Indian industry's confidence has risen enormously despite security problems and the non-transparency that still prevails to some extent in legal and administrative structures in Africa.[60]

Conclusion

Both sides in the India-Africa relationship should not conclude that there is no scope for improvement in relations — most certainly there is. From an Indian perspective, a powerful triad of government, the private sector, and civil society can take the India-Africa relationship to a much higher level of strength and vitality. Can India's Africa policy do better? The answer is an unequivocal 'yes'. The only question mark that remains is: does India have the will to execute this policy and does it have the stamina to sustain it?[61] Political cooperation between India and Africa in building governance institutions at both the macro and micro levels, such as local government authorities and CSOs, should intensify. Engagement by the Indian government sector is likely to see an increase in capacity-building and human-resource development, based on the knowledge economy in which India is very competitive. Also, India's engagement with Africa should move from a passive request-based approach to a more aggressive involvement by the Indian private sector.[62] The government in New Delhi should vigorously encourage Indian industry to partner with their African counterparts. There has been some rise in private sector involvement since the first summit, but India must do more: from free trade agreements with various African regions to developing strategic investment plans that would facilitate Indian companies getting the best return on their investments in key focus areas such as agriculture and the ICT sector.[63]

From historical ties and large diaspora communities to goodwill earned through peace-keeping operations and 'soft power' in the form of educational links and the film industry, New Delhi has many advantages in Africa. The importance of building on these is self-evident — securing energy sources in Africa, cementing defence and security co-operation in the Indian Ocean region, and getting in at an early stage of what could be a crucial growth story for the African continent in the coming decades. Again, it has been a good beginning; but whether this will mature into a mutually beneficial relationship and a real partnership will depend on New Delhi's capability to forge economic links tempting enough for Indian companies to utilise.[64] India needs to recognise that the unfolding scenario in Africa is complex, that its pace is rapid and inconsistent, and that competition for Africa's potential markets and natural resources has become increasingly intense. Hence, there is a need for a fresh evaluation of policies, the removal of constraints on the implementation of past decisions, and the fast-tracking of new initiatives. New Delhi needs to deepen its engagement and interaction with Africa with the specific goal of fulfilling Africa's needs and aspirations in accordance with India's own capabilities and interests. It will require more resources — human, technical, and financial — faster implementation and, above all, a change in the conventional Indian mindset (Bhatia, 2010). Indeed, India has always been seen as 'the latecomer' in Africa — it, therefore, needs to do some soul-searching as to why it does not hold more appeal for Africans.[65]

Finally, more specific research on India-Africa relations is essential as there is often little realisation of how different India's approach to Africa is from that of China and other countries. Although India and Africa have had long-established political and economic (especially, trade) links, there has been too little debate on, and analysis of, India's role in Africa.[66] Therefore, Indian academics and researchers have to make a concerted effort to reach out to, and establish greater engagement with, African universities and research institutions. It is important for this engagement to be robust, and to diversify by reaching out to other disciplinary areas beyond sociology, the political sciences, and economics. This will be a huge challenge, given the dire state of much of the higher education system and research institutions in Africa. Nevertheless, together an agenda needs to be defined in order to produce joint knowledge that could be turned into a policy dialogue in which government, private sector, and civil society can all participate.[67] There is also a need for the Indian government to create new policy synergies by opening its doors to a small but talented community of Africanists working in, or affiliated to, the African Studies Association of India (ASAIndia), the Institute of Defence Studies and Analyses (IDSA), the Indian Council of World Affairs (ICWA), a few other institutions, and some of the major Indian universities. Taken together, they represent an extremely valuable source of expertise outside government circles. The media can also play a role in enhancing public interest through an increased focus on Africa; they should inform and educate, as developments in Africa are often fascinating, besides having a profound bearing on India's national interests.[68]

References

1. Bhatia, Rajiv, 'India's Africa Policy: Can We Do Better?', *The Hindu* (New Delhi), 15 July 2010.

2. *Ibid.*, Jain, Payal, *India-Africa Relations* (Politics and Government), 17 May 2008, http://artic les.maxabout.com/politics-government/India-africa-relations/article-7017 — accessed on 26 May 2011).
3. *Ibid.*
4. Vines-1, Alex., 2010, 'Indian Peace and Security Policy in Africa', in Chatham House, *Two Years on from the Forum Summit: The Future of Africa-India Engagement* (Report of a conference held at the Royal Institute of International Affairs, Chatham House, on 9 April 2010), p. 21.
5. Jain, Payal, *op cit;* Vines-2, Alex, *India's Africa Engagement: Prospects for the 2011 India-Africa Forum* (Programme Paper, AFP 2010/01) London: Royal Institute of International Affairs (Chatham House), December, p. 9.
6. *Ibid.*, pp. 7 and 14.
7. *Ibid.*, quoted, p. 14.
8. Chand, Manish, 'Comparing China with India in Africa', in Chatham House, *Two Years on from the Forum Summit: The Future of Africa-India Engagement* (Report of a conference held at the Royal Institute of International Affairs, Chatham House, on 9 April, 2010), p. 22.
9. Vines-2, *op cit*, p. 11.
10. Bhatia, *op cit*.
11. Jain, *op cit*.
12. Cheru-1, Fantu, 'Evolving China-India-Africa Relations: Potential Benefits and Risks', in Chatham House, *Two Years on from the Forum Summit: The Future of Africa-India Engagement* (Report of a conference held at the Royal Institute of International Affairs, Chatham House, on 9 April 2010), p. 4.
13. Obi-1, Cyril, 'Energy', in Chatham House, *Two Years on from the Forum Summit: The Future of Africa-India Engagement* (Report of a conference held at the Royal Institute of International Affairs, Chatham House, 9 April 2010), p. 5.
14. Chatham House, 2010, *Two Years on from the Forum Summit: The Future of Africa-India Engagement* (Report of a conference held at the Royal Institute of International Affairs, Chatham House, on 9 April 2010), pp. 1-2.
15. Chand, Manish, *op cit;* Vines-2, *op cit,* p. 4.
16. Beri, Ruchita, 'Locating Africa in India's Energy Policy', in Chatham House, *Two Years on from the Forum Summit: The Future of Africa-India Engagement* (Report of a conference held at the Royal Institute of International Affairs, Chatham House, 9 April 2010), p. 18.

17. Chatham House, *op cit*, p. 6.
18. Patey, Luke, 2010, 'Sudan and India', in Chatham House, *Two Years on from the Forum Summit: The Future of Africa-India Engagement* (Report of a conference held at the Royal Institute of International Affairs, Chatham House, 9 April 2010), p. 12.
19. Vines-2, *op cit,* p. 7.
20. *Ibid,* pp. 2 and 6.
21. Beri, *op cit,* p. 19.
22. Bhatia, *op cit.*
23. Vines-2, *op cit,* pp. 2 & 5; Kanungo, Anil Kumar, 2011, 'India's Sense of Urgency on Africa Welcome', *Sunday Times of India* (New Delhi), 22 May 2011.
24. Vines-2, *op cit,* p. 6; Kanungo, *op cit.*
25. Bhatia, *op cit;* Kanungo, *op cit;* Vines-2, *op cit*, p. 6.
26. Cheru-1, *op cit,* p. 4.
27. Patey, Luke, 2010, 'Sudan and India', in Chatham House, *Two Years on from the Forum Summit: The Future of Africa-India Engagement* (Report of a conference held at the Royal Institute of International Affairs, Chatham House, 9 April 2010), p. 12.
28. Price, Gareth, 2010, 'Panel Discussion: The Future of India-Africa Relations', in Chatham House, *Two Years on from the Forum Summit: The Future of Africa-India Engagement* (Report of a conference held at the Royal Institute of International Affairs, Chatham House, on 9 April 2010), p. 26.
29. Vines-2, *op cit,* pp. 4 and 7.
30. Chatham House, *op cit,* p. 17.
31. Obi-2, *op cit,* p. 16.
32. Sidiropoulos, Elizabeth, 2010, 'South Africa and India', in Chatham House, *Two Years on from the Forum Summit: The Future of Africa-India Engagement* (Report of a conference held at the Royal Institute of International Affairs, Chatham House, on 9 April 2010), p. 13.
33. Bhatia, *op cit;* Chatham House, *op cit*, p. 1.
34. McCann, Gerard, 2010, 'Kenya and India', in Chatham House, *Two Years on from the Forum Summit: The Future of Africa-India Engagement* (Report of a conference held at the Royal Institute of International Affairs, Chatham House, on 9 April 2010), p. 8.
35. Jain, *op cit.*
36. McCann, *op cit,* pp. 8-9.
37. Vines-1, *op cit,* p. 20.
38. McCann, *op cit*, pp. 9-10.

39. Vines-2, *op cit,* pp. 1 and 7.
40. Sidiropoulos, *op cit,* pp. 13-15.
41. Price, *op cit,* p. 26.
42. Vines-2, *op cit,* pp. 1 and 7.
43. Mawdsley, Emma, 2010, pp. 19-20.
44. Obi-2, Cyril, 2010, 'Discussant', in Chatham House. *Two Years on from the Forum Summit: The Future of Africa-India Engagement* (Report of a conference held at the Royal Institute of International Affairs, Chatham House, on 9 April 2010), p. 15.
45. Chand, *op cit,* p. 22; Modi, Renu, 'Discussant', in Chatham House, *Two Years on from the Forum Summit: The Future of Africa-India Engagement* (Report of a conference held at the Royal Institute of International Affairs, Chatham House, on 9 April 2010), pp. 22-23.
46. Jain, *op cit.*
47. Bhatia, *op cit.*
48. Vines-1, *op cit*, pp. 20-21; Vines-2, *op cit*, p. 8.
49. Vines-1, *op cit*, p. 21; Vines-2, *op cit,* pp. 9-10.
50. Bhatia, *op cit.*
51. Vines-1, 2010, 21; Vines-2, 2010, 1 and 7-8
52. Bhatia, *op cit.*
53. Dubey, Ajay, 'Panel Discussion: The Future of India-Africa Relations', in Chatham House. *Two Years on from the Forum Summit: The Future of Africa-India Engagement* (Report of a conference held at the Royal Institute of International Affairs, Chatham House, on 9 April 2010), pp. 25-26.
54. Cheru-2, Fantu, 2010, 'Panel Discussion: The Future of India-Africa Relations', in Chatham House. *Two Years on from the Forum Summit: The Future of Africa-India Engagement* (Report of a conference held at the Royal Institute of International Affairs, Chatham House, on 9 April 2010), p. 26.
55. Chatham House, *op cit,* p. 2.
56. Vines-2, *op cit,* p. 1.
57. *The Times of India*, New Delhi, 23 May 2011.
58. Kanungo, *op cit.*
59. *The Times of India*, New Delhi, 26 May 2011.
60. Kanungo, *op cit.*
61. Bhatia, *op cit.*
62. Dubey, *op cit,* p. 25.
63. *The Times of India*, New Delhi, 26 May 2011.
64. Ibid.

65. Vasudevan, Parvathi, 2010, 'Nigeria and India', in Chatham House, *Two Years on from the Forum Summit: The Future of Africa-India Engagement* (Report of a conference held at the Royal Institute of International Affairs, Chatham House, on 9 April 2010), p. 11.
66. Chatham House, *op cit,* p. 1.
67. Cheru-2, *op cit,* p. 27.
68. Bhatia, *op cit.*

2

India and Africa: Which Partnership for Which Research and Development?

Carlos Cardoso
*CODESRIA, Dakar**

1. Taking Stock of the Development of Social Science in the Global South

Although the title of the chapter suggests a development with a broader scope, our focus will be directed more to the status of social sciences in Asia, the continent where India is located, and Africa. Each of the two continents is of course diverse, but for our purpose, we treat them as an entity. Although they also belong to Global South, in this paper we will leave aside countries like China and Brazil, because of their geographical and demographical size. The data, resources and information are derived mainly from the recently published 2010 World Social Science Report (WSSR).[1]

Despite the differences that we might encounter amongst the countries in the South and perhaps in different regions of a certain country, the social sciences in the South have experienced a considerable development in recent years. This does not, however, mean that the social-science institutions and social-science researchers

* Council for the Development of Social Science Research in Africa, Dakar, Senegal.

in the South are devoid of problems and challenges. Just to mention a few, they encounter insufficient public subsidies, deterioration of the scientific profession, changes in the modes of knowledge production, a relative decline in the number of books and articles produced, and on top of everything else, brain drain. More importantly, in our view, is the lack of political will to change the situation. Some governments, mainly those countries belonging to the emerging countries (China, India and Brazil) have started to change their attitude toward social sciences, but this new attitude takes time to be converted in a seat of real politics and practices.

In Sub-Saharan Africa and South Asia, there is what the authors of the WSSR called a 'deinstitutionalisation' of research (Mouton), i.e., a situation where the landscape is characterised by an increase of short-term applied research conducted outside universities by consultancy firms and non-governmental organisations, at the request of international donors or private foundations. The broad themes that unite social-science research in Asia and the Pacific Region are unemployment, social mobility and equity, security and safety, education, population, health, globalisation, adaptation to climate change and the governance required to manage these matters.

The progress made worldwide and in those particular countries in terms of information and communication technologies are shaping the social-science environment and practices, as well as, the whole conditions of knowledge production. These technologies have allowed young scholars (more strongly in Asia but also in Africa) to be aware and better connected to the progress of social science in the world than ever before on the diversity, overlap, commonalities and dilemmas of current social-science themes and topics. They are no longer privileged information available only to the elites. The younger generation of scholars is given the opportunity to travel for research and exchange purposes.

In India, South Asia, this development has been nurtured especially in the centres of excellence in social-science research, resulting among others, in the emergence of new research fields and topics.

In Africa, the social sciences went through tremendous changes with different regional and national impacts, characterised by disparities, imbalances and divides. To prove this disparity, it should suffice to cite the WSSR, which states that 75 per cent of academic publications in the web of science database come from South African, Nigerian and Kenyan social scientists, and from only a few universities. Similar disparities in the knowledge-production process and concentration in major universities and research centres can be found in other regions.

1.1 The Status of Research in Africa

Social-science research in Africa is often at crossroads. Paradigms that inform beliefs and thoughts are multiple. They build a very complex net, and vary from tradition on one extreme to modernity on the other. In their way of thinking and action, it is possible to discern an overlapping of two models of knowledge, which coexist and yet ignore each other, namely, the indigenous and the modern.

Kane's[2] work published in 2003, drawing on the works of two African thinkers, Mudimbe[3] and Appiah[4] showed that in post-colonial Africa there are at least two intellectual traditions of knowledge production on Africa, namely, Anglophone and Francophone. Shockingly, Kane notes that both of them offer us a Eurocentric reading of knowledge production in Africa and on Africa. Mudimbe[5] argues that the writings that contributed to the invention of Africa and the idea of Africa have primarily been produced by Europeans during the colonial period which he calls the 'colonial library'. As for Appiah the bulk of writings produced in Sub-Saharan Africa are in Portuguese, English and French and, consequently, most intellectuals in Sub-Saharan Africa are 'Europhones'.[6] He added that historically Third-World intellectuals (including Sub-Saharan Africa) are products of the encounter with the West.[7]

Kane has shown that next to the 'colonial library', which is essentially Eurocentric and Europhone, the other includes the 'Islamic library' where many intellectuals have contributed their shares. These can by no means be classified Europhone. The space of Islamic meaning (sense) is part of these plural spaces. According to Kane, it is a space that is structured, around beliefs and Islamic practices (Islamic learning esoteric and exoteric religious practices: prayer, fasting, proselytisation, pilgrimage to holy places). This space of meanings influences considerably the populations, particularly the heavily Islamised areas of Africa. The gradual establishment of this area of meaning happened after over a thousand years of slow and gradual

Islamisation, during which the Arabic language and culture gained citizenship rights in many corners of the Sub-Saharan Africa.[8]

But most Arabizantes African intellectuals are not only unknown to Europhones, but also to a considerable number of Arab and Orientalistic authors who compiled works on the Arabophone intellectuals. Here one can mention names such as Abd al-Karim al-Maghili (died 1504), whose contribution is linked to the idea of coming in every century of a Muslim reformer versed in religious sciences who orders what is permissible, forbids what is not allowed, presides over the destinies of men and resolves disputes.

The above-stated ideas influences the many political movements from the seventeenth, eighteenth and nineteenth centuries led by Muslim scholars, including the creation of Muslim theocracies.[9] Reference is made to the city of Timbuktu, which in the past was a great intellectual centre of Islam, where universities flourished in the medieval sense of the term, and a community of teachers and students lived together for the purpose of transmitting or acquiring religious knowledge and benefiting from the privileges granted by the king and the religious authorities.[10]

More recently, we could mention names like Mohamed Abd al-Jabri, an Arabophone Moroccan intellectual who devoted most of his time to the study of the Arabic intellectual 'patrimoine', trying to solve the dilemma of modernity/tradition, and to construct a model and a project of Arabic thought. Cheikh Yassine of Berber origin is another intellectual who belongs to the Islamist Khalifat. He was the only knowledge producer within his movement, which was well structured and followed a pedagogical approach that is based on his experience in the administration of the education system.[11]

Kane said that it is imperative to rethink the near monopoly claimed by Western languages and order in the epistemological process of 'understanding reality in Africa'[12] not only because of the numerous recent studies that show vigorous debates in written or oral non-Western languages, but also because there is a space of post-colonial sense (meaning) that is common to intellectuals emerging from the fusion between Europhone and non-Europhone traditions. He ends it by quoting Zaki Laidi who says that 'there is not only an epistemological order, but several spaces of meaning in Africa'.[13]

The Africanisation of our intellectual agenda implies the resolution of many contradictions, i.e., the contradictions between the different intellectual traditions in the continent, between the colonial library and Islamic library, as well as between indigenous knowledge and modern knowledge.

Basically, it is a struggle against the fragmentation of knowledge that is produced on the continent and about the continent. It is this question that CODESRIA has tried to address since its inception in 1973. As stated in its various documents, and drawn mainly from across the social-science faculties and research centres of African universities, the founding members of CODESRIA were propelled by a determination to combat the dispersal and fragmentation of knowledge production on the continent. Hence, they created a forum where autonomous, Africa-based networking on a continental scale could be fostered and made to flourish. Equally important in the thinking of the founding members was the desire to break the disciplinary and linguistic-geographical barriers to scholarship in the African social-science research community. The latter concern brought the goal of decolonising knowledge and promoting an endogenous scientific conversation to the fore.

Nowadays, fragmentation and division are still part of the landmark of the social sciences worldwide. The last World Social Science Report was dedicated to precisely address this knowledge divide, the one between countries and regions.[14] Similar to the economic order, the current knowledge order is characterised by a number of inequalities and imbalances that impact upon the capacity of the South to compete with the Global North in terms of knowledge production. And it must be stressed that this kind of divide is undermining the strength, quality and efficiency of the social sciences in general.

Higher education is in progress in Africa. There has been a boom in terms of the number of higher learning institutions on the continent in the last decades. While we witness the proliferation of institutions, a number of questions pertaining to the philosophy, objectives and political orientation of these institutions remain either unanswered or the answers are inadequate to explain or respond to the challenges. Many African universities have been assigned the task to contribute to development, which in the first instance seems to be a good thing. In order to be relevant, institutions of higher learning ought to be grounded on the national realities and are expected to contribute their part to the development of the society in which they are located. In short, the objective of the university should go beyond a mere utilitarian role.

When we speak about research on development issues, of course, we should not aspire universities and research centres to come back to the early post-colonial state, when universities were conceived to provide the 'manpower' necessary for material development; where original knowledge production was seen as a luxury. Universities should also be conceived as a place where knowledge production is for knowledge sake. For instance, we need to conceive PhD programmes as the training of the next generation of African and Indian scholars who will become creative and critical thinkers. With this objective in mind, I think Indian and African institutions might have some common interests in the field of social-science research.

Therefore, the question that this paper tries to answer is whether India and Africa have convergent interests in the area of social science research, and if so, what are they and what platforms and mechanisms can be envisaged to not only make the cooperation possible but also fruitful. After analysing the structuring of the social sciences in both India and Africa, the paper will benchmark the status of social sciences in each of these areas of the globe and propose ways forward through a fruitful cooperation among countries in the South. The paper proposes ways by which the barriers that have contributed to the fragmentation of the social sciences in the South and to the persistence of an epistemology, whose dominant paradigms are not fully reflective of the realities of these parts of the world, could be overcome.

India is important because it is part of the emerging countries whose economy has recorded performances never seen before, presenting a sustainable growth rate that could put the country among the top ten large economies of the world in the next ten years. The vitality of Indian society is not limited to economic field; it also offers a good example where science and technology is contributing to the advancement of society and meeting the vital needs of its inhabitants. Also, the social-science research contributes to public policy, providing rational explanations and offering solutions to problems afflicting society. Hence, keeping abreast of matters in social-science research is important in India.

Indian researchers and research centres have worked on many of the current challenges confronting African societies. Many of these issues are common to both, Africa and India. Issues that are in the research agenda of African researchers and research centres – HIV/AIDS pandemic, climate change, transformative social policy, pervasive marketisation of higher education, corruption and political succession and political and economic integration of the African continent — can find inspiration in the ways Indian researchers have dealt in their own context. The search for ways of responding to and rolling back neoliberalism seems indeed to be one of the most important issue African social-science research faces in the twenty-first century. Related to that question is the issue pertaining to who sets the research agenda and the issue of autonomy that are central in African context.

1.2 CODESRIA's Experience in Nurturing South-South Cooperation

The Council for the Development of Social Science Research in Africa (CODESRIA) has been instrumental in implementing a very dynamic academic South-South cooperation, contributing to the advancement of social science in the South in general and in Africa in particular. The council retains its role in serving as a bridge not only across the barriers that militate against networking in Africa but also between Africa and the rest of the world; a role which it has played credibly since its inception and in which it has accumulated a great deal of experience. In an age where much pressure is exerted towards forging a new global partnership, CODESRIA's experience would be invaluable in paving the way for the African social research community both through its own initiatives and by playing a facilitation role for others.

This contribution has benefitted through cooperation with institutions in the South by promoting social-science research across multiple programmes - South-South exchange programme for research on history of development (SEPHIS), the Latin American Council of the Social Sciences (CLACSO) and the Asian Political and International Studies Association (APISA). SEPHIS was established in 1994 to encourage researchers located in the South to establish links with their colleagues in other parts of the South. Under the general theme of 'Historicizing modernity and development', SEPHIS has focused its activities on two sub-themes which run through histories of national and local development: identity and equity. One criticism of the programme is its funding from Netherlands' Ministry of Development Cooperation though it has received funds from other organisations too. The critics feared that such a dependence on Netherland could undermine the sustainability of research programmes. Strangely, as we are analysing this kind of cooperation the existence of SEPHIS seems to be threatened because the Netherlands' authorities have decided to withdraw the funds. If we were asked to propose a programme for South-South cooperation, our choice would be to reproduce a programme like SEPHI. The paper will revert to the issues of the thematic areas that are of interest for a hypothetical cooperation between India and Africa in terms of research projects and exchange of researchers and academy.

For a start, it suffices to say that the two themes - identity and equity — seem to be very pertinent and timely. In the framework of SEPHIS programme, identity focuses on colonial and post-colonial construction of 'national' and 'community' identities, cultures and histories and asks questions about the differential access of various groups to citizenship, human rights and possibilities for political and cultural expression. The second theme, equity, focuses on the historical dimensions of economic marginalisation related to class, community, gender and religion, as well as differential access to the fruits of development. These issues are discussed in detail later.

In a joint venture with other sister organisations in the South, CODESRIA contributed to the capacity building of young scholars within the framework of the CODESRIA-SEPHIS Extended Workshop. The workshop was organised around the comparative experiences of Africa, Asia, the Caribbean and Latin America. It brought together twelve young social researchers in the field of history for three weeks of joint reflection, knowledge building and training. The researchers shared their experiences, attempted to improve theoretical and methodological quality of their work, and deepen their comparative insights. The participants were offered practical support in sharpening their skills on how to write an article, plan a research project, and submit a research proposal for funding. The discussions tried to link the research interests of the participants with the progress of their work.

The last workshop of this kind took place in Dakar from 2 to 12 November 2010, where some scholars from India were present.[15] More importantly in this context, two of the resource persons, including the director of the workshop, came from India.[16]

In collaboration with the Asian Political and International Studies Association (APISA) and the Latin American Council of Social Sciences (CLACSO), CODESRIA organised an annual South-South Summer

Institute, which is primarily designed to offer advanced research training opportunity to younger scholars on the diverse problems and challenges facing the countries of the South, and the theoretical and methodological perspectives that might be appropriate for gaining a full understanding of the specific situation of the countries and peoples located outside the core of the international system as it is presently structured. The main premise of this effort is the inadequacy of the theories and methodologies developed in the North, crystallised in the mainstream social sciences, to provide the required instruments for the attainment of a sound understanding of the problems confronting the countries of the South. In doing so, it hopes to promote a revival and expansion of comparative thinking and cross-regional networking among a younger generation of Southern scholars. The different sessions of the institute are rotated among the three continents where the lead collaborating institutions are located. This helps the participants in the institute, who are also drawn from all the three continents, get exposed to the socio-historical contexts of other regions of the South; as an input it helps to broaden their analytical perspectives and improve the overall quality of their scientific engagements.

CODESRIA's Programme for Training, Grants and Fellowship is well-suited for building capacity and strengthening institutions. It is multidisciplinary in orientation and tallies well with the council's overall commitments, including its pan-African orientation and its emphasis on gender, generation, region, and linguistics diversity. The focus on 'social issues' of continental relevance is responding well to the needs of the African research community. The programme is complementary and supportive of the training that takes place within the institutions of higher education. Decentralisation is an important feature involving universities throughout the African continent, promoting an African expertise.

This process of programmatic expansion was intercepted by an onset of the crises in African higher education system that required CODESRIA to invest in more basic tasks that would contribute to the reproduction of the social-science research community. The serious constraints African universities faced have turned into a full-blown crises and still grappling to resolve it. The necessity for the adaptation of the CODESRIA programmatic strategy to the requirements of the time was further underscored by the fact that the 1980s marked the beginning of the coming of age of the second and third generations of

African social scientists, generations that knew varying degrees of difficulty in exercising and/or even developing their scholarship on account of increasing difficulties in the environment of knowledge.

Many of the interventions of the council in the African intellectual milieu between the 1970s and 1990s were driven and shaped by a desire to contribute to strengthening of the African higher education system, especially the universities and centres of advanced research.

2. Why does Cooperation between Indian and African Research Institutions Matter?

India-Africa scientific cooperation is more concentrated in fields of medical and natural sciences. The experience reveals how far this cooperation can go and what Africa can gain by establishing and nurturing this kind of cooperation. Keerti Pradhan, a health management specialist, went to Africa for the first time in 2000. Since then, he has become passionate about applying India's success in the eye-care sector to Africa. He has been helping Africans improve their vision through low-cost Indian technology. And with Indian private companies now flocking to Africa, Pradhan hopes one of them will adopt his pet project as a community initiative and spread it to the rest of the continent. 'Among all its health programmes, India has done very well in the national programme for controlling blindness,' Pradhan says. A key indicator, the cataract surgery rate, which is the number of cataract operations done per million population each year, has increased from 1,500 to 4,500 within ten years in India. In contrast, sub-Saharan Africa has an average cataract surgery rate of 700. 'I realised that healthcare was dominated by the Western model, where the donor agencies pump in a huge amount of money.... It was like giving a person biryani when they can only eat dal and rice' (Pradhan, as told to IANS). The Western model of eye care is unsuitable, he realised, for African conditions, which has minimal infrastructure and human resources. The technology and method of delivering healthcare in India is much lower to the Western model. 'In the Western model, for each operation, the entire set-up, starting with the table, is changed. In the Indian model, only the clothes are changed,' explained Pradhan. The difference in the cost of each cataract operation is therefore sharp – \$15 for the Indian method, compared to \$75 for the Western model.[17]

Coming back to the field of social sciences, it must be stressed that both India and Africa are part of the South, a world region that is confronted with Western paradigms that is designed to dominate other regions. Both regions remain, to various degrees, at the periphery of the North American and European circles of social-science production. Therefore, both Africa and India have interest in challenging the philosophical foundations of an epistemology that intends to be universal and an epistemological order that tends to be hegemonic. In both regions, scholars are asked and required to critically engage and interrogate the existing theories and corpus of Eurocentric and European social sciences and re-link them critically with the corpus of knowledge produced by our peoples and societies. Alvares states, 'Even where academic work in Asia and Africa may nowadays reflect local issues due to efforts of individual researchers who wish to do meaningful, independent work, the methodologies applied and theoretical frameworks still remain firmly Euro-American in character.'[18]

2.1 Areas of Cooperation

CODESRIA is still the only genuinely Pan-African social-science research institution, one which remains dedicated to the goal of consciously transcending all barriers to research and combating the fragmentation of knowledge production whilst drawing participation in its programmes from Central, Eastern, North, Southern, and Western Africa, as well as the diaspora. The access that flows from this status places CODESRIA in a good position to broker sustained policy dialogues bringing researchers and policymakers together on issues of concern to the South-South in general and the African continent in particular.

CODESRIA is looked upon by many not solely as the lead voice for African social researchers, but as a 'model' the example of which could be emulated by others. This advantage is one which is critical in a period of uncertainty and flux which Africa is currently experiencing. All these things, in turn, position the council to offer leadership in academic matters as well as in questions related to institution-building. CODESRIA continues to enjoy the advantage of being an institution that can afford to be at the cutting edge of innovative responses to the crises of higher education and advanced research in Africa.

CODESRIA came to assume an early role as a site for experimentation in the knowledge production process for which the university system was not adapted. In the context of the changes taking place globally and regionally which call for innovative thinking, CODESRIA has a possibility to maintain and enhance its role as a credible site of experimentation. The council retains its pioneering work in serving as a bridge not only across the barriers that militate against networking in Africa but also between Africa and the rest of the world; a role which it has played credibly since its founding and in which it has accumulated a great deal of experience. In an age where greater pressures are mounting for the forging of a new global partnership, CODESRIA's experience would be invaluable in paving the way for the African social-science research community both through its own initiatives and by playing a facilitation role for others. The council also has the distinct advantage of having in its networks, a diverse collection of scholars drawn from different disciplines and also reflecting the four generations of African social scientists. The council is also the only research organisation with a continental reach and an active presence in forty-two countries spanning Anglophone, Francophone, Lusophone and Arabophone Africa.

1. Taking into account all that has been stated above, the following areas of cooperation in capacity building can be identified: adoption of ICT as key tools in the production and dissemination of knowledge;
2. Since CODICE, the CODESRIA documentation centre, is working with the view of creating a virtual library, emphasis should be placed on a human highly-specialised working team made of a librarian, a web master and people in charge of digitalisation;[19]
3. Capacity building for research programming/ planning and administration;
4. Regional networking in the area of joint or cooperative research;
5. Inauguration of a programme for the study of China, India and Russia in the context of the emergence of new international geo-political and developmental architecture;
6. Reinforcement of CODESRIA's South-South Programmatic Partnerships through an extension to India of the relations of scientific collaboration which are already in place with CLACSO and APISA and the building of new ones;

7. Call for continued innovations in the mode of programme delivery that would allow for a carefully managed expansion;
8. PhD programmes on issues that are of Indian and African interest;
9. Programme on exchange of researchers.

2.2 Themes that might be of Interest for both India and Africa

As it has been stated above, on account of several common problems facing the two societies, African and Indian social scientists have also some themes on which they could collaborate and work together. Some of these themes include:

(*a*) Poverty
(*b*) Equity/Social Inequalities
(*c*) Population growth and management of cities
(*d*) Health and healthcare
(*e*) Citizenship and political participation
(*f*) Theoretical framework within which the university is taught both in Africa and India.

References

1. World Social Science Report, 2010, UNESCO/ISSC, Paris.
2. Kane, O. Intellectuels non-europhones, Document de travail No. 1, 2003, CODESRIA, Dakar.
3. Mudimbe, V. *The Invention of Africa. Gnosis Philosophy and the Order of Knowledge*, Bloomington and Indianapolis, Indiana University Press, 1988.
4. Appiah, K.A., *In My Father's House: Africa in the Philosophy of Culture*. London: Methuen, 1992; New York: Oxford University Press.
5. Mudimbe, V., *op cit*.
6 Appiah, K.A., *op cit*, p. 68.
7. *Ibid*.
8. Kane, O., *op cit*.
9. *Ibid*, p. 12.
10. *Ibid*, p. 9.
11. Chegraoui, K. (2005), Idéologie, religion et ethnocentrisme au Maghreb, in *Intellectuels, nationalisme et l'idéal panafricain. Perspective historique*, Sous la direction de Thierno Bah, CODESRIA, Dakar.
12. Copans, J. (1993), "Intellectuels visible, intellectuels invisibles", *Politique africaine*, 51, octobre, pp. 7-25.

13. Laidi, Zaki (dir.) (1998), Géopolitique du sens, Paris, Desclée de Bowwer.
14. World Social Science Report, 2010, UNESCO/ISSC, Paris.
15. Balram Uprety, Department of English, St. Joseph's College, Darjeeling - North Point, *Construction of Gender and Sexuality in Nepali Folklore*; V. Kalyan Shankar, Department of Economics, University of Pune, Pune, *The History of a Geography. Evolution of Red Light Areas as Urban Spaces in India.*
16. Rohini Sahni, Department of Economics, University of Pune, Pune; and Charu Gupta, Department of History, University of Delhi, Delhi.
17. South-South Opportunity, http://www.southsouth.info/profiles/blogs/better-vision-for-africa-with
18. Alvares, C. '*A critique of Eurocentric Social Science and the Question of Alternatives*', paper presented at the International Conference on 'Academic Imperialism in Higher Education and Islamic and Non-Western Countries' organised by the Centre for International Scientific Studies and Collaboration (CISSC) and Iranian Higher Education Association, Tehran, 2010, pp. 1-2.
19. CODICE is designed to keep African scholars abreast of new ideas. It maintains a rich documentary collection of social-science information and research findings. This comprises books and periodicals as well as numerous reference works, reports, conference papers, press dossiers, thesis and dissertations. CODICE manages and updates the following databases: Bibliographic databases; the Database of CODESRIA publications, the database of African Social Scientists and the Database of Periodicals.

SECTION 1

ISSUES OF INDIAN DIASPORA

3

Diplomacy of the Diaspora: Harnessing Diasporas in Kenya's Foreign Policy

Makumi Mwagiru

Introduction

One of the most rapidly growing aspects of diplomacy and foreign policy in Kenya is the diplomacy of the diaspora. This diplomacy factors the country's diaspora in foreign policy decision making, and in the implementation of the country's diplomatic strategy. The entry of the diaspora into Kenya's foreign policy is based largely on its size and economic strengths, but also on the potential contributions it can make in Kenya's electoral politics and outcomes. In the latter case, presidential aspirants in the 2012 elections have gone out to woo the diaspora which is estimated to constitute a third of the eight million unregistered voters in Kenya, and a voting bloc of 15 per cent of the total registered voters in 2012.[1]

The new-found interest in Kenya's diaspora in its foreign policy earlier based on economic dimensions has thus taken on a political tinge. This politicisation of the diaspora will help to mainstream diaspora diplomacy in Kenya. This paper investigates the problems and prospects for that diplomatic and foreign policy mainstreaming of the diaspora. It argues that while well intentioned, it nevertheless gives room for the development of various conflicts in the country, and should hence be approached with greater care.

The paper also argues that while the mainstreaming of the diaspora in Kenya's foreign policy is long overdue, there is, however, a missing link in Kenya's diplomacy of the diaspora. The missing link is the lack of attention to the diasporas of other countries in Kenya. It is suggested that Kenya's foreign policy would be strengthened by factoring in other countries' diasporas. This would enable Kenya to strengthen its bilateral diplomacy with the countries from where this other diaspora comes. The paper maintains that this foreign diaspora can be used to leverage Kenya's security, economic and other relations, and can through negotiation, harness it in ways that have not been secured before.

Framework for Analysis

An analysis of Kenya's (or any) foreign policy towards diasporas- either Kenyan or foreign – is based on certain understandings of the anatomy of diasporic communities. Members of a diaspora are essentially migrant communities. But their migration does not delink them from the communities that they came from. Ties with those home communities remain, and hence the diasporan community is bilateralised. In the language of diplomacy, it has characteristics of bilateral diplomacy because there is an active link between the receiving community (even state) and the sending community or state. The two sides in this bilateral formulation are connected by a 'corridor' – 'a cultural space that transmits people, money and information in both directions ... such corridors can be visualised as extensions of the hometown that embraced men far away, realms of interests and affections that could extend over great distances; they were both connective links and living cultural spaces.'[2] The migrant community creates a *niche* in the receiving community: an occupational speciality or social role in which to survive or prosper. As Kuhn observes:

> Where a 'niche' is a liveable space for a particular migrant group in a new environment, 'corridor' is an extension of the migrant's old environment. It is a skein of connections that keeps the migrant embedded, in significant ways, in his old village, lineage, or region. We can distinguish it from a 'myth of return' or a longing to go home again, because, in certain respects, the migrant has never left home. He has preserved various models of belonging (economic, cultural, kinship) so that he can remain oriented firmly toward his

> society of origin, even while sustaining himself in the society where he is physically living. Maintaining corridors is the essence of sojourning. The migrant has not committed himself mentally or behaviourally to a permanent break with the old country, its culture or its people.[3]

This is the background against which the diplomacy of the diaspora revolves, or should revolve. Recognising the roles that diasporas can play in a country's foreign policy essentially means adopting a policy of recognition of the diaspora. If foreign policy based on the recognition of the diaspora is enshrined, it leads to the diaspora responding with loyalty. The consequences of loyalty include investment in the country to help it meet its economic, political and other interests. These aspects have been observed, for example, in the interactions between China and overseas Chinese communities.[4] However, while the government's policy towards the diaspora should be innovative, it must also be flexible. It needs especially to avoid generating conflicts between the diaspora and the local communities in the country. Such conflicts arise where the diaspora is treated in policy as a distinct group, and is given preferential treatment. While this is often understandable, it runs the concurrent danger of actually marginalising the diasporic group through differential treatment, for example through offering tax breaks as an incentive to invest.

States need to engage a wider level of the diaspora beyond just their own. Currently, Kenya's foreign policy defines the diasporic frontier very narrowly by identifying it only as the Kenyan diaspora. If, however, other national interests of Kenya were taken into account, then the definition of the diaspora must be enlarged. One of the key national interests for Kenya is regional security especially the security of the Horn of Africa region. This aspect of national security is closely tied to the Somalian diaspora in the country, and their interactions with the Kenyan Somalia community and other Kenyans. It is evident that the Somalian diaspora in Kenya can be nurtured in ways that can contribute to Kenya's security nationally and regionally. But this cannot happen if the definition of the diaspora that undergirds Kenya's foreign policy is unduly restrictive, and recognises only Kenyan diasporic communities. To be completely functional as a foreign policy that harnesses the diaspora, it must engage not just Kenya's diasporic community, but the community of other countries' diasporas that also create corridors between their home communities and Kenya.

Diaspora Communities in Kenya

Kenya is home to the diaspora communities of various countries. These diaspora communities can be divided into those of non-African origin, and those of African origin. The diasporas of non-African origin in Kenya are the Europeans, specifically British, Indians and Arabs. The emergence of these diasporas is historical. The British diaspora emerged with the establishment of colonialism dating back to the turn of the 19th century. Many of them arrived in the country as part of the demobilisation process after the First World War; these were later joined by those demobilised after the Second World War. They were seen from where they came from as frontiersmen. They obtained large tracts of land at concessionary rates to enable them to settle in the country.[5] They settled in the Rift Valley,[6] and in parts of central Kenya, whose climate was conducive. During the colonial period, they were famous for their social exploits in the so-called 'happy valley' which has entered into historical and fictional notoriety.[7] In the post-independence period in Kenya, a few of them left for South Africa and other colonies, but a substantial number remained and formed the core of the British diaspora in Kenya. They remained partly as a result of the assurances of Kenya's first president Jomo Kenyatta, that the new (black) government would respect their property rights, and would forgive, though not forget the colonial excesses and experiences. Their relationship with black Kenyans has been mixed, but nevertheless they have become part of Kenya's social, cultural, economic and political fabric.

The Indian diaspora emerged during the colonial period, as the colonial power searched for labour in building the East African railway. These early labourers were employed on contractual terms. At the end of their contracts, some remained, and formed the core of the Indian diaspora that has since become entrenched in Kenya's political, economic and social life.[8] They were active in trade and trade unionism, while some entered professions such as law and medicine, teaching, and the civil service.

There is also a substantial Arab diaspora in Kenya, which again has historical roots beginning even before the colonial period. This diaspora has thrived in Kenya, and become part of the social, cultural, economic and political life in Kenya. The entrenchment of this diaspora is highlighted during election periods in Kenya. During these times, some electoral participants are often accused of being 'foreigners' from Dubai, the Emirates and so on.

Some of the other diaspòras in Kenya emerged after Independence, as a result of political problems and schisms in other countries. Among this group are members of the Ugandan, Rwandese, Sudanese and Ethiopian diasporas in Kenya. Those from Uganda emerged as a result of the despotic rule of Idi Amin. These Ugandan refugees settled in Kenya during the 1970s and 1980s. They contributed much to Kenya especially in the education sector, since many of them were well educated, and took up jobs at the public universities, and secondary schools. Their contribution in this sector was notable, and there is at least some anecdotal evidence that on their mass return to Uganda, they left the Kenyan secondary school sector experiencing gaps especially in subjects such as mathematics and English. However, not all of them returned to Uganda. A similar case exists for the Rwandese, a substantial number of whom took up residence in Kenya. Like the Ugandans, these were engaged in the education sector as teachers, and a large number of them also engaged in business. Again a good number of them remained after the normalisation of life in Rwanda, and formed the core of the Rwandan diaspora in Kenya.

The Sudanese diaspora in Kenya was created by the long-running conflict in Sudan. That conflict in Sudan divided the country into two opposing groups of the south and the north. In this conflict, the South Sudanese found succour in neighbouring states, of which Kenya became perhaps the largest host of Southern Sudanese. Although some came into the country as refugees, a large number were allowed to settle in Kenya. Apart from this, Kenya offered opportunities to them in education and jobs. Although quite a number of South Sudanese have gone back to South Sudan after its independence, a substantial number still remain who have settled in the country, and form the core of the Sudanese diaspora in Kenya.

The Ethiopian diaspora in Kenya is also a result of the conflicts experienced in Ethiopia over a long period. Ever since independence, there has always been an Ethiopian diaspora in Kenya, many of whom are engaged in business. Because of the shared borders and communities between the two countries, there is also a large number of Ethiopians who cross the border areas into Kenya, where they have kith and kin. But with that Ethiopian diaspora, as with the Sudanese and Somalis who are neighbours of Kenya, the relationships in the border areas have often been characterised more by conflict than cooperation.

Of the other African diasporas in Kenya, the Somalis form a large part of the diaspora population in Kenya. The Somalia diaspora's relationship with Kenya is however more complicated than with the other diasporas. Somalis in Somalia have been dispersed to all the neighbouring countries of Somalia, like Kenya, Ethiopia, and Djibouti. Part of Somalia's foreign policy has articulated the dream of consolidating these dispersed populations into one united Somalia, causing many foreign policy problems for the countries neighbouring Somalia. On the other hand, there is a substantial Somali population who are Kenyans. Thus, the Somalis in Somalia are part of their kith and kin: and for them territorial borders do not exist. While there is a large number of Somalia diaspora in Kenya, it is difficult to know which of them are Kenyans legally and which belong to the diaspora. Members of a diaspora have three distinct memberships and different links.[9] That Somalia diaspora has ethnic relations with Somalis in Kenya; national links with Somalis in Somalia, and civic links with both Somalis in Kenya and Somalia. This reality has created a very compiex relationship between Kenya and the Somalia diaspora. This was most graphically illustrated during the Somalia National Reconciliation process that took place in Kenya in 2002-05. In that process the venue for the negotiations was chosen at Eldoret to make sure that only genuinely Somalia Somalis participated. But the venue was later changed to Mbagathi in Nairobi. The negotiators at Eldoret were moved to Nairobi by road. While they were *en route* from Eldoret to Mbagathi, a large number of Somalis residing in Nairobi at Eastleigh, moved into and occupied the venue at Mbagathi. By the time those *en route* from Eldoret arrived, the venue was occupied by these diverse Somalis: some of whom were Kenyans, and the rest were members of the Somalia diaspora in Kenya. This derailed the whole reconciliation process,[10] which eventually failed.

Kenya's Diaspora Abroad

Kenya is thus a host of various diasporas. However, Kenya also has a substantial diaspora in other parts of the world. In particular, Kenya has a substantial diaspora in other African countries, the Middle East, the United Kingdom, the United States, Canada, Australia, and South Africa. These Kenyan diasporas are not historical in the same sense as other diasporas in Kenya are. It has been argued that the most important reason for this shift in migration patterns is the deterioration of the Kenyan economic performance. While the first two decades witnessed high economic and employment growth with new opportunities opening up for Kenyans in all sectors, the situation has been reversed over the past 25 years, especially in the 1990s.[11]

For the most part, Kenya's diaspora abroad is made up of those who originally left in search of education, but decided to settle in those countries after completing their education. This is particularly true of the Kenyan diaspora in the United States of America. Other members of the Kenyan diaspora in the USA emerged through the 'green card' process, and their children were born in the USA. In Canada and Australia, the diaspora arose from the fairly liberal immigration policies in those countries that enabled foreigners to settle and invest there. There are now four generations of Kenyan diasporas in Europe and USA: the first generation left in the 1960s on education scholarships and decided to stay; and the second generation left in the 1980s for investment opportunities in Europe and USA, which were opened up significantly. A third generation, the children of the second generation is also a significant number, although their ties to Kenya are increasingly diminishing. However, since the new constitution of Kenya (2010) allows dual citizenship, these will also have closer legal links to Kenya than they would have under the single citizenship system. The fourth generation, which is in the making, constitutes those who are currently finding their way to the USA for education purposes, and those who keep leaving under the green card framework.

Apart from this European and American based diaspora of Kenya, there is also a Kenyan diaspora in Africa. A large part of this diaspora is to be found in South Africa and South Sudan. The Kenyan South Africa-based diaspora left Kenya after the end of the apartheid system. They left Kenya in search of business and investment opportunities; but also a good number left in search of educational opportunities in the south. Some in this latter group finished their education but decided to settle in South Africa, where the feeling was that the grass was greener. Other groups of Kenyan settled in other South African regions like Botswana and Swaziland, where they were employed mostly in the professional sector as doctors, nurses, university lecturers, engineers and the like. Hence Kenya's diaspora in the Southern African region while not overwhelming, is substantial enough. In Southern Sudan, there has been an exodus of Kenyans especially in the five years since the South Sudan became semi-autonomous, and has increased since its independence. Kenyans have moved into South Sudan to take advantage of the many opportunities to do business and to invest in the new republic. Others have gone there to provide professional services, especially as teachers, and in the non-governmental sector. The number of Kenyans in South Sudan is substantial, and stands at more than half a million.

The Kenyan diaspora abroad has made many inroads in Kenya's development in many sectors. Its largest contribution is the remittances it sends back home. These remittances are estimated to be between shs. 54.5 billion to shs. 220 billion in 2010 alone. There is a controversy about the figures. But these controversies are not about the fact that there are hefty remittances from Kenya's diaspora, but about the computation of these remittances. The Central Bank of Kenya estimated the remittances to be shs. 54.5 billion in 2010; the World Bank estimates this to be shs.150 billion per year; the Kenyan diaspora organisation abroad estimates the figure as 220 billion. The central bank figures are lower than the rest because it only captures remittances through banks. The World Bank and diaspora figures include informal remittances such as a Kenyan visitor abroad being sent to deliver some money to family members back home. Whichever of the figures is used, there is clearly a large contribution by the Kenyan diaspora to the economy. These remittances are used in various sectors, but most of it goes to real estate investment: construction of houses, purchase of land and business. What is even more significant in these figures is that the incomes of the Kenyan diaspora abroad surpass those from tourism and agriculture, which are Kenya's highest foreign currency earners.[12]

The Kenyan diaspora abroad is engaged in many activities. Some are academics, teaching and researching in universities abroad. A large number are employed in business and other organisations. An equally large number of them are gainfully employed in small organisations where they perform general tasks and duties; and many of these hold more than one job at the same time. And a large number are engaged in business activities in these countries. As an observer noted, in Canada and the USA, the Kenyan diaspora occupies 'almost every profession and jobs as engineers, businesspeople, professors, doctors, nurses, technicians, factory workers, baby-sitters and watchmen.'[13] Thus, from the perspective of the countries where these diaspora members are resident, they are not people living on the taxpayers' money, and hence not being a burden.

Foreign Policy of the Diaspora

Partly because of the significant amounts of remittances that the Kenyan diaspora remits to the country each year, the government recognised the potential of the Kenyan diaspora abroad. But the government has also recognised that the Kenyan diaspora can be influential actors, playing crucial roles in Kenyan life. In the last electoral period in Kenya, the Kenyan diaspora was engaged politically in the elections. They funded political parties, and organised for contending politicians to address them on the electoral platforms of their parties. They also participated actively in the debates on the new constitution; they indeed lobbied for the inclusion in the new constitution of a provision on dual nationality, which is now part of the constitution, much to their benefit.

In particular, the ministry of foreign affairs has factored the diaspora in Kenya's foreign policy. In both its statement of Kenya's foreign policy and in its strategic plan, the ministry of foreign affairs recognises that Kenya has a diverse and large diaspora abroad, which amongst other things offers opportunities for the better marketing of Kenya abroad, and contributes substantially through its remittances to the country. From these perspectives, the ministry is engaged in strategies to create a framework for the engagement of this diaspora in the articulation of Kenya's foreign policy, and in domestic political activities like voting and in the larger political processes. For Kenya therefore, there has been a movement from general dissociation with its diaspora, to active association. But this current active association has not emerged from negotiations between the diaspora and the government. It has been largely resulted from unilateral concessions on the part of the government, fuelled by the realisation of the economic potential of the Kenyan diaspora.

This strategic trend in formalising relationships between Kenya's foreign policy and the diaspora, was concretised in the creation of a department for diaspora affairs in the ministry of foreign affairs in 2008. The argument has *even* been canvassed that since diaspora incomes exceed those of the ministries of agriculture and tourism, which are major foreign income earners for Kenya, and which have their own government ministries, there should also be a ministry for diaspora affairs in the country. The recognition of the role that the Kenyan diaspora can play in Kenya's foreign policy and other sectors is an important and fresh component of Kenya's foreign policy.

Potential Conflicts in Kenya's Diaspora Diplomacy

In articulating that policy, a *caveat* about likely conflicts that it is likely to generate in the country should be borne in mind. In African countries there have always been conflicts arising between those who stayed and those who left, only to return when things were better and the fights against tyranny had been won. This was the kind of conflict that happened in Uganda, after the ouster of Idi Amin[14] and is happening in post-independence South Sudan.[15] There were those who had chosen (or had no option) to stay at home, and keep the country - especially the civil service - running. And there were those who went into exile, only to return later, and demand jobs and recognition in the new dispensations. This is a difficult conflict to manage because both sides contributed to the emergence of the new dispensation, albeit in different ways. But this kind of conflict can lead to slowing down the pace of reconciliation and the creation of conducive environments for all citizens to contribute in the new dispensation.

This sort of conflict could arise from Kenya's handling of the resource of the diaspora. There is a risk that the diaspora could be treated inequitably in the country, by either disregarding them, or by giving them larger opportunities than Kenyans at home are offered. At some stage in Kenya, the realisation of the role and contribution of the diaspora led to people in the diaspora being offered many jobs, including in diplomatic missions and the public service, seemingly at the expense of Kenyans who had remained in Kenya: or who having gone outside for education, returned to Kenya to build the nation through the hard times including through dictatorial regimes. Those who stayed make the case that they should have first option in government appointments. Those who left argue that they had no choice but to leave, and that in any case they also made contributions to the country while abroad. If this kind of conflict is not managed well, it can lead to the souring of relationships between the diaspora and Kenyans in Kenya. This souring of relationships can lead to perceptions about each other that are not healthy for creating strategies and systems in which both can feel appreciated and fulfilled.

Kenya's foreign policy on the diaspora seems to operate only on the basis that the diaspora must remain abroad. This is conditioned by the core belief that the benefits of that diaspora to Kenya lies mainly with its capacity to send remittances back home. As long as this is the operational framework, the conflicts and negative perceptions will remain. Kenya's vision of the diaspora needs to be enlarged in this perspective by taking into account a returned diaspora. The concept of a returning diaspora ought to be encouraged more, because a returned diaspora would have much to offer the country in various aspects. The returned diaspora captures many different Kenyans and captures different elements of Kenyan *haigui* (in China this means those who went abroad for various reasons and return having stayed abroad for different periods of time): those studying abroad and returning after their education; those scholars who return home after conducting research abroad; those who went to study abroad but decided to stay on and even obtained permanent residence abroad; those who went abroad as students but stayed on and became citizens in countries abroad; and those who migrated abroad in other circumstances like skilled workers, business people and who subsequently obtained permanent residence or citizenship abroad.[16] Enlarging the Kenyan diasporic community in this way would help to reduce tensions and conflicts, and condition responses to policies targeting them.

Diaspora and National Interest in Kenya

The real issue that arises is how the diaspora can be used to promote the interests of the country, without at the same time raising these kinds of conflicts. These conflicts arise because the foreign policy administration of the diaspora is centred on the wrong basis. Currently, the perception of the Kenyan diaspora is coloured largely by the financial contributions of the diaspora to Kenya. This economic and financial-based perception can lead to reifying the diaspora on a very narrow base. It bears restating that although the total amount of remittances are significant, these cannot, for example, be compared to the earnings of the tourist industry or agriculture. In the latter cases, there is a clear amount of money that enters the coffers of the government and which can be quantified and budgeted as such. In the diaspora earnings, the money involved is dispersed among individuals-normally family members; and sometimes it goes into activities such as construction of family homes, purchase of flats and the like. This is of course significant for the economy as it is, and cannot be avoided. But the basis of policy should take this into account.

The argument that the remittances of Kenya's diaspora are far greater than those from tourism and agriculture combined should be taken with a pinch of salt because it is based on a wrong conceptual basis. While it may be true that the actual *gross incomes* of Kenya's diaspora are greater than the earnings from tourism and agriculture, the real issue should be about the percentage of that income that is remitted to the country. And it is unlikely that on this basis the case can be made that diaspora remittances exceed those from tourism and agriculture. The other pertinent issue is that while the amount of Kenya's diaspora remittances is substantial, those remittances go to the individual accounts of members of the diaspora and their families. This is not money that the government has any access to, and which it can use to leverage its interests internationally or regionally. Hence these remittances clearly touch the shores of Kenya, but they do not touch or promote its wider national interests.

Although the argument about diaspora earnings being larger than the combined earnings from tourism and agriculture is thus a *non sequitur*, the question arises about what a useful alternative could be. A useful alternative would be if these remittances could exist in a form – when they arrive in Kenya – that the country could use to leverage some of its core national interests. This can only happen if those remittances passed through an account that can allow Kenya to leverage them. For example, if the remittances were coming into pension or retirement funds, it would kill two birds with one stone. It would be to the benefit of the members of the diaspora to save in this format. But it would also benefit the country because, as such, those funds and their management would enable Kenya to negotiate internationally with those from whom it borrows money, and who impose stringent conditions for repayment. But unlike the Indian diaspora which has directed its remittances in this way, Kenya's diaspora has been reluctant to remit in nationally useful ways. This offends a basic principle of the relationship between diasporas and their home country: that they must have a commitment to building the country.

It is true that many analysis of the diaspora take only the economic/financial aspects into account. But, 'equally important are the social remittances, namely the flow of ideas, technologies, theories, beliefs, world views, and new ways of doing things.'[17] While this is true, it can create the risk of policy making based on the diaspora alone on the assumption that they being 'from abroad' have better knowledge to offer, and that they are better at whatever enterprise they engage in. This trend of thinking is common especially with the older generation who perhaps because of colonial experiences reify the white man – and other foreigners. They believe, like Mr Green in Chinua Achebe's *No Longer at Ease*, that the African has structural problems, and is corrupt through and through, and that he has been sapped mentally and physically by the climate and tropical diseases. It is this mental makeup that has led to some policies in Kenya that have increased conflicts between the Kenyan diaspora and Kenyans living in Kenya. For example, a few years ago in the last tenure of Daniel arap Moi, 'the dream team' consisting of a group of Kenyan diasporics was appointed to run ministries as permanent secretaries. Some of these were from the Kenyan diaspora, working in international organisations abroad like the IMF and others. They were hired, over the head of Kenyans in Kenya, and paid grossly inflated salaries, often five times as much as their Kenyan counterparts. Eventually, that dream died because they did not deliver. There were other instances where diaspora Kenyans were appointed to diplomatic posts even though they were not trained for them. Again they were hired over the head of Kenyans who had spent long years in the diplomatic service, but who were now required to work under these diasporans.

The point is that engaging the diaspora does not necessarily require that they be absorbed in the formal sector, particularly the civil service. Those who can contribute to the civil service could be allowed to apply for the jobs on offer, rather than be headhunted. Such headhunting creates grounds for the generation of perceptual and other conflicts, and is not the best way forward. Headhunting also gives an unfair advantage in that those head-hunted are able to negotiate salaries that go beyond the normal range of remuneration for technocrats doing the same jobs. Headhunting also means engaging in a one-sided dialogue with an interlocutor that is not interested in negotiating. In this framework, concessions are made – at the expense of generating local conflicts between the diaspora and Kenyans living in Kenya; and it also entrenches the negative perceptions about the diaspora. What makes this unilateral dialogue even more unsatisfactory is that as soon as the jobs for which they were headhunted end, the concerned individuals wash their hands of the country and return to the diaspora. This has two repercussions. It means that those members of the diaspora who were headhunted, and took the jobs for a while, are no better than expatriates in their own country. It also offends the principle that one cannot be both at home and remain a member of the diaspora. In other words, one cannot have one's cake and eat it too, since both are mutually exclusive.

The Missing Link in Kenya's Diplomacy of the Diaspora

There has nonetheless been an important shift in Kenya's foreign policy, where recognition of the status and role of Kenya's diaspora has been one of its important developments. This realisation has also shaped in some way the management of Kenya's diplomacy, which will never again be the same on this aspect of diaspora relations. This realisation that the Kenyan diaspora can be harnessed in promoting Kenya's foreign policy and even in articulating it was a new breath in Kenya's foreign policy. However, because this realisation is recent, strategies of affecting it are still being developed, and it is understandable that mistakes will be made. It is also understandable that because of its recent origin, some policies which can be dysfunctional for other relationships in the country may be tried only to be later revised. In particular, the issue of the perception between the Kenyan diaspora and Kenyans in Kenya will have to be marshalled carefully; otherwise the whole emerging diplomacy of the diaspora in Kenya may founder.

There is, however, a missing link in this diplomacy of the diaspora in Kenya. Kenya's diplomacy so far has identified only one side of the coin of the diplomacy of the diaspora. That side of the coin is inward looking in the sense that it has begun to engage Kenya's own diaspora in the articulation of foreign policy and its implementation. The other side of the coin of this diasporic diplomacy is equally important. This side of the coin relates to how Kenya's foreign policy and diplomacy can engage the diasporas of the other countries. The engagement of other countries' diasporas in Kenya's foreign policy and diplomacy has two elements. The first concerns how that diaspora can be harnessed to promote Kenya's foreign policy and diplomacy. The second concerns how that other diaspora can be harnessed to improve general bilateral relationships between Kenya and the other countries. Apart from this dimension of diaspora diplomacy, another is how Kenya's diplomacy can make use of the contributions of others with links with Kenya. These are people who earlier belonged to other countries' diasporas in Kenya, but who have since returned to their countries. As Ghai notes:

> the country can also derive benefits from the contributions of others with links to Kenya. The latter include former long- and short-term residents of Kenya and those with 'blood connections' through their mother or father or other relatives...quite a few former residents even though they never acquired Kenyan nationality, cherish deep sympathies and sentiments for the country and would wish to contribute to national development and the well-being of Kenyans.[18]

These aspects of the diplomacy of the diaspora, especially the first type, have not been factored in. This is clearly a missing link in Kenya's diplomacy of the diaspora.

Kenya has considerable diasporas of other countries living in Kenya. The most prominent of these are the diasporas from the United Kingdom, the Arab world, India, Somalia, Uganda and Rwanda. Amongst these the diaspora communities from the Arab world, the UK, and India would be a good platform for Kenya to launch this other part of the diplomacy of the diaspora. Of the other diasporas – those from Rwanda, Uganda and Somalia – the harnessing occurred because many from these diasporas returned home to hold senior government positions; in that capacity they have been able to bring their understanding of Kenya and Kenyans in formulating their countries' relations with Kenya.

Harnessing the diasporas of other countries in Kenya to promote better relations between the countries is more challenging than harnessing Kenya's own diaspora in promoting its foreign policy and diplomacy. It is challenging because of the perceptions that exist in Kenya about those diasporas and their loyalties, and perceptions of those diasporas about Kenya and its intentions towards their countries. While the level and problem of perceptions of the three diasporas that are the subject of this discussion are different, nevertheless there are serious perceptual bridges that will first have to be crossed.

Perceptual Challenges for Diaspora Diplomacy in Kenya

There are four main perceptions that need to be addressed. The first is the perception of the government towards these other diasporas.

The second is the perception of Kenyans about them; the third are the perceptions of these 'other diaspora communities' about Kenyans; and the fourth is their perceptions about the government, and its intended diplomacy of the diaspora.

The first challenge will only be met by 'selling' the idea of the diplomacy of the diaspora in this sense to the decision makers in Kenya, especially the ministry of foreign affairs. Now that the entry of the diaspora into Kenya's diplomacy has been attained at the policy level, this may not be a very difficult thing to achieve. The second challenge is to sell the idea of this diplomacy to the authorities of those other countries represented by this diaspora. This may be more difficult to do. A lot of these diasporans are Kenyans, and as such the other countries may find it difficult to engage with them, especially when they see them purely as Kenyans. These other countries would also have to take into account likely conflicts between their own citizens and their diasporas. These conflicts are likely to arise because citizens may feel that the diasporic community is receiving more and even better attention. Selling the idea of diplomacy of the diaspora in this context is a difficult, but not insurmountable problem. It involves dealing with perceptions and harmonising them in a way that allows this diplomacy of the diaspora to have an entry into bilateral relationships between the countries. The idea behind this selling diasporic diplomacy in this sense is that if it is not done, policy makers may establish this element of diasporic diplomacy, but later find that they cannot re-enter into their constituents' environment. Because the basis of this challenge is perceptual, it can be addressed through the media (to whom also this idea must be sold first), and through confidence building measures such as seminars and workshops that bring all these different actors together— the governments, members of the relevant diaspora, and Kenyans of different sectors.

The second challenge will be to bring members of these other countries' diasporas into the framework of the formal diplomacy between their countries. This, however, is much easier to do once the perceptual confidence building has been achieved. Bringing the members of these diasporas into the diplomatic framework entails three different perspectives. The first one involves engaging them in the formal frameworks of diplomacy in the context of diplomatic appointments. This is difficult to do and might also raise the same kind of conflicts as those arising between Kenyans in Kenya and

Kenyans in the diaspora. The second perspective involves bringing them into the diplomatic framework in semi-formal contexts. This is much easier to do, because these semi-formal contexts are such that no other Kenyan could be engaged in the same way. These semi-formal frameworks include, for example, making more creative use of the institution of consular diplomacy, especially the institution of honorary consuls. Honorary consuls do not cost the appointing country any finances, or if it does it is minimal. Consuls are appointed because of their personal standing in different enterprises such as business. If both countries agree on this *modus operandi*, it would significantly improve the content and context of diasporic diplomacy between them. The third perspective entails bringing them into the diplomatic frameworks unofficially. This is much easier to do because it does not entail any competition with other citizens. It involves, for example, including members of these other diasporas in official delegations, both forma and *ad hoc*, in engagements where the two countries are involved. These kinds of engagements include, for instance, trade delegations, tourism promotion delegations, educational delegations and the like. In some areas of engagement they could also be included in delegations that are sent out to negotiate certain issues between the two countries, for example, bilateral air services delegations which negotiate routes and traffic rights between the two countries involved.

The third challenge is to bring members of these other diasporas into the non-official framework of the diplomacy between the two respective countries. This is far easier to do than bringing them into the framework of official diplomacy. The non-official aspect of this is important because it realises that much of the diplomacy that is likely to make a difference in the relationships between countries is not official diplomacy alone, but the other type of diplomacy. This component has many elements based on the different sectors in which peoples and countries may engage each other. These elements involve areas like trade and business, religious aspects, sports, education and tourism. Some of these aspects such as trade are already factored into the processes of official diplomacy. But the other aspects are best conceptualised as people-to-people diplomacy, which involves engagements in which citizens are engaged together in different activities. People-to-people diplomacy creates the frame in which relations between two countries can be nested. There already exists a lot of this kind of diplomatic interactions among citizens of different countries. However, these have not always received any kind of official blessings, and hence the impact of their role and existence has not been gauged.

People-to-people diplomacy has different strands, each of which is useful in establishing the contours of diaspora diplomacy. On the one hand it is about the diasporas of the same country in different states in the region beginning to deal with each other on a more structured basis. This surely is important for those countries, and is a benefit that they should help to promote. It is also about the different citizens of the states in the region being brought even closer together as a result of the structured diaspora relations of their different foreign diasporas. Often overlooked is the third component: a diaspora community which is functioning in a more structured way can enable members of that diaspora to engage in meaningful relations with the citizens of their countries of origin. And the members of that diaspora, in so doing would be the link between the citizens of their countries and the citizens of their adopted homeland. The diplomacy of the diaspora that is functional can, therefore, become the fulcrum on which these diverse relations are centred and built on.

Many of the foreign diasporas in Kenya also exist in the other East African countries. The problem has been that these have not been able to come together in a framework that would enable those other regional countries to benefit from this wider diaspora. In this context, the diplomacy of the diaspora needs to develop a regional perspective. In the East African region, such a regional perspective can be developed through the East African Community. The East African Community is developing a common diplomacy amongst its member states. This common diplomatic framework would be considerably strengthened were it to include the diplomacy of the diaspora from an East African perspective. This regional diplomacy of the diaspora would engage not only the diasporas of East African states in each other's countries, but also the significant diasporas of non-East African countries.

Conclusions: Harnessing Diasporas in Kenya's Foreign Policy

The diplomacy of the diaspora has not been practised for long in Kenya. However, there have been useful beginnings in bringing it into the foreign policy framework of the country. This current foreign policy framework of diaspora diplomacy however addresses only one aspect of the components of this diplomacy. While concentrating on the Kenyan diasopra abroad is likely to enhance the foreign perspective of Kenya, it needs to be broadened to include other diasporas and how they can be harnessed into the service of Kenya's national interest. This is because essentially, a diplomacy or foreign policy of the diaspora should be geared towards 'the quest for resources, business opportunities, diplomatic initiatives, and strategic partnerships'[19] and to enhance peaceful coexistence and national security.

Concentrating on Kenya's diaspora has helped to begin the process of entrenching the diaspora into Kenya's diplomacy. This is a new perspective in Kenya's diplomacy. The practises of this diplomacy of the diaspora need, however, to be widened and enlarged to include and involve the diasporas of other states in Kenya. Because of the history of East Africa, there is a shared foreign diaspora among the East African countries. This shared diaspora can be harnessed by countries in the region to promote a common diplomacy - and later foreign policy - amongst them. In doing so, a framework will have been laid for developing this diplomacy into a regional context, where these diasporas of other countries also exist.

In developing this fresh framework for foreign policy and diplomacy, Kenya has opened up areas of its diplomatic front that can only yield more benefits. Enlarging this diplomacy would even lead to yielding of higher benefits. But fully establishing the diplomacy of the diaspora in Kenya will require careful foreign policy formulation, and challenge further the management of diplomacy in the country. The diplomacy of the diaspora that is in the process of entrenchment in Kenya is, however, a complex type of diplomacy, that will require intense consultations amongst stakeholders and constituents of Kenya's foreign policy and diplomacy. It will also call for concentration between Kenya and its regional partners, especially those who share a common diaspora.

Kenya has made a step in recognising that its diaspora can be a useful resource in terms of implementing and articulating its foreign policy. It has made an important leap in officially recognising and reflecting this role of its diaspora in its foreign policy strategising. However, this process of active association with its diaspora has happened on a unilateral basis. It is unilateral because it has not been based on a serious negotiating framework in which both sides have negotiated their interests in the partnership and created rules about how those interests can be met, preserved, and mutually promoted. The framework of this relationship has been highly distributive, and resulted in a win-lose framework. And yet, the relationship between

Kenya and its diaspora needed to be conceptualised along an integrative framework. In this kind of framework, both parties agree that they are both pursuing interests that can be mutually realised in a win-win framework. In such a framework, both sides must recognise that they are sitting on the same side of the table, to face a common enemy.[20] The common enemy in this context is the harsh international and economic environment, which both can deal with more easily if they work together.

Kenya has not got round to this aspect of the diplomacy of the diaspora. It must, sooner rather than later, engage these other diasporas. When it does, it should do so on the basis of an integrative approach to negotiating emerging relations with these other diasporas. This would strengthen its practises of the diplomacy of the diaspora. It would eventually lead to strengthening bilateral relations with the countries of those foreign diasporas. It would also strengthen relationships between subregional and regional organisations and those other countries. And it could also lead to strengthening relationships between sub-national groups (such as the home towns and cities where the foreign diaspora members originally hailed from) and those of the towns and cities in Kenya where they now live and work, through strengthening the corridors in which cultural and other interactions take place.

References

1. Ndegwa, Alex, 'Why diaspora vote could be game changer', *The Standard on Saturday* (Nairobi), 19 November, 2011, pp.1, 9.
2. Kuhn, Philip, 'Why China Historians Should Study the Chinese Diaspora, and Vice Versa', *Journal of Chinese Overseas*, Vol.2, No. 2.
3. *Ibid*, pp. 168-69.
4. Cangbai, Wang, Wong Siu-Lun & Sun Wenbin, 'Haigui: A New Area in China's Policy Toward the Chinese Diaspora?', *Journal of Chinese Overseas*, Vol. 2, No. 2, 2006, p. 305.
5. Van Zwanenberg, R.M.A., *Colonial Capitalism and Labour in Kenya, 1919-1939*, East African Literature Bureau, Nairobi, 1975.
6. Kiwanuka, S., *From Colonialism to Independence*, Kenya Literature Bureau, Nairobi, 1973.
7. Nicole, Christopher, *The Happy Valley*, Sheridan Book Co., Reading, 1994.

8. Singh, Markhan, *History of Kenya's Trade Union Movement to 1952*, East African Publishing House, Nairobi 1969.
9. Naujoks, Daniel, 'Diasporic Identities: Reflections on Transnational Belonging', *Diaspora Studies*, Vol.3, No. 1 (2010), p. 5.
10. Kamudhayi, Ochieng, *Negotiations in Civil Wars: A Case Study of the Somalia National Reconciliation Process, 2002-2005*, Ph.D Thesis, Institute of Diplomacy and International Studies, University of Nairobi, 2010.
11. Ghai, Dharam, 'How Can Kenyans Abroad Contribute to National Development?' *Development in Practice*, Vol.15, No. 5, 2005, p. 668.
12. Ng'etich, Jacob, 'Kenyans missing the point on remittances', *Saturday Nation* (Nairobi), 7 May 2011, p. 34.
13. Ochwada, Hannington, 'How Kenyans in the diaspora are shaping their motherland's Destiny', *Daily Nation* (Nairobi), 6 May 2011, p.12.
14. Mwagiru, Makumi, *Conflict, Diplomacy and Mediation in Uganda*, IDIS and Ngatho Publications, Nairobi: 2004, pp. 65-66.
15. Mwagiru, Makumi, 'Tiger's Eyes in the Dark: Potential Post-Referendum Conflicts In South Sudan', paper presented at the Foreign Service Institute, Ministry of Foreign Affairs, *Seminar for Professional Diplomats*, Mombasa, 19 November 2010.
16. Cangbai, Siu-Lun and Wenbin, *op cit,* p. 296.
17. Chaturvedi, Sanjay, 'Diaspora in India's Geopolitical Visions: Linkages, Categories, and Contestations', *Asian Affairs*, Vol. 32, No. 3 (2005), p.148.
18. Ghai, Dharam, *op cit,* p. 670.
19. Phan, Peter, J., 'India's Expanding Relations with Africa and Their Implications for U.S. Interests', *American Foreign Policy Interests*, Vol. 29, 2007, p. 341.
20. Lewicki, R.J., D.M. Saunders and J.W. Minton, *Essentials of Negotiation*, Irwin/McGraw-Hill, Boston, MA, 1997.

4

India and Indian Diaspora in Africa

Ajay Dubey

During the colonial period a large number of people of Indian origin (PIO) were taken to African countries in different capacities - as indentured or railway worker, artisans and slaves. This forced migration of PIO under colonial rule was part of the British policy to take Indian labour all over the world to replace black slaves after their emancipation.

There are more than twelve million PIO spread in 136 countries.[1] Majority of them are located in Africa, Caribbean and Oceania. They immigrated in different bursts and different capacities. During ancient times, they went as merchants from western India to Africa and the Middle East. From eastern part of South India, they migrated to Burma (now called Myanmar), Indonesia and other countries of Southeast Asia. This group derived its livelihood from international trade and still maintained international kinship and economic network.[2] Some south Indian rulers had sent successful expedition to Southeast Asia. Largely Indians migrated to Far East and Southeast Asia to spread Buddhism.[3] The previous small-scale movement of Indian people turned into mass migration. They went under three different capacities: (*i*) the indentured worker in sugar colonies of Caribbean, Oceania and Africa,[4] (*ii*) under *Kangani* / maistry system to Malaysia and Ceylon,[5] (*iii*) and free or passenger Indians primarily to East Aftica.[6]

The free Indians went in small number to many other places as well. In the third phase, during twentieth century, Indians emigrated as skilled and semi-skilled workers to (*i*) Europe, North America and Oceania and (*ii*) the Middle East. However, they were not allowed to have citizenship in Gulf countries.

Among all these regions, Africa is an important area because of various reasons. It is a region where Mahatma Gandhi, an Indian leader, raised the issue of discrimination of PIO. A large number of Indians migrated to South Africa, Indian Ocean countries and East Africa in different capacities - as traders, indentured workers, free-passage Indians. After India's Independence, they went as contract skilled workers. It is a region that witnessed the best status of PIO as in Mauritius,[7] and the worst kind of crisis of PIO in Uganda. It is also a region towards which Indians leaders before Independence, and later the Government of India, actively engaged itself both for association and disassociation with and for PIO.

This paper examines the issues of PIO in African countries - their problems, their crisis, their constraints and aspiration - to understand the policy response by India. In times of crisis PIO naturally turn to India. To understand the Indian diaspora in a comparative international perspective, two aspects need to be analysed - the contextualisation and positioning of PIO in their countries of adoption; and second, the international force or support to which they relate themselves for their identity and safety. In the absence of an organised and effective force like GOPIO, India despite its weakness and limitation remains a single such source. This paper tries to capture both factors - the concrete reality that PIO face in Africa, and the imperatives and constraints of Indian policy towards PIO - in order to arrive at some trends, issues and concerns of PIO.

Indian Policy Towards PIO in Africa

In the last fifty years, there has been a major transformation in India's policy on the issues of People of Indian Origin (PIO) in Africa. Yet there is a thread of continuity that exists. The Government of India did not take up the PIO cause as their concern until the formation of BJP government in 1998. Indian settlers who represented 'mini India' or were 'ambassadors of India' promoting goodwill for India in Africa, became a non-issue or a sensitive issue, if not a liability. South African Indians, for whom Mahatma Gandhi struggled in South Africa, whose cause India took to the UN even before becoming independent and sacrificed its substantial trade relation with South Africa was a very special issue for India. For this, even Nehru made deviations from his strongly-held policy on Indian settler's abroad but now it became a better-to-avoid issue between India and South African interactions. At the same time cultural identification of PIO, the informal interaction of Indian visitors, holy men, fund collectors and religious activists from Swayam Sewak Sangh still goes on intensely. The following sections attempts to analyse and highlight the experience of interaction between Indians policies and PIO issues in Africa during the last fifty years after India's independence.

In the late nineteenth century the discriminatory treatment in a racially-structured society of South Africa led Mahatma Gandhi to fight it out legally and thereby veered him into active politics. Later, Indian nationalists of all shades started to demand improvement in working and living conditions of Indians settled abroad. The PIO's protest began to be articulated in East Africa also. East African Indian National Congress, based on the model of Indian National Congress, was founded in 1914. A.M. Jeevanjee went to the extent of advocating 'the annexation of African territory' (Tanganyika) to the Indian Empire 'arguing that it had been an Asiatic kingdom in ancient times'.[8] Indians in Africa formed the middle section in the three-tier society, whites at top and blacks at the bottom. However, their presence was more apparent to Africans as they came directly in contact with them through their retail shops and business. At the same time, they were aggressive in commercial sector. Elspeth Huxley once observed, 'In all countries the backbone of the country is small man, the White colonialist with small means, but there is no place for him in the country when once the Asiatic is there...It means, if open competition is allowed, the small White colonialist must go to the wall.'[9]

Evolution of Indian Policy on PIO

Jawaharlal Nehru is responsible for evolving India's policy towards Indians settled abroad. His focus area was Burma, Malaya and Srilanka,[10] and as far as Africa is concerned, he visualised the clash of interests of Indians and Africans. In 1927, he outlined the policy of Indian National Congress (INC) regarding Indian settlers in other colonial countries: 'an Indian who goes to other countries must cooperate with people of that country and win for himself a position by friendship and service.... The Indians should co-operate with

Africans and help them, as far as possible, and not claim a special position for themselves.'[11]

However, not all agreed with this policy of INC. The other stream of Congress members - C.F. Andrews, Srinivas Shastri, H.N. Kunzru, M.M. Malaviya, B.G. Gokhale - were mainly concerned with discrimination of Indians and wanted for them a parity with the white settlers. It was on the same lines of Mahatma Gandhi in South Africa. Thus, it became a sentimental issue for Indian nationalists. Nehru, who represented left wing of the Congress, differed with the conservative wing. He asserted cooperation between Indians and Africans. This contrasted with his general policy of India's support to the combined struggle of Indian settlers and Africans in which African cause was paramount. In a message to INC of South Africa, Nehru wrote in 1939, 'India is weak today and cannot do much for her children abroad but she does not forget them and every insult to them is a humiliation and sorrow for her. And a day will come when her long arm will shelter and protect them and *her strength will compel justice for them.*'[12] It is this duality between Nehru's policy and the presence of two wings (conservative and left) in Congress, which helps us to understand the change and continuities in Indian support to Indian settlers in Africa. By early 1950s, it was Nehru's policy towards Indians in East Africa and South Africa that ultimately prevailed.

Indian National Congress had set up an overseas department in 1929 and a slender contact was established with the local Congress organisations in South and East Africa. In the interim nationalist government formed on 2 September 1946, Nehru, who had taken over the charge of foreign relations, took the issue of discrimination of Indians in South Africa to United Nations. After Independence, Nehru, in the Constituent Assembly on 8 March 1948, said: 'Now these Indians abroad what are they? Are they Indian citizen - are they going to be citizen of India or not? If they are not, then our interest in them becomes cultural, humanitarian and not political. Either they get the franchise of the nationals of the other country or treat them as Indian minus franchise and ask for them the most favourable treatment given to an alien.' He advised the Indian immigrants, 'If you cannot be, and if you are not friendly to the people of that country, come back to India and do not spoil the fair name of India.'[13]

Nehru farther clarified in 1950, 'In many parts of Africa – East, West, South – there are considerable number of Indians, mostly business people. Our definite instructions to them and to our agent in Africa are that they must always put the interest of indigenous populations first. We want to have no vested interests at the expense of the population of those countries.'[14] He continued to emphasise the same view about the Indians abroad, 'if they adopt the nationality of that country we have no concern with them. Sentimental concern there is, but politically they cease to be Indian national.'[15] In 1953, Nehru asserted, 'About Africa and Indians there, I may tell you, the policy we have pursued for many years...We have told them very definitely and precisely that we as government do not encourage or support them in anything they might want and which goes against the interests of the Africans. We have made that perfectly clear.'[16] Nehru was clear that any overt move by the Indian government for the PIO would do more harms than good to them. He was not against people-to-people contacts or non-governmental associations. 'During Indo-Chinese war India welcomed contributions from Asians of East Africa to help boost its defence efforts.' When questioned on this Nehru told a foreign journalist, 'Indians overseas have dual loyalty, one to their country of adoption and other to their country of origin.'[17] India deplored it as an act of disloyalty when it found that Asians were selling and promoting Chinese-made goods at the cost of Indian goods.

For the Asian Relations Conference, two South African Indians – Y.M. Dadoo and G.M. Naicker – were invited but there was no black participant from South Africa. When Nehru was the prime minister and the question of racism in South Africa was taken up at the United Nations (UN), it was only the discrimination of Indians in South Africa that was India's concern, though soon India had to change its policy to include black Africans also. This caused great misgivings in Africans.[18] During 1960-66 the gulf between India and Indian settlers abroad widened as India started to perceive them as more of an obstacle than an asset in its diplomatic relations with Africa. As compared to the seriousness of the Chinese attack of 1962, the discrimination faced by the PIO lost its significance.

Before Independence when Nehru formulated India's position on Indians overseas, most of the Indians in Africa were in British colonies. The intention was to make British rulers of our country responsible for the welfare of overseas Indians and securing for them fair treatment and justice in relation to white settlers. Immediately after India's independence, Government of India was not in a position to assert for full justice to Indian settlers in Africa. Moreover, the leaders of white settlers in Kenya and South Africa saw India as a threat to British rule in Africa. They called Nehru a Hindu communist who wanted to replace European rule by Indians.[19] Their propaganda about India's sinister design on African colonies where Indians were in a substantial number and their image as an exclusive community whose only interest in Africa was economic exploitation, made Indian leaders very sensitive on question of Indians overseas. Nehru had other priorities, like mobilising the Afro-Asian countries to keep them away from cold war rivalries.[20] Hence, the issue of PIO was not emphasised in Africa.

Nehru's policy of exhorting Indians to identify themselves with Africans in East Africa was not based only on his ideological commitment. In Kenya, the presence of Indian settlers was larger than the European community and the latter wanted to keep Kenya as a white-man's country. The whites pursued a strong anti-Indian campaign in Africa and several riots broke out in Kenya, Uganda and South Africa involving Indians and Africans during 1944-49.[21] If Africa's struggle was to be weakened and divided there was every likelihood that the white Kenyan settlers could have extended the South African model in East Africa. Therefore, it was prudent for Indian settlers to join hands with blacks in opposing the white settlers; sometimes even sacrificing their short-term gains.

The fears of British settlers in Africa and the close watch of British government on independent India's relations with Indian settlers in Africa became clear in appointment of Apa B. Pant as India's high commissioner to East Africa. The British government received a cable from Sir Philip Mitchell of Kenya that he had been informed by a retired ICS officer, now a resident of Kenya, that Pant was 'far from being desirable...and is most likely to cause trouble if he comes to East Africa. Indeed I am told that it is not beyond the realm of possibility that he is being sent here for that purpose.'[22] However, Pant was given clear instruction by Nehru to exhort East African Indians to identify themselves with Black African cause and not to seek special privileges. Pant's appointment was not welcomed by the British government or colonial governments in East Africa. It was obvious from the very beginning that his pronouncements would be closely watched and scrutinised.

It was to allay this sort of fear that Nehru, in the constituent assembly on 9 August 1948, said: 'The Indian Commissioner will not be entitled to discharge consular function in respect of Indians who may not be considered to be (Indian) national, that is permanent resident in those territories or to act as spokesman of such Indians.' When Mau Mau rebellion (1952-53) broke out in Kenya very few Indian settlers in Kenya sided with the British; they were accused of being with the rebels. 'There were few Europeans in Kenya who do not insist that New Delhi, through its official and non-official representatives in Africa, has encouraged the rebellion of Mau-Mau.'[23] Apa B. Pant was charged in British Parliament for fomenting Mau-Mau trouble.[24] Under pressure, India took a soft stand and recalled Pant.

During the late 1950s, Indians of East Africa were considered as hurdles in consolidating Indo-African relations. But after the Indo-Chinese war of 1962 when Indian isolation was exposed in Africa, Indira Gandhi, in her capacity as official delegate, toured African countries in 1964. She continued to emphasise that Indian settled in Africa must identify themselves completely with the African people and make their fullest contribution to the societies in which they lived. However, as seen by her tour programme in Africa, besides her official engagements, she made it a point not to miss the Indian settlers, leaders and members of the community though in certain small location their number did not exceed even fifty.[25] She also called Indian settlers as 'ambassadors of India' in Africa. It shows a subtle departure from Nehruvian policy; the Indian settlers then became a useful instrument for generating goodwill for India. Their position as 'ambassadors of India' implied that they were no longer excluded from policy considerations of India.

These shifts became more noticeable in many areas when Indira Gandhi became the Prime Minister of India. By the second half of 60s, there was an increasing realisation that Indians in Africa, whatever passport they may hold, should not be put outside India's Africa policy. This also suited the Indian move of economic diplomacy in Africa and other developing countries as Indian settlers in East Africa had requisite capital and will to share it with Indian economic initiatives in African countries.

PIO in East Africa

In 1967, the Government of Kenya started the Kenyanisation of its economy when all non-citizens, largely Indians, were asked to take work and residence permit. It allowed them to trade only in restricted areas and items. Though it was a purely an internal policy of Kenyan government, Indian diplomats mobilised the PIO to surrender British passports and obtain local citizenship. Not many responded to this advice. PIO were not willing to migrate to England because of social insecurity and degeneration of their children in Western culture. Going back to India and being trapped in vicious trap of poverty, filth and unemployment was out of question.[26] Partly, Indian policies did not allow them to forget their old links, it appealed to them thrice in two years for financial help for defence fund to contain China and Pakistan. Religious leaders, fund collectors for charity, and politicians kept the contact alive, which strengthened the feelings of mutual dependence.

When they were in crisis this time India did not react favourably.[27] Indian Parliament discussed the issue at length; Indira Gandhi intervened to assure the members that the government was monitoring the situation.[28]

Indian Minister of State for External Affairs B.R. Bhagat carried a personal message from Indira Gandhi to President Kenyatta. When Bhagat arrived at Nairobi, his prior appointment with Kenyatta was cancelled, and he was unable to deliver the letter that he was carrying. He met some other officials including the vice-president. On his return, he reported to the Parliament about the fear in Kenya that India was trying to interfere in the internal affairs of Kenya and 'he was going there to ask them to slow down their policy'.[29] Indian Parliament interpreted the cancellation of Bhagat's appointment as a snub to India, and they suspected the British for this malicious propaganda about India's role.[30] Public was enraged in India as well as in Nairobi. *Times of India* stated, 'But if the implication is that president Kenyatta fell into a trap laid for him by a third party, it does little credit to his political acumen.'[31] Justifying the cancellations of the appointment, *Daily Nation* (Nairobi) criticised Bhagat for not handing over the message for Kenyatta to somebody else and called his conduct as bad tempered.[32] The then Indian High Commissioner, Prem Bhatia, later narrated the incident in his book, 'My opposition made no difference. I was informed that move was based on political decision and that it had already been announced as a government commitment. In the event I had no alternative but to prepare myself to make the best of a bad job.'[33] Nevertheless, the Government of Kenya extended the permit to non-citizen for a longer period varying from one to two years with prospect of renewal.

Indian government started some economic initiatives at a bilateral level to bring the Indian settlers in Kenya within the policy framework of India. It proposed to establish Africa-India Development Corporation with Kenyan PIO, the aim being to seek integration of the Indian community in the economic life of Kenya, thus fortifying the foundation of a multiracial society.[34] It indicated a shift in India's stand but the policy did not materialise.

When Idi Amin came to power in January 1971 in Uganda, he wanted to put the entire Ugandan economy in the hands of Ugandans of African origin. He said that the 80,000 Asians in Uganda were sabotaging the economy and encouraging corruption and therefore there were no rooms for them in Uganda.[35] All PIO whether they were Kenyan citizens, British or Indian passport holders had to leave within ninety days by 8 November 1972. Amin called the expulsion of PIO 'as part of the war of liberation'.

Indian Deputy Minister of External Affairs said in Parliament, 'We are in touch with the Ugandan authorities and I can assure the house that we shall do everything we can to protect the interest of Indians there.' The Indian president while in Lusaka denounced the expulsion and stated, 'The happenings in Uganda have a heavy clouds of doubt and uncertainty over the minds of many people of Indian origin in several countries of Africa...The pernicious doctrine of racialism may permeate even free Africa.'[36]

Public opinion was aroused in India but it strongly refuted and ridiculed Amin's allegation that India was planning to invade Uganda along with Tanzania and Zambia. However, India made it clear that it was going to support any international move, which would persuade Amin to extend the expulsion deadline. India did not take a tougher stand because: Indian move against a purely racial issue would have been interpreted as Indian interference and design in Africa; India supported Afro-Asian solidarity; and more importantly, since 'there is nothing to be gained by using strong words, if they cannot be backed by meaningful action in Uganda, any show of strong sentiment may trigger off an anti-Asian wave.'[37] Years later India faced the same constraints when Bavadra government was dismissed in Fiji and an anti-PIO move started there.

The Ugandan crisis made India realise that the leadership and political system of African states vary considerably from country to country and Indian support to Afro-Asian solidarity had to be qualified by longer national interests. These expulsions brought home another point to India. Despite India's consistent support to African decolonisation and Afro-Asian solidarity none of the African countries, howsoever friendly to India and opposed to Idi Amin's action, offered to accommodate expelled Indians even in small number as a gesture of sympathy with India.[38] The Government of India made special provisions and gave incentives to Asians to resettle in India with their savings and assets. Despite the offer, almost none of them opted to return to India. The restraint approach of India succeeded in getting Amin to agree to pay compensation for business and properties of Indian passport holders, which was not given to Indians of other nationalities.

PIO in South Africa

Indian settlers in South Africa were a separate issue for India. Long before Mahatma Gandhi used his tactics of noncooperation, civil disobedience, *satyagrah* and peaceful protests in India's freedom struggles in 1920, he had evolved and made maiden use of many of these methods in South Africa in the late nineteenth century. The personal insult heaped on him and his strong feelings against racial discrimination of Indians in South Africa became a sentimental issue for the followers of Gandhi. Their cause always remained high in India's foreign policy consideration.

The Asiatic Land Tenure Act also known as Ghetto Act became law in June 1946. It was directed against Indians confining them to specified areas only.[39] In United Nations General Assembly session that started on 3 September, Indian representative Chhagla articulated India's concerns in the UN subcommittee. He condemned South Africa's 'discriminatory treatment of Asiatic in general' as a denial of human rights and the Ghetto Act, both of which impaired friendly relations between India and Africa. The Franco-Mexican resolution – calling for treatment of Indians in South Africa to be in conformity with international obligations and charter of United Nations – was passed.

In March 1946, Nehru recommended termination of trade agreement and breaking up of diplomatic ties with South Africa.

Lord Wavell, the Indian viceroy, executed it right away.[40] This strong step was taken when India was still fighting for its independence and needed economic support from all quarters. This step cost India five per cent of its trade revenue. India's special support to Indian settlers in South Africa lasted until late 50s. Till then the resolution of Indian National Congress that supported the Indian and the non-Indian settlers' cause in South Africa applied.[41]

Based on the human rights clause of non-racial treatment, India raised the issue of South African Indian settlers exclusively within the UN. Because of the provisions, India had to extend support to all groups and communities subjected to racial discrimination in South Africa. Further, the policy of exclusively supporting Indian settlers was in contrast to Nehru's policy of advising Indian settlers in other parts of Africa, where he counselled the Indian settlers to integrate themselves with African cause and aspiration and not to seek special position or privilege. Meanwhile the Group Area Act of 1950 had formally institutionalised the apartheid policy affecting Indians as well as Black Africans.

President Dr. Rajendra Prasad, in his address to the Parliament in 1952, explained the shift, 'The question is no longer merely one of Indians of South Africa; it had already assumed a greater and wider significance. It is question of racial domination and racial intolerance. It is a question of African more than that of Indians in South Africa.' India raised the question of apartheid policy and succeeded in appointment of a UN commission to study the racial situation in South Africa. From then onward it became an issue of apartheid policy in South Africa that involved both, Indians as well as black Africans. India worked for establishment of majority rule in South Africa.

In central African territories, the strength of Indians was small and they did not strive for a special position. They were exhorted from the very beginning by Apa B. Pant and his successor, India's High Commissioner Nirmaljit Singh, to fight along with black African nationalist. In Zimbabwe in the fight against the White rulers, Indian settlers fought along with Africans in demolishing the racist regime. Their relation with Africans was one of trust. There were inter-African riots but Indian settlers were hardly ever target or issue. However, it was different in the case of Zambia Military and police under Kaunda administration; time and again they intimidated the Indian business community.

The defeat of India in Indo-Chinese war of 1962 and its isolation in Africa changed India's priorities.[42] Diplomatic support vis-a-vis China and Pakistan became the most important consideration. By the time India overgrew its inferiority complex by becoming self-sufficient in food, creating Bangladesh, detonating atomic bomb and launching satellites, it also emerged as a country having the third largest skilled and trained manpower. Its economic consideration became paramount in third world countries like Africa where its technology and skills could be sold at very competitive prices. The South-South umbrella suits India to sell its manufactured and value-added goods in Africa.[43] The issue of PIO receded into background as it does not fit in or helps in contemporary concern of India. The current euphoria of India on the end of apartheid is not just because Indian settlers and Blacks have become free from racialism. It is also largely because India wants to convert its goodwill in South Africa, this time, into a favourable access to its large and strong economy.

Both domestic and international changes have altered the priority and agenda of India's policy towards Africa. With abolition of colonialism, both internal and external, the struggle for equal privileges for PIO does not exist. Second, in post-colonial phase of Africa, India by its experience realised that expectation of 'dual loyalty' and inclusion of PIO in policy framework neither wins them over for Indian investment or other economic needs nor does it please African governments who have to deal strongly with PIO according to their domestic imperatives and pressures. The PIO, after their experience in Zanzibar, Uganda, Zambia and other countries, have realised that support for their protection is limited because of India's own limitations. Third, PIO have historically and politically become a part of African states and no longer an issue of major concern. Therefore, the Indian government had other priorities during 1970s and 80s.

India learnt through its East African experience that it is unrealistic and counterproductive to expect South African government to favour Indian settlers as a reciprocal gesture for India's contribution in their struggle against apartheid. It is to be seen how Indian settlers share the burden of economic and social restructuring programme in South Africa. Such pressures and demands from black groups have already started surfacing openly. However, because of the long isolation of South Africa from India they will not have, unlike East African Indians, a 'dependency' attitude towards India. But it does not mean that PIO have no place in Indian policy.

Since early 90s again there is a proactive interest of Indian government in the Indians overseas. The foreign remittance from NRIs in Gulf region and North Africa provided meaningful addition to India's foreign reserve requirements. After liberalisation of the economy in 1991, the Government of India has promised many incentives to attract foreign direct investment from the NRIs and others settled abroad. The Congress government was cautious dealing with the PIO. Bharatiya Janata Party (BJP) favoured this segment when they came to power. Historically Rashtriya Swayam Sewak Sangh (RSS), a support base for BJP, had maintained close people-to-people contact through its branches among Hindu overseas settlers. It organised the first ever conference of PIO in New Delhi.[44] The PIO cards issued to them provided substantial advantages compared to other foreign nationals.[45] The attitude of PIO became positive too.

By mid 90s, except in South Africa, PIO got long enough time to prove their loyalty to the country of their adoption. They emerged from isolation at home and emerged as a confident identity group. It also emerged as one the most prosperous and organised ethnic groups in their countries. Many countries have successfully used the presence of different diasporic community to mobilise economic and diplomatic support for their country.[46] By 1990s diasporas - Black, Jewish, European, Chinese or Indian - are not centrifugal, sectarian force that need to be contained or crushed, rather it has emerged as a secular, acceptable identity force at the international level. In such a changed scenario the proactive interest of India in 90s does not have any element of imperialist design or racist preference as was likely to be construed during the Nehru period.

Concerns and Issues of PIO

What does the African experience of the Indian diaspora inform us about the People of Indian Origin in general? First, the PIO even in Africa are not a monolithic lot. They have wide divergences based on language, religion and geographical regions from which they emigrated. They arrived in different capacities, e.g. as indentured worker, free passenger, as trader or businessmen. In a way, they are microcosm of Indian diversity. Second, though they have multiple diversity but all of them have identity of being ethnic Indians. People of Indian origin around the world have a feeling of oneness among themselves and feel a part of greater Indian society.[47] The countries of their adoption treat them as ethnic Indians. Third, almost all of them, whether indentured worker, free passenger, semi-skilled or skilled worker or business community, have done economically and professionally quite well.

Though prosperous and confident of their identity the PIO suffer from being a minority, except in Mauritius. The prosperous minority faces subtle or obvious *hostility of the less-prosperous majority community especially when the former has not successfully integrated with the indigenous groups*. Because of its domestic positioning, lack of networking and absence of strong global organisation, the Indian diaspora has failed to mobilise its resources and strength when it faced crisis in Uganda or Fiji. Its feeble impact in international area is the weak position of the origin country. Despite its large population India is not strong economically or militarily and therefore, it can neither help effectively nor do PIO look towards it for vital support during crisis. This is in contrast to Israel, China or Europe who respond aggressively if its diaspora are adversely affected. Despite vital contribution, the host country may not take the PIO seriously as they do for other diaspora[48] whose origin countries are powerful in world affairs.

Diaspora has started to be recognised as an international force. The race for globalisation has created an environment to look beyond rigid national boundaries for economic and other aspiration of people. The emerging science and technological advancement has reduced distance, cost and broken the communication barrier. Along with the favourable opportunities, Indian diaspora has threats as well. In most countries, PIO are a minority and any visible attempt to foster external loyalties, however innocuous it may be for domestic system, may invite suspicion and hostility if done without taking the local leaders into confidence. A confident and economically networked PIO will prove a better asset for the country of their adoption rather than an isolated, sulking and vulnerable PIO. Indian diaspora focuses on business links and fails to extend it to other sections of the society – businessmen, professional, cultural and political leaders and most importantly common people. Business should be a propelling force for people to come together not a sole end in itself. The formation of GOPIO is timely but it needs to make use of its strengths.

Having discussed the socio-economic political and international positioning of PIO one needs to answer as to what should be done to enable Indian diaspora to emerge as an international force? What are the roles and tasks of different stakeholders – the government and people of India, the leaders and business community of PIO, the academician, the media, etc? These are questions that need answers. It becomes clear after scanning the literature on overseas Indians that it has remained focused on micro socio-political and economic issues and justifiably so because that was the main concern of marginalised immigrants in their new countries. Academics should describe, analyse and intervene on issues like (*a*) Indian diaspora as a player in world identity politics and (*b*) Indian diaspora as an international force in world system. Anthropological and sociological micro studies on trial and tribulation, folklore and *dalpuris* are important but in order to understand the new emerging nature of Indian diaspora, and to compare and contrast the competitive edge of it, the frameworks of international relations/ studies must be used now.

References

1. For earlier estimate, see Jain, P.C., 'Indians Abroad: A current Population Estimate', *Economic and Political Weekly*, 17 (8) 1982. The recent figure has been compiled from different sources: *Europa World Year Book* and other Region and Country specific year books.
2. Tinker, Hugh, *A New System of Slavery*, OUP, London, 1979; and Mangat, J.S., *A History of Asians in East Africa*, Oxford, 1969.
3. Thapar, Romila, *A History of India*, Penguin, 1966.
4. Tinker, Hugh, *A New System of Slavery,* op cit.
5. Sadhu, Karnail Singh, *Indians in Malaya: Some aspect of their immigration and settlement 1786-1957*, OUP, 1969.
6. Ghai, Y.P., Dharam Pal Ghai, *The Asian Minorities of East and Central Africa*, London, 1971.
7. Dubey, Ajay, *Government and Politics in Mauritius*, Kalinga, Delhi, 1997.
8. Jeevanjee, A.M., *An Appeal on Behalf of Indians in East Africa*, Bombay, 1912.
9. *Selected Works of Jawaharlal Nehru,* Vol. 2, Delhi, 1992, pp. 353-62.
10. The cause of Indians settled in Africa and other places was taken up by Sapru, Shastri, Kunjru, Maharaj Singh and others.
11. *Selected Works of Jawaharlal Nehru,* New Delhi, 1972, pp. 353-68.

12. *Selected Works of Jawaharlal Nehru*, Orient Longmans, Delhi, Vol. 9, 1976, p. 618.
13. *Ibid.*
14. Chhabra, H.S., *India* and *Africa*, New Delhi, p. 15.
15. *India's Foreign Policy* 1946-61, p. 130 (Nehru's reply to debate on foreign policy in Lok Sabha, 2 September 1957).
16. Chhabra, H.S., *India and Africa,* New Delhi, p. 15.
17. Gupta, Anirudha, 'India and Asians in East Africa' in Twaddle, Michael (ed.), *Expulsions of Minority: Essay on Ugandan Asians*, Univ. of London, 1975, p. 134.
18. Dubey, Ajay, 'Nehru and India's role in African liberation struggles (1947-64)', *Africa: Journal of African Studies Society of India,* July 1989, p. 27.
19. Brigg, Group Captain I.R., the conservative White settler leader in Kenya asserted that India wants to squeeze them out and make it an Indian colony, *The Times*, London, 4 August 1954. South African High Commissioner in London stated in 1954, 'If Nehru could weaken European influence in Africa, then it will mean Africa for Indians', in McKay, V., *Africa in World Politics*, New York, p. 170.
20. Dubey, Ajay, 'Nehru and Africa in Afro-Asian Solidarity', *Ind-Africana*, Delhi University, Vol. 2, No. 2, pp. 38-46.
21. Sadiqu Ali, Shanti, *India and Africa,* pp. 32-33, 51-52.
22. Tinker has given a documented account as how Pant's appointment had to face hurdles and delays, for his alleged subversive intentions. Tinker, Hugh, *The Banyan Tree: Overseas Empire from India, Pakistan and Bangladesh*, London, 1977, p. 318.
23. Blundell, Michael, *New York Times*, 19 July 1953.
24. Lord Alport raised the question concerning 'the contribution made to prevailing conditions of transition and unrest in Kenya during Mau-Mau rebellion by the staff of Indian High Commission office'. Alport demanded that Government of India should be asked to withdraw its staff from Kenya. *Britain: House of Commons Debates,* Vol. 5 1 8, 29 July 1953.
25. See Gopal, Ajit S., The Indian Journalist who covered her entire safari, *World Focus,* No. 53, October 1984, p.15.
26. For a detailed discussion see Gupta, Anirudh, *'India and the Asians'* op. cit. p. 130.
27. Nehru used to say that if they are not ready to become citizen and not welcomed there they should come back to India.
28. Indian parliament was told that there were 186,000 people of Indian origin in Kenya. Out of this 130,000 were British citizen, 44,000 Kenyan and only 4,000 were Indian nationals.

29. *India Lok Sabha debate,* Series 4, No. 29, 25 March 1968, pp. 101-14, col. 3003.
30. *Ibid.*, col. 3002.
31. *Times of India*, New Delhi, 26 March 1963.
32. *Daily Nation* wrote - 'The head of state is a busy person with many calls on his time and Mr. Bhagat should have been quick to appreciate this fact. Cancellation of the appointment however did not imply refusal to receive the message. He declined, preferring to return to India, with the message. He may argue that he was right in his decision. That is his right. We respect it. We feel that his decision was wrong and his conduct bad tempered.' *Daily Nation*, Nairobi, 27-3-68, reproduced in *Africa Diary*, Vol. VIII, No. 20, 1968, pp. 3921-22.
33. Bhatia, Prem, *Indian Ordeal in Africa*, New Delhi, 1973, p.130.
34. *AICC Economic Review*, New Delhi, October 1966.
35. *Africa Digest*, Vol. 19, No. 57, October 1972, p. 96.
36. Quoted in Gupta, A., 'Uganda Asian, Britain, India and Commonwealth', *African Affairs* (1974), p. 322.
37. *Times of India*, Delhi, 6 October 1972.
38. Dubey, Ajay, *Indo-African Relations in the Post Nehru Era*, Kalinga Publication, Delhi, 1990.
39. Dubey, Ajay, 'Identity Politics of Indian South Africans: Democratisation and governance of South Africa', paper presented at ICSSR-HSRC seminar on *The Dynamics of Social Identity in India and South Africa: Its Implications for Democratisation and Governance* held at Bungler between 20-22 October 1998.
40. Indian High Commissioner did not return to South Africa since 1946 when Ghetto Act was passed. But India used to maintain a small office in Durban which was finally closed in 1954 and thereafter all direct links between India and South Africa ceased.
41. See *Indian National Congress Resolutions on Foreign Policy*, AICC New Delhi, 1946-66.
42. For detailed analysis of this change, see Dubey, Ajay, 'India and Africa: Changing Priorities and Styles of Diplomatic Interactions in the post Nehru Era (1965-1985)', *Foreign Affairs Report*, Delhi, May-June 1988, pp. 29-44.
43. For economic diplomacy, see Dubey, Ajay, 'Indo-African Economic Relations (1965-85): A Case of South-South Interactions' *Africa Quarterly*, Vol. XXVII, Nos. 3-4, pp. 41-79.
44. This conference was organised by Indian Council of International Cooperation, New Delhi.

45. By paying one time fee of US$ 1,000 they can get multiple entry visas for twenty years. PIO cardholders have almost all commercial rights as Indian citizens except in case of purchase of agricultural property and right to vote.
46. Mauritius used the presence of Indian, European, African and Chinese diaspora for economic and diplomatic gain.
47. The first global meet of the People of Indian Origin concluded, 'There is growing awareness in the overseas Indians in the Caribbean, Fiji, Mauritius, Africa, and Far East, that is echoing back to rekindle patriotism in Indians living in India.'
48. In both Mauritius and South Africa, the majority communities go out of way to accommodate European settlers feel at home because otherwise the European countries may adversely affect the country concerned through aid and diplomacy.

SECTION 2

NON-TRADITIONAL SECURITY ISSUES

5

India's Energy Security and its Relations with Oil-Rich African Countries

Aparajita Biswas

In recent times, the issue of energy security has attracted the attention of leading scholars in India. This is in the backdrop of the country's escalating demand for oil and gas, which is in tune with its rising economic growth. It may be noted here that the current total energy requirement of India ranks it among the world's highest. This increase in energy needs is due predominantly to India's growing population and its rapid industrialisation. Over the next twenty-five years, this demand is expected to more than double. I shall be focusing on oil – one of the sources of energy that is the subject of maximum concern for India.

Taking the general switchover of India's relations with Africa as a starting point, this article reviews its increasing engagement with oil-rich African countries. In fact, the factors that have led India to recast its foreign policy in the 1990s include its rapid economic growth and its efforts to achieve a more secure supply of resources (especially oil and gas) for its industrial production. Another factor relates to its search for new emerging markets. In this changing scenario, Africa is considered an important neighbour by India, with oil-rich African countries being regarded as a high-priority area in its foreign policy. At present, about a quarter of India's crude oil imports are being sourced from Africa. Given that the continent is expected to contribute approximately 25 per cent of the growth in the world's petroleum and LNG supplies by 2012, there is enormous potential for India to increase its volumes of crude oil imports from African countries in the future.

This article approaches India–Africa relations in the energy and resource sectors from a different angle, by focusing on the linkages of India's domestic development and its foreign policy behaviour.

India's Domestic Development and Energy Scenario

India embraced the era of globalisation when it introduced its programme of economic liberalisation in 1991. It abandoned the model of mixed economy of earlier years and integrated the country into networks of globalisation through a new export-oriented policy, opening of the national economy, financial deregulation, increasingly mobile foreign investment and a loosening of governmental control over firms or markets. In foreign policy matters, economic affairs and the concept of energy security have gained new importance. As a result, India along with China has emerged as the growth engine of the world economy.

The other aspect of the liberalisation of India's economy is the initiation of a debate on energy security. India's overall energy scenario shows that its vibrant economic growth over the past ten years has stimulated a huge upsurge in its demand for oil. Oil accounts for 31 per cent of India's total energy consumption, and there is unlikely to be any significant scaling down of dependence on these fuels in the next five to ten years.[1] Consequently, its growing hunger for more and more energy and natural resources is leading to massive extractive activities both inside the country and across the world. It need not be emphasised that a fast-growing economy typically requires more energy and India's liberalisation drive has produced a manufacturing structure that requires huge increases in energy consumption.

According to the projection of the World Energy Outlook, India's energy needs are likely to balloon over the coming decades. These needs will be driven by its quest to maintain the high levels of economic growth (around six to seven per cent annually) that it has enjoyed since 1994. Recent data indicates that internal production actually accounts for only a quarter of its energy demand or less.

Despite the global financial crisis, India's oil consumption significantly expands due to secular growth from rapid industrialisation. As per the report published by Platts, India is now the second biggest consumer of crude oil in Asia and its demand continues to grow. The demand for gasoline in India is inelastic partly because of its fast growing automobile industry that has recorded an increase in car sales by 30 per cent.[2]

Such a heavy demand for energy and raw materials has led to two major structural imperatives for India. One is to undertake dramatic reforms in the hydrocarbon sector, such as deregulation of the market-driven oil and gas industry, allowing participation of the private sector, both Indian and foreign, in upstream and downstream activities and a multipronged strategy to ensure future oil supplies from overseas oil and gas properties. The other is to diversify energy imports and to acquire equity oil by India's state-owned oil companies. The Oil and Natural Gas Corporation (ONGC) of India and its export arm, the ONGC Videsh Limited (OVL), received particular support from the Indian government in overseas investments and acquisitions in various oil-rich countries. The Government of India has also encouraged ONGC to look for income and rent from the upstream sector (exploration and production).

At a relatively rapid pace, ONGC of India and its export arm the ONGC Videsh Limited (OVL) announced investment in offshore gas fields in Vietnam, as well as energy projects in Africa, Iran, Russia, Algeria, Kazakhstan, Indonesia, Venezuela, Libya and Syria. At present OVL is active in fourteen countries and has twenty-three projects. The urgency for such an external push was prompted by high energy and commodity price. Given Africa's rich endowment of energy, minerals and other key resources, it was only natural that India would see the continent as a new frontier.

India's Energy Scenario

Let us take a cursory look at India's energy scenario. While it has significant reserves of coal, it is relatively poor in oil and natural gas resources. India's energy mix is coal dominant, with coal accounting for more than half of primary commercial consumption and oil accounting for almost a third. However, if consumption follows the current trajectory, India is projected to run out of coal, its primary source of energy, in forty years. Its oil reserves amount to 5.9 bn barrels – only 0.5 per cent of total global reserves.[3] The majority of

India's oil reserves are located in offshore Bombay and onshore in Assam.

In terms of gas, India currently accounts for 0.4 per cent of global reserves and just over one per cent of production. While most of the developed gas is in Bombay High, major discoveries by a number of domestic companies hold significant medium- to long-term potential, with Reliance Industries, state-controlled ONGC and Gujarat State Petroleum Corporation (GSPC) all confirming significant deepwater finds that are now under development or in early-stage production.

India's oil and gas sector is dominated by state controlled enterprises, with ONGC being the largest upstream-oriented oil company, dominating the exploration and production (E & P) segment and accounting for roughly around three-quarters of the country's oil output. Its downstream segment is also dominated by state-controlled entities, although private companies have increased their market share. Indian Oil Corporation (IOC) is the largest state-controlled downstream company, operating ten of India's seventeen refineries and controlling about three-quarters of the domestic oil transportation network.[4]

India has always been an oil-importing country, with about 80 per cent of its crude oil requirements being met by imports, which accounts for approximately 31 per cent of its total imports. Its crude oil imports have more than doubled in the last ten years, touching 159.26 m tons in 2009-10. It can be reasonably assumed that, if the price of crude doubles within a decade to around $230 per barrel, India will import 4 m bbd corresponding to an annual oil import bill of $335 bn by 2021-22.[5] About 70 per cent of its oil imports are from West Asia which accounts for four per cent of its gross domestic product (GDP).[6] At current rates of economic growth, this figure is likely to rise to as much as five million barrels per day by 2020. Unless India obtains or develops alternative sources of energy, in fifteen years it will have to import close to 90 per cent of its petroleum needs.

One of the important consequences of this scenario is that India's dependence on the international energy market will increase – thus making it more vulnerable against external shocks. In fact, factors like the 9/11 terrorist attacks on the US, the predominantly American 'war on terror' and the military interventions in Afghanistan and Iraq have all heightened India's sense of insecurity and vulnerability. The other cause of anxiety is that there are few or no viable energy alternatives currently existing: India's civilian nuclear programme has regularly fallen behind schedule and large-scale development of hydroelectricity generation facilities has been stymied. It is working on securing alternative sources of energy in cooperation with other countries. These efforts are focused on oil, natural gas and nuclear energy. However, each of these potential sources presents complicated geopolitical challenges.

India's Oil Strategy in Africa

Since the late 1990s, India's policy towards Africa has been very closely linked with its energy security policies. The African continent holds ten per cent of the world's oil reserves, with five countries dominating its upstream oil production. Together they account for 85 per cent of the continent's oil production and are, in order of decreasing output, Nigeria, Libya, Algeria, Egypt and Angola. Other oil-producing countries are Gabon, Congo, Cameroon, Tunisia, Equatorial Guinea, the Democratic Republic of the Congo, and Cote d'Ivoire. The region has increased its output by 36 per cent in ten years, compared with 16 per cent for the rest of the world. Angola and Nigeria are now the two best African producers, who rank before Algeria and Libya even though they hold the largest oil reserves (56 bn barrels estimated).[7]

Moreover, according to the report of the US Energy Information Administration (EIA), West Africa may become an important non-OPEC oil-producing region within a decade. Africa's oil surplus has grown over the past decade, and at the same time the light, sweet crudes of West Africa was found to be well suited to refineries.[8] The Gulf of Guinea, an arm of the Atlantic Ocean, has a large amount of hydrocarbon energy resources. Eleven African countries, including Ivory Coast, Ghana, Benin, Togo, Nigeria, Cameroon, Gabon, Equatorial Guinea, Democratic Republic of Congo, and Sao Tome and Principe share its continental shelf. Among them, Nigeria, Gabon and Cameroon are major petroleum producers. With a reserve estimated as 49.405 bn barrels and proven natural gas reserve at 194.975 trillion cubic feet (TCF), this area is likely to become the world's leading deep-water offshore production centre. Over the next twenty years, it could become Africa's third largest producer with 740,000 barrels a day. Moreover, new oilfields have been explored in Equatorial Guinea, Chad, Sa, Tome and Principe. Together with Africa's traditional oil producing countries, like Gabon and Congo-Brazaville, these new discoveries could bring Africa's oil output to a million barrels a day within the next ten to fifteen years.[9]

The region is a magnet for investment where competition for influence is fierce between European, US, Chinese, Indian and other Asian interests. According to the United Nations Trade and Development (UNCTAD) World Investment Report, FDI inflows to the region were concentrated in a few industries such as oil, gas, and mining. Six oil producing countries (Algeria, Chad, Egypt, Equatorial Guinea, Nigeria and Sudan, in descending order of the value of FDI) accounted for about 48 per cent of inflows to the region.[10] The sources of these inflows includes Asian Foreign Direct Investment (FDI) which accounts for ten per cent of the stock of the FDI in the world. In absolute terms, Africa's share of Indian FDI outflows increased from US$243 m in 2000 to US$2.4 bn in 2008. Most of its investments are in the energy sector.[11]

On the one hand, Namibia and South Africa show strong prospects of oil and on the other hand, oil has recently been found in countries like Mauritania, Uganda, Kenya, Tanzania, Somalia and Mozambique. In Uganda, as much as one billion barrels of oil in reserve has been confirmed in the Lake Albertine Graben region, between Uganda and the Democratic Republic of Congo (DRC). If extracted, oil resources will catapult Uganda among the top fifty oil producers of the world.[12]

India imports oil mainly from Nigeria, Sudan, Republic of Congo and West African States. It has an investment of US$ two billion in the energy sector in Africa, with Nigeria being the leading supplier of oil from Africa. India imported 13.2 m tonnes of crude oil from Nigeria in 2009-10. According to the report, it has been decided in the India Nigeria Joint committee meeting held in New Delhi in 2012 that India's annual requirement of Nigerian crude oil would be around 18 m tonnes per annum from 2012-13 onwards (PIB Bureau, GOI, 2012). Meantime, Indian Oil Corporation (IOC) signed a term contract with the Nigerian National Petroleum Corporation for importing 40,000 barrels of crude oil per day at the official selling price, for a period of one year, to begin with.

In 2004, IOCL signed an MOU with Nigeria's Edo State to erect an oil refinery, in return for Nigeria's offer of a stake in an oilfield in Edo. The participation of ONGC Videsh Ltd (OVL) in

Nigeria's upstream sector has forged significant energy ties between India and Nigeria.[13]

Besides OVL, Indian multinationals are also active in the oil-rich African countries. For example, in 2005 ONGC-Mittal Energy Ltd (OMEL) entered into oil-for-infrastructure deal with the Nigerian government worth $6 bn, to establish a refinery and power plant and lay railway lines in Nigeria. The Nigerian government had awarded exploration rights on two oil blocks (OPL 279 and OPL 285) to OMEL. In 2010, OMEL discovered hydrocarbons in a Nigerian deepwater block. The joint venture completed drilling of the first well in OPL 279 block.[14]

OMEL has also managed to secure almost 15 m tonnes of LNG supplies from the Olokola LNG project in Nigeria, which is being developed by Chevron Texaco, British Gas and Shell. The OMEL deal 'is seen as one of the first examples of India's new approach in West Africa'. In the same year, OVL struck a US$31 m deal for exploration of highly potential oilfields in the North Ramadan Block No. 6 area of Egypt. The block had a potential to produce oil of more than 600 m barrels. However in 2007, it decided to relinquish its oil block in Egypt as it did not find the discovery commercially viable. In 2008, OVL and its partner IPR Red Sea Inc made a significant oil discovery in offshore Egypt. The discovery was made in the first exploration well North Ramadan-1A in the North Ramadan block in Gulf of Suez. Total potential resources in the block exceed 200 m barrels of oil.

In a major breakthrough for the state-run Oil India Limited (OIL) in securing oil and gas assets abroad, the company and its partners have entered into an agreement with National Oil Corporation of Libya for four exploration blocks in that country, estimated to hold two trillion cubic metres (tcm) of gas reserves.

In 2008, Essar Energy Overseas, an Essar Oil subsidiary, signed an agreement to acquire 50 per cent stake in Mombasa-based Kenya Petroleum.[15] In 2010, it was reported that British Oil and Gas giant, BP Plc, had talks with Indian companies — Reliance Industries and Essar Oil — over a potential sale of its assets in Africa. BP's assets in Africa are estimated to be pegged at about $500 m, and the sale is in line with the company's strategy that seeks to sell about $30 bn worth of assets in the next eighteen months to enable it cover the costs of the Gulf of Mexico Oil spill crisis.

Lately, Sudan too has emerged as a small but fast-growing oil producer. It did so first with the help of American and European corporations and, more recently, with investments from Chinese, Indian and Malaysian companies. With its daily oil production of about 500,000 barrels a day, Sudan is earning the kind of wealth that will ensure prosperous times for its economy. However, this country is divided today, which could lead to unprecedented challenges, especially in the demarcation of the border which is in the proximity of conflict zones.

In the light of the above, the major issue in Sudan is that, the majority of proven reserves are located in southern Sudan, in the Muglad and Melut Basins. Southern Sudan accounts for between 75-80 per cent of Sudan's daily crude oil output. The technology and infrastructure to extract and export this oil is based in Port Sudan which is in North Sudan, on the Red Sea.[16] One can consider this to be a highly paradoxical situation, given that South Sudan is reliant on Khartoum (North Sudan) to transport the oil and share the profits, whereas Khartoum is reliant on South Sudan for most of its oil exports. It goes without saying that North Sudan is no longer in possession of 75 per cent of its oil production sources.[17]

The disagreements between Sudan and South Sudan cover issues of distribution of oil revenues, demarcation of their 1,800-km (1,200-mile) border, division of national debt and the status of citizens in each other's territory. Predictably, these differences soon turned into an armed conflict, with Sudan resorting to use might by sending fighter jets to bomb South Sudan troops and also its oilfields.

Foreseeing the split of Sudan, India went on a diplomatic offensive by making efforts to befriend South Sudan. It has invited Sudan's officials and politicians for training and exchange programmes from 2006 onwards. This was followed by the opening of its consulate in Juba, among the first countries to do so. Moreover, given its investments in Sudan's oil sector – it is undivided Sudan's third largest partner in the oil sector – India naturally has a great stake. The Indian government and individual companies account for a 25 per cent stake in the Greater Nile Oil Project which produces 280,000 bpd. Sudan offers Indian investors – most of them in the oil and gas sector – attractive incentives and preferential access to Arab countries. OVL, an Indian company, expanded its activities in Sudan after the withdrawal of Western oil companies due to US sanctions on the issue of Darfur crisis and human rights. Along with CNPC of China and Petronas of Malaysia, OVL capitalised on the opportunity left by US and Western multinational oil companies in Sudan. Its initial investment of US$1 bn in the hydrocarbon sector soon increased to US$3 bn in 2012.

In 2004, OVL agreed to construct a 741 km oil pipeline from the Khartoum refinery to export terminals at Port Sudan. Sudan, in turn, offered an investment destination for Indian oil service companies, with the Mumbai-based Dodsal Group carrying out the pipeline's construction at a cost of almost US$194 m. The oil refinery company, Indian Oil Corporation (IOC), was later brought in to train Sudanese engineers to operate the pipeline.[18] The oil sector also boosted Indian exports to Sudan with the pipe manufacturer, PSL Ltd, winning a US$190 m contract to supply 785 km of pipeline for the Melut Basin Oil Development Project.[19]

OVL has stakes in several wells with a daily production of 160,000 barrels. Out of this, 100,000 barrels per day of production are from wells that now fall within South Sudan. India gets one million tonnes of crude oil per year from here, which, in equity oil parlance, would mean a growth rate of 12 per cent of the $750 m Indian investment. Incidentally, China is investing about US$300 m to increase the capacity of the Khartoum refinery.

And now, the matter of South Sudan deciding to suspend its oil production and shipment for the next one year due to disagreements with Sudan over the issue of oil tariffs, has undoubtedly threatened the oil companies of India, China and Malaysia. To protect its oil interests, India has appointed a special envoy to broker peace between the two countries, both of which are crucial to its pursuit of oil and other hydrocarbon resources in Africa. An offshoot of the uncertain conditions prevailing in Sudan and Syria is that OVL's production this year has gone down considerably (about four per cent).

Besides oil India has gone in to developmental sectors like infrastructure, agriculture, human resource development, information and communications technologies, and small and medium industries in Sudan. India has successively increased its trade investments, with statistical records showing that it is now the sixth largest exporter to Sudan, with its bilateral trade volume in 2010 touching around $900 m, while extending credit worth $1 bn. In fact, it extended an EXIM Bank Line of Credit of US$50 m to contribute to the economic development of Sudan.[20]

Promoting Oil Diplomacy in the African Countries

To promote oil diplomacy in the African countries, India has taken number of initiatives to woo African countries. As a part of the strengthening relations, India for the first time hosted a high profile two-day 'India-Africa Hydrocarbon Conference' in New Delhi in the first week of November 2007. Oil ministers from ten African countries and delegations from sixteen other countries attended the conference, in which a road map was drawn up to identify the broad areas of cooperation in the hydrocarbon sectors between India and African countries. At the conference, External Affairs Minister Pranab Mukherjee said, 'India is increasingly looking at taking its partnership with Africa to a position which would be mutually beneficial to both sides. We are a natural market for Africa's rich hydrocarbon resources.'[21]

In 2004, India pledged $500 m in the form of concessional credit facilities to eight energy and resource-rich West African countries: Burkina Faso, Chad, Equatorial Guinea, Ghana, Guinea-Bissau, Ivory Coast, Mali and Senegal – to help private Indian firms carry out development projects (Team -9).[22] It is reported that $280 m worth of projects have already been approved against concessional Lines of Credit. These include $970,000 for the construction of a national post office in Burkina Faso, $30 m for rural electrification in Ghana, $4 m for a bicycle plant in Chad, $12 m for a tractor assembly plant in Mali, and $15 m for potable drinking water projects in Equatorial Guinea.

Even as a part of its oil strategy, India has cooperated with China and started its oil investments in states on the fringes of the international community, such as in Sudan, Libya, and Angola, in the late 1990s. It is to be noted here that China has massive investments in Africa's oil sector. As discussed earlier, in Sudan, both ONGC and CNPC were active in oilfields after American and Canadian firms withdrew from Sudan in the mid-1990s due to a combination of security and human rights concerns. Though the international community repeatedly accused Sudan of gross human rights violations, this did not deter China and India from reaching for Sudan's natural resources to feed their burgeoning energy needs. Rather, both countries are busy wooing Sudan for acquiring a maximum share of its oilfields.

Interestingly, in spite of cooperation between Indian and Chinese oil companies in African oilfields, there is also fierce competition between them to acquire oilfields. Indian companies lost out many lucrative deals to other companies (often Chinese) on a number of bids to acquire oilfields.

However, what distinguishes China's involvement in Africa from that of other nations is that it is accompanied by a clear government policy in support of African commercial ventures, abundant financing and tax benefits for Chinese firms operating abroad, and robust diplomacy toward the region. State-owned Chinese companies can depend on the Ministry of Commerce which manages most Chinese aid programmes, to add sweeteners to bids for African government contracts or assets. There is also a widespread feeling that India lags behind China, and a perception that Chinese companies get the benefit of quicker decision making. When OVL lost out to KNOC in Nigeria, officials blamed the government for not clearing its $1.4 billion bid on time. Thus, although some analysts in India's strategic community do harbour hopes of potential cooperation between India and China in their global quest for energy resources, these hopes represent the triumph of fond wishes over harsh realities. India is in a fundamentally competitive, if not a conflicting, relationship with China.

Conclusion

However, in spite of rivalries and cooperation between India and China in African oil fields, India's ONGC-OVL or China's National Oil Companies (NOCs) are minor actors among foreign investors. They lag far behind the International Oil Companies (IOCs) in terms of asset value and production. They produce less oil and gas compared to USA and Western multinational oil companies. It is impossible for them to compete with IOCs such as BP, Exxon Mobil and Shell as they do not have the technology necessary when it comes to some of Africa's most desirable blocks, including those located in the deep waters of the Gulf of Guinea.

However, the investment of Asian countries in Africa is undoubtedly different from US or Western engagements. Asian countries take into account the interests of African countries and their desire to promote economic development, which gives them an advantage over US and Western countries. African countries have benefited enormously from the concessional loans provided by India and China in infrastructural projects. In the recently held India-Africa Summit in May 2011, India has committed to provide grants and aid to contribute to capacity building in the socio-economic sectors, infrastructure, SMEs and agriculture sectors to the African countries. Thus, India's investment in Africa has now gone far beyond oil and natural resources. Nevertheless, it is obvious that in the energy sphere, India is gradually extending its footprint in Africa and attempting to reduce its dependence on West Asian countries.

References

1. EIA, India Energy Profile - EIA, 2010.
2. India Overtakes Japan in Crude Oil Consumption, http://indiatransportportal.com/2010/09/india-overtakes-japan-in-crude-oil-consumption/
3. IAGS, Energy Security, *India's Energy Security.Challenge, http://www.iags.org/n0121043.htm*
4. *Oil and Gas overview, www. kpmg.com.in*
5. 'How India can beat the oil crisis', *The Economic Times, http://articles.economictimes.indiatimes.com/2012-04-07/news/31304968_1_oil-imports-import-bill-shale-gas Apr 7, 2012, 11*
6. EIA, Top of Form Bottom of Form EIA, *India's Oil and Gas Profile, abarrelfull.wikidot.com/india-oil-and-gas-profile*
7. ADB, *Africa Economic Outlook,* 2010.
8. *Ibid.*
9. International Energy Agency, *Oil Market Report, 2006, http://www.eia.doe.gov/oiaf/ieo/pdf/o*
10. *Ibid.*
11. India's Economic Engagement with Africa, *Africa Economic Brief,* Volume 2, Issue 6, 11 May, 2011.
12. Kathman, Jacob and Megan Shannon, 'Oil Extraction and the Potential for Domestic Instability in Uganda', *African Studies Quarterly*, Vol. 12, Issue 3, Summer 2011.
13. *Nigeria: Refinery: Edo Signs MOU with Indian Firm, http://allafrica.com/stories/200409131043.html*
14. ONGC and Mittal Signs MOU in Nigeria 5. ONGC Videsh, *IRP Red Sea strike oil in Egypt, http://www.sify.com/finance/ongc-videsh-irp-red-sea-strike-oil-in-egypt-news-default-jegvxQabhga.html*
15. Essar Oil picks 50% in Kenya Petroleum, TNN, Jan 16, 2008, *http://articles.economictimes.indiatimes.com/2008-01-16/news/27720829_1_kprl-kenyan-refinery-essar-energy-overseas*
16. Rodgers, Michael, AUGU 'Sudan's Projected Oil Production and Revenues Summary', *PFC Strategic Studies*, August 2002.

17. Gordon, Anthea, 'Oil in Sudan: An Independent Problem?', 24 October 2011, *http://thinkafricapress.com/south-sudan/oil-sudan-independent-problem.*
18. Large, Daniel and Luke Patey, 'Caught in the Middle: China and India in Sudan's Transition', *DIIS Working Paper,* No. 36, 2010.
19. *Ibid.*
20. Ministry of External Affairs, 'India-Sudan Joint Statement', 22 October 2003, *http://meaindia.nic.in/mystart.php?id=55037273*
21. India- Africa Hydrocarbon Conference and Exhibition, *http://india.merinews.com/catFull.jsp?articleID=127560*
22. India commits $500 million aid for West Africa, *http://www.siliconindia.com/shownews/India_commits_ 500_million_ aid_for_West_Africa___-nid-23233.html 01 March 2004.*

6

Why China Beats India in Competition for Angolan Oil?

Alex Vines

Over the last decade Angola has become increasingly important as a source of oil for China, though far behind India. This chapter assesses how China has accessed Angolan oil and its future prospects; also compares China with India's efforts to obtain further oil concessions.[1]

The Angolan Context and the Success of China

After the end of its civil war in 2002, Angola posted the highest increase in oil output (ahead of Russia, Azerbaijan, Brazil, Libya and Kazakhstan, among others). From 2004-05, Chinese oil companies began to secure oil blocks in Angola. Angola is today a key player in Africa's oil industry as a major producer and exporter, and in 2008 Angola briefly surpassed Nigeria as the leading sub-Saharan oil producer. In 2010 China's imports of crude from Angola stood at 18 per cent of the total (the same as Saudi Arabia), and for the period from January to June 2011, Angola was China's second most important supplier of crude oil (after Saudi Arabia and ahead of Iran).[2] Exports to China of Angolan oil was 45 per cent while the US was the destination of 23 per cent of Angolan oil.[3]

The success of the relationship between Angola and China is marked by two important features. The first is the success of Chinese oil strategies in Angola through the interlinking of state-directed businesses and diplomacy. Business vehicles established by Hong Kong-based private interests in partnership with the China Petroleum and Chemical Corporation (Sinopec), and the Angolan national oil company, Sonangol, have served the Chinese well in building up a portfolio of joint ventures with the Angolan leadership that have extended beyond oil to construction, aviation and real estate across the world. The second is that in contrast to the reluctance of Western donors to finance Angola's essential post-war reconstruction, China was quick to provide oil-backed loans for infrastructure.

Oil and Reconstruction after the War: The Contribution of China

After the war ended, rapid reconstruction became the Angolan government's top priority. China, which established diplomatic relations with Angola in 1983, has played a particularly important role in assisting these efforts. Chinese financial and technical assistance has engaged in over 100 projects since 2004 in a number of areas, including energy, water, health, education, telecommunications, fisheries and public works. On the occasion of Chinese Prime Minister Wen Jibao's visit to Angola in June 2006, President dos Santos described bilateral relations as being 'mutually advantageous', and partnerships as being 'pragmatic', with no 'political preconditions'.[4]

By 2009, China had facilitated loans to Angola amounting to at least US$13.4 bn (or, according to some estimates, up to US$19.7 bn). In 2009-10, a further US$ 10 bn worth of credit lines were signed.[5] President José Eduardo dos Santos visited Beijing twice in 2008, underlining the importance of this relationship for Angola. In return, China's Sinopec group initially obtained oil equity through the Sonangol Sinopec International (SSI) business vehicle in a valuable deepwater block, and later obtained equity stakes in three further offshore blocks and in pre-salt blocks (see below). President dos Santos touched the core of this in November 2007 when he stated that 'China needs natural resources and Angola wants development'.[6]

The visit of vice-president, and likely future secretary general of the Chinese Communist Party, Xi Jinping, to Luanda in January 2011 further cemented the relationship. During Jinping's visit new agreements were signed in the transportation, mining and construction sectors and an extension of credit lines was agreed. Jinping noted that at that time that Chinese loans had 'reached US$10 bn'.[7]

'Angola Mode': Oil-Backed Loans for Infrastructure

Having become a net oil importer in 1993 Chinese demand for oil is growing exponentially. As a result of this increasing demand, since 2003 Chinese National Oil Companies (NOCs) have tried rapidly to acquire stakes in exploration and production projects in Angola, as well as purchasing more Angolan oil on the spot market. In early 2004, Sonangol opened its Sonasia office in Singapore, aimed at promoting the trade of Angolan crude oil to Asia.

The China Construction Bank (CCB) and Exim Bank provided the first funding for Angolan infrastructure development in 2002. The Angolan Ministry of Finance had little input into these arrangements since funding was provided directly to Chinese firms. Financial relations between China and Angola grew further in November 2003 when a 'framework agreement' for new cooperation was formally signed by the two governments. On 21 March 2004, the first US$2 bn financing package for public investment projects was approved. Since 2004 Angola has agreed to at least two oil-backed loans for Chinese financial assistance for key public investment projects in infrastructure, telecommunications and agro-businesses under the National Reconstruction Programme. China's EximBank is increasingly making use of this deal structure – known by the World Bank as the 'Angola mode' or 'resources for infrastructure' – whereby repayment of the loan for infrastructure development is made in natural resources.[8]

There are questions, however, regarding the quality and of the infrastructure delivered in return for oil as well as the timelines involved. There were some stoppages in Chinese construction projects in late 2007 and in 2008 linked to the China International Fund (CIF, see below). For example, the Benguela railway line project was subject to a series of contractual revisions that followed the discovery by the Angolan authorities of 'irregularities' by Chinese firms. As a result, the Angolan government decided to let the Chinese companies continue to lay the railway lines, but to invite other competitors to tender for complementary projects.[9]

The assistant director of the Benguela Railway Company confirmed that sixteen Chinese camps had been dismantled and revealed that the contract had been cancelled.[10] Work on the railway has however restarted in October 2010. The project has grossed US$1.8 bn to date and reconstruction is set to be completed towards the end of 2012, by which time an estimated four mn passengers and 20 mn tons of goods will be transported along the line. Ambitious plans also exist to extend the line to DRC, Zambia and Zimbabwe.[11]

Sinopec's First Steps: SSI and the Block 18 'Ground-Breaking' Deal

Following the opening of China's first credit line to Angola in March 2004, Sinopec acquired its first stake in Angola's oil industry in July of the same year - 50 per cent of the BP-operated Block 18. Sonangol Sinopec International (SSI) was created to explore the stake on the block.[12] It is a joint venture majority-owned by Sinopec (55 per cent stake) with Beiya (now Dayuan) International Development Ltd., and China Sonangol International Holding Ltd. (CSIH) holding 31.5 per cent and 13.5 per cent of SSI respectively.[13]

SSI obtained a seven-year loan that is covered by a pre-completion guarantee from Sinopec during construction. Sonangol had prepared the way for this deal with a previous US$3 bn corporate deal signed in September 2005, sold in the Hong Kong market under Hong Kong law through Calyon.[14] This was the largest pre-export finance facility ever and Trade and Forfeiting Review called it 2005's Deal of the Year. It came about because of contractual restrictions on Sonangol at the time for seeking new credit. The deal also marked a new structure, with funds provided directly to China Sonangol International Holding (CSIH) rather than a special purpose vehicle (SPV). CSIH was able to raise the funds on the back of the long-term off-take agreement the crude trader China International United Petroleum and Chemicals (Unipec).[15]

This was the first Sonangol deal to involve a Chinese off-taker; it amounted to a US$3 bn loan that was to be paid back over a seven-year period by the delivery of Angolan crude to Unipec (at a rate of 40,000 b/d for the first three years).[16] Once this loan was syndicated, CSIH participated in the SSI project finance facility through its 31.5 per cent equity stake of Dayuan International Development. This arrangement suits Sinopec well, enabling it to benefit from major technology transfer from the Western companies leading the operations (BP is the operator in Block 18) while still being granted a large share of the oil from these licences.

Sinopec's Growth in Angola

In March 2005, during Chinese Vice-Premier Zeng Peiyang's visit to Angola, nine cooperation agreements were signed, mostly related to energy. Sonangol also entered a long-term uplift agreement to supply oil to Unipec, which *Africa Energy Intelligence* estimated could result in Sinopec (as the parent company) lifting up to 100,000 b/d.[17] Additionally, the two parties signed an MoU to jointly study plans for the exploration of the shallow offshore blocks 3(05) and 3(05A) (previously known as Block 3(80) - see above) that had been withdrawn from Total in late 2004.[18] Later that year, Sonangol agreed that CSIH would acquire the 25 per cent stake.[19] CSIH does not have any Sinopec participation but the CSIH stake was handed over to SSI (where Sinopec holds a 55 per cent interest) in 2007.

In April and May 2006, Sonangol announced the winners of exploration licences for seven shallow and deep-water concessions that had been put out to tender in November 2005. SSI acquired three new Angolan offshore oil blocks. It offered US$750 mn for 20 per cent of ENI-operated Block 15 after failing to win the operatorship. SSI also made a record US$2.2 bn signature bonus payment ($1.1 bn for each block) for the relinquished offshore Blocks 17(06) (27.5 per cent) and 18(06) (40 per cent). This signature bonus payment is a record for Angola and suggests that Sinopec felt it needed to pay over the odds to secure this acreage despite the ongoing Chinese loans to the Angolan government. From these Angolan acquisitions SSI hoped to add approximately one bn barrels of equity oil from production over the next five years. Sinopec believed that Blocks 15(06), 17(06) and 18(06) have proven reserves of 1.5 bn, 1 bn and 700 m barrels of oil respectively.[20]

Since 2004, China has obtained equity partnerships in Angolan deepwater oil blocks through Sinopec's majority in Sonangol Sinopec International Limited (SSI) and in shallow-water blocks through the China Sonangol International Holding Limited (CSIH), a joint venture between Sonangol and Hong Kong-based private business interests. SSI was awarded equity in deepwater Block 18 in 2004 and CSIH was awarded equity in Blocks 3(05) and 3(05A) in 2005. This was, however, turned over to SSI by 2007. SSI was awarded further equity in Blocks 15(06), 17(06) and 18(06) (with Agip-ENI, Total and Petrobas being the respective operatorship winners) in the May 2006 oil licensing awards (although this was subsequently handed over to CSIH to hold, before being returned to SSI eventually - see below).[21] In the most-recent pre-salt round (2011), CSIH consolidated its foothold in Angola (see Table 1).

Table 1

Block (s)	*Company*	*Year Acquired*	*Share (%)*	*Partners*
19	CSIH	2011	10	BP [OP]
20	CSIH	2011	10	Cobalt [OP] (40%)
36	CSIH	2011	20	Conoco-Phillips [OP]
38	CSIH	2011	15	Statoil [OP]

Inter-Chinese Rivalry

Increasingly it is impossible to speak of 'China' as a unified homogeneous actor in Angola. This becomes clear when analysing the increasing number of different interests and actors that exist in the oil relations between Angola and China.

Sinopec Corporation's director and chairman of the third session of its Board of Directors, Dr Su Shulin, visited Luanda in April 2008. This was followed by a delegation from Zhen Hua Oil (an affiliate of NORINCO) who arrived in Luanda in March 2008 to sign an MoU with Sonangol.[22] Chinese NOCs seem to be competing abroad.

This became much clearer in the 'Marathon saga': On 17 July 2009, it was announced that Marathon International Petroleum Angola Block 32 Ltd, a subsidiary of Marathan Oil, had entered into a definitive agreement with CNOOC and SINOPEC. Both companies were said to purchase an undivided 20 per cent participating interest in the production-sharing contract and joint-operating agreement in Block 32 for US$13 bn, effective from 1 January 2009. Marathon Oil would have retained a ten per cent working interest. The companies expected to close the transaction by year-end 2009, subject to government and regulatory approvals.[23] Unusually, China's CNPC also made a separate bid. As it turns out, CNOOC and SINOPEC both lost out, as did CNPC. Sonangol decided to exercise its right of first refusal and offered the stake to CSIH.

For the first time Chinese companies were openly competing among themselves for Angolan concessions and the biggest winner so far in this story was CSIH. Efforts also by CNOOC to partner up in 2011 with other Asian national oil companies like Indonesia's Pertamina for Angolan oil concessions have yet to show success.

Chinese Opportunities in the Financial Crisis of 2008

Angolan officials admitted that falling oil prices in the wake of the international financial and economic crisis of 2008 have forced them to cut back on some of their US$42 bn infrastructure plans for 2009. Not yet cash-strapped, but nevertheless concerned, President dos Santos visited China in December 2008 to seek guarantees that it would honour its Angolan loans and beef up its bilateral cooperation by extending new loans, and on 17 December 2008 Li Ruogu, the chairman and president of China Exim Bank, announced: 'We are planning to expand our cooperation with the Angolan Ministry of Finance.'[24]

Shortly after this pledge, China's commerce minister, Chen Deming, paid a two-day visit to Angola in January 2009 bringing with him a commitment from the China Development Bank to extend an additional loan to Angola worth at least US$1 bn. This was confirmed by Chen Yuan, president of the China Development Bank, on 12 March 2009, following yet another meeting with President dos Santos.[25]

An initial agreement was signed in August 2008 and negotiations concerning the implementation of the agreement have continued into 2009. This deal includes construction of social housing, agriculture, transport and telecommunications. The former vice prime minister of Angola, and former head of the National Private Investment Agency (ANIP) Aguinaldo Jaime, confirmed in September 2008 that this loan would not be oil-backed.[26] He also told the Chinese media in January 2009 that President Dos Santos had 'already received the president of the China-Africa Development Fund twice, clear proof of the degree to which Angola values its alliance with China.'[27] More loans from the Chinese Exim Bank are likely.

China's (then) ambassador to Angola, Zhang Bolun, met President dos Santos on 17 February 2009, after which he signalled that China was considering further financial assistance for infrastructure that would be 'properly implemented and protected from the world crisis'.[28] It is clear that since the legislative elections in 2008 the Angolan government has new priorities. Rapid post-conflict infrastructural development is less. At the fourth session of the bilateral Angola–China Commission in March 2009, officials[29] committed themselves to increased financial cooperation by agreeing to put in place an investment guarantee scheme (emulating an earlier US agreement to the same effect). At the meeting China also offered a grant worth US$34.15 mn.

Chinese government officials believe that oil-backed loans are the most beneficial arrangement as they offer the greatest security, and have regularly indicated this preference to their Angolan counterparts. The Angolans, however, seem to continue to want to move away from the 'Angola mode' approach. China is clearly seeking to secure more oil concessions but it is at the same time under pressure to provide better local content provisions in contracts for its companies.[30] Despite these differences the bilateral relationship seems to be solid.

India and Angola

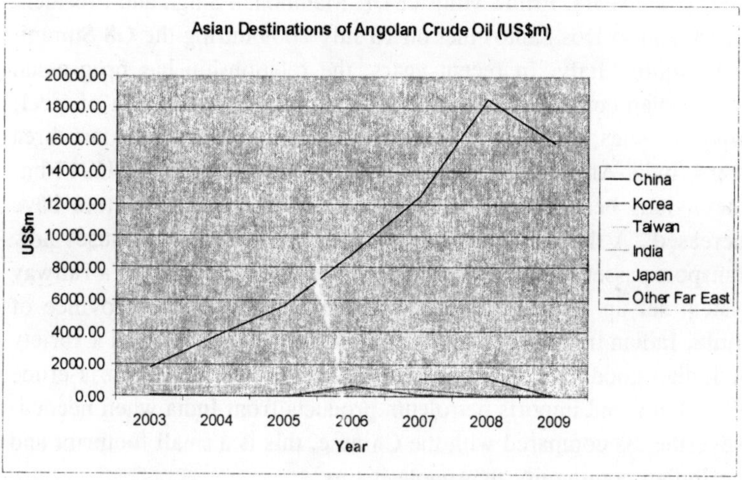

Although India was one of the first countries to recognise the MPLA government in 1975, following support of nationalist movements against Portuguese colonialism, its footprint is tiny in Angola compared with China. India set up its resident mission in Luanda in September 1986 and Angola its Embassy in Delhi in 1992. Despite this bilateral visits have been slow. President José Eduardo dos Santos visited India in April 1987 and a series of officials have visited India since, more regularly since 2005. João Miranda, Foreign Minister of Republic of Angola visited India from 10 - 13 May 2006 and met Shri Anand Sharma, minister of state for External Affairs, Shri Kamal Nath, minister of commerce and industry, and Shri Murli Deora, minister for petroleum and natural gas. He will also meet a cross-section of businessmen at a meeting arranged by the Confederation of Indian Industry and visited the facilities of several leading companies engaged in the software, automobiles, agricultural equipment, transportation, railways, energy and mining sectors.

India's Prime Minister Shri Rajiv Gandhi visited Angola in May 1986 but visits by Indian officials to Angola have been subsequently slow until around 2005. In June 2007, Shri Anand Sharma, minister of state for external affairs visited Luanda to discuss cooperation in the fields of oil, geology and mining, agriculture, health, education and tourism. Trade with India has been small mainly meat, pharmaceuticals, dairy products and machinery. After a gap of twenty-two years, Prime Minister Dr. Manmohan Singh and President Jose Eduardo Dos Santos met on 10 July 2009 during the G8 Summit in L'Aquila, Italy. In recent years, the relationship has progressed fast. Indian companies have invested in Angola in the area of steel, paper, plastics, pharmaceuticals, drinking water, etc. In the last three years, India-Angola trade has quadrupled to reach close to US$2 bn, interactions between our governments and the private sectors have increased. A thousand specially designed Ashok Leyland buses now transport passengers and goods in the provinces of Angola, a railway system set up with Indian credit line is running in the province of Huila, Indian tractors are a popular brand in the country and a variety of Indian goods are now exported to Angola. Angola exports crude oil to India and imports petroleum products from India when needed. Nevertheless compared with the Chinese, this is a small footprint and the Indian community in Angola is tiny.

Lines of Credit extended by India, include $40 mn for rehabilitation of Angolan Railways by RITES, $10 mn for purchase of tractors and $5 mn for the agriculture sector by credit extended by the Exim Bank of India.

India has tried to get oil acreage in Angola. For example, ONGC's bid for an Angolan oil block failed at the last moment in 2004 when its offer of $310 mn for infrastructure development could not compete with a massive $725 mn from China. However, India hopes to do better in the 2009 Angola licensing round and in July 2008, India's oil minister announced that ONGC had qualified to bid as an operator in the next licensing round and would consider jointly bidding with Angola's national oil company Sonangol. ONGC was also interested is bidding for a 20 per cent stake in an Angolan oil field that US energy firm Marathon Oil Corp sold, but as discussed above this concession eventually went to China Sonangol.

In 2010-11, ONGC once more bid for a 25 per cent stake of block 31 being relinquished by Exxon. Indonesian state energy firm Pertamina initially tried to bid for this concession jointly, but the joint effort collapsed and made a $3.5 bn offer alone. Even so, it seems that Sonangol will claim right of first refusal and Pertamina said in November 2011 that if that happened Pertamina would withdraw its offer. Once gain Angolan politics and outbidding, undercut Indian oil diplomacy.

In May 2007, President dos Santos also offered India a 30 per cent stake in the Lobito oil refinery when the Minister of State for External Affairs, Anand Sharma, visited Luanda. This offer has not been taken forward but ONGC-Videsh has been designated as the company to deal with oil issues.

Indian state oil company, Indian Oil Corp (IOC) has been more successful than winning concessions and purchased 1.6 million barrels of oil for delivery in June 2011 from Angola, making Angola the main African oil supplier to India that month. This purchase was part of an acquisition of 2.6 million barrels due for delivery in June in Africa, and Nigeria provided the remaining one million barrels of oil.

In the first quarter of 2011, India and the US were the main buyers of Angolan oil. Until the end of 2010, India imported around seven per cent of Angola's oil production and the outgoing Indian ambassador to Angola has stated his country's interest in increasing the amount of oil it buys from Angola. 'We would like to get to ten per cent. We have eighteen refineries and import around 70 per cent of the oil we need,' the ambassador said.

India's diamond diplomacy seems more successful. The Angolan state diamond company, Endiama has agreed to do business directly with the large Indian diamond industry, while India is looking at opening an institute for jewellery manufacturing in Luanda. India's Minister of State for Commerce, Jairam Ramesh, visited Angola in April 2009 to set up an initiative of direct import of diamonds. India seeks direct links with supplier countries, cutting out the middlemen.

As part of diversifying and beefing up supply of rough diamonds, Jairam Ramesh visited the CEO of Endiama, the state-owned Angolan diamonds company, which promised to send a team to Mumbai to begin the process of setting up an office there. This would enable direct sales of rough diamonds by Endiama to Indian companies in 2009. Endiama has also invited Indian mining companies to explore and develop diamond mines in Angola.

The China International Fund, the GRN and Local Politics

Obtaining oil concessions from Angola has been complex for Chinese companies and Indian policy makers should reflect on this. From its genesis, oil-backed borrowing became an increasingly effective tool by which the Angolan presidency could secure spending priorities, bypassing the inefficiencies of the traditional financial system. It has become central to the exercise of power, and the *Gabinete de Reconstrução Nacional* (GRN) became its epicentre.

The GRN was set up in 2005 to manage large investment projects and ensure rapid reconstruction of infrastructure prior to national elections. Initially headed by a military adviser to the president, General Helder Vieira Dias 'Kopelipa', GRN was designed to provide work for the demobilised military in order to bring new dynamism to the reconstruction effort. It was also created on the assumption that the ministries would not have the capacity to manage the large inflows of money directed to the National Reconstruction Programme. GRN was designed to kick-start major prestige projects such as three railways, including the *Caminhos de Ferro de Luanda* railway project, drainage systems in Luanda, studies on a new city near Luanda, social housing, administration, and the construction of a new Luanda International Airport at Bom Jesus. Many of these project have been delayed (see below) and are still due to be completed. The GRN is exclusively accountable to the Angolan presidency.

China International Fund Ltd (CIF), a private Hong Kong-based institution, was meant to provide the funds to undertake these projects. According to a senior government official close to the presidency, GRN projects are valued at somewhere around US$10 bn. In April 2007, the World Bank published an Angolan Ministry of Finance estimate of the loan as being $9.8 bn at Libor plus 1.5 per cent.[31] The US Department of State 2008 Investment Climate Statement on Angola estimates the CIF loan figure between $2.9 bn and $9 bn.[32] These figures broadly fall into the figures mentioned by Chinese vice-president Xi Jinping when he visited Luanda in 2011 (US$10 bn - see above). However, according to the former Angolan ambassador in Beijing, João Manuel Bernardo, total credit lines from China to Angola for the purposes of national reconstruction stood at US$6 bn in September 2010. The ambassador also stated that US$2 bn from the 2004 credit line had already been used up.[33]

While there is uncertainty regarding the exact figures, it is also unclear how these funds were allocated across projects.

Throughout 2007 and for much of 2008 many GRN projects came to a standstill, provoking a lot of media speculation. Although it was reported that CIF had some difficulties in raising funds to complete the projects, a GRN technician admitted that a lack of planning on the part of the GRN also contributed towards the failure of many construction projects even to start. As he explained: 'We went ahead with projects pressured by strict time deadline and did not take into account the forward planning that is required in a country like ours.... We overlooked crucial elements such as the fact that our ports would not be able to cope with the increased amount of material being imported for these projects.'[34] Chinese construction firms also complained about CIF cajoling contractors into taking part in projects in Angola, routinely delaying payment for completed work and keeping rates as low as possible.[35] As a result, some of the funds from the second EximBank loan were used to continue the major programmes of GRN, but the Ministry of Finance was forced to raise US$3.5 bn in domestic funding by issuing treasury bonds in 2007. This was a new departure as Angolan funds are being used for the first time to finance Chinese firms to ensure completion of these projects.

In May 2010, Manuel Hélder Vieira Dias 'Kopelipa', the former head of the GRN, was replaced by President dos Santos with António Teixeira Flor, ex-vice-minister of Urbanism and Housing. This was followed by a presidential decree in September 2010 which saw the GRN disbanded and the various responsibilities of the GRN redistributed. The development of the Luanda areas of Kilamba Kiaxi, Zango e Cacuaco were transferred from GRN to 'Sonangol - Real Estate and Property' (Sonangol Imobiliária e Propriedade - SONIP)[36] and the son of José Eduardo dos Santos, José Filomeno dos Santos 'Zenú', has taken over the oversight of the construction of the new airport. Despite the decentralisation of the GRN there is however no indication that the control of core aspects of the GRN has been ceded by the presidency.

What is CSIH and CIF?

CIF was created in 2003 and appears to be the construction arm of Beiya International Development Ltd, a parent company of China Angola Oil Stock Holding Ltd, which trades Angolan oil and is linked to CSIH.

According to Sonangol, CSIH is a joint venture that 'was established in mid-2004 and has its HQ in Hong Kong'. Its business activity is 'exploration and production of oil and gas'. The CSIH website states that the company engages in crude oil trading and has oil blocks in Angola and 'the ultra-deep waters off Nigeria'.[37] According to the Hong Kong registry of companies, CSIH was set up in September 2004 and is 70 per cent beneficially owned by Beiya International Development Limited and 30 per cent by Sonangol EP. New Bright appears to have taken over the share of Beiya, which has since renamed itself, Dayuan.

CSIH is one of the many companies associated with the Angolan-Chinese joint venture and the Cayman Islands registered SSI. The ownership of SSI changed in March 2010, when it was acquired by a subsidiary of Sinopec Corp from a subsidiary of China Petrochemical Corporation (which is also the controlling stakeholder of Sinopec Corp, with a 75.84 per cent share). It appears that SSI engages exclusively in deep-water acreage off Angola (exploration and production), while CSIH is active in shallow water/onshore as well as ultra-deep water sites. As shown in the previous section, China Sonangol, while still firmly entrenched in Angolan oil exploration, has diversified its business as well as its geographical radius of action. This has happened in conjunction with, and sometimes under the aegis of, the China International Fund (CIF). More information on the set-up of these and other related companies, as well as persons attached to these networks can be found in the Chatham House Report 'Thirst for African Oil: Asian National Oil Companies in Nigeria and Angola'.[38]

Chinese officials have denied any link between CIF and the Chinese government but acknowledge that the company has contributed to the development of Angola.[39] Indeed CIF's brand new skyscraper head office, the 25-floor CIF Tower, dwarfs Angola's nearby National Assembly building in central Luanda.

Chinese officials have distanced themselves from the company at various points. A spokesperson from the Chinese embassy in Angola said, 'We are not familiar with [CIF's] background, but all their projects have been built in Angola are not good,'[40] and a commercial counsellor from the Chinese embassy in Angola said, 'We are not the direct department in charge of Chinese–Angolan economic cooperative efforts, but we never saw [CIF] merge in any of the public exercises and meetings between the Chinese government and the Angolan government.'[41]

CIF seems to have successfully positioned itself between the Chinese and the Angolan governments (and between Sonangol and Sinopec) and controls access to Angolan resources. This is even the case for Angolan oil contracts for Sinopec – they are controlled by CIF.[42] CIF was able to get into this position by initially organising a team of four well-connected business people who were close to some Chinese government agencies. Through their connections the contracts kept coming, and CIF's position as the bridge to Angola became virtually unassailable.

The CSIH and CIF company web includes some illustrious personalities, and reaches into the highest echelons of the Angolan presidency. For example, José Filomeno dos Santos, the son of the president of Angola, is the official Sonangol representative at CSIH, and the CIF delegation to Guinea included Manuel Vicente - the CEO of Sonangol and step-nephew of the president of Angola.

Although the Sinopec Group has indicated that overseas operations will be transferred to its publicly-listed subsidiary (Sinopec Corporation), it has not added its Angolan equity production numbers to the latter's disclosures. To add to the confusion, in Angola's *Ministry of Petroleum Report on Petroleum Sector Activity in 2007* (published 11 June 2009), SSI (and CSIL) is referred to as a 'national, privately owned oil company'[43], while at the same time, it was recently reported on the Chinese National Development and Reform Commission website that: 'The [Chinese central] government has approved Sinopec's $983 m acquisition in March [2011] for Total's five per cent stake in Angolan oil block 31 via China Sonangol International.'[44]

Far from being limited to Angola, CSIH and CIF are expanding into other African markets. The story seems to be the same everywhere. Upon news stories of Chinese investments into the country in question, the inevitable disclaimers that CSIH and CIF has nothing to do with the Chinese state follow from the Chinese embassies. The nature of CIF and CSIH only gets more complex instead of clearer the more one analyses it.

Conclusion

From both the Angolan and the Chinese perspective, this relationship is pragmatic and strategic. Chinese financing was provided when concessional funding was not available for Angola. Integral to this cooperation is China's need to access energy resources. In the construction sector, Angola is a particularly favourable market for many Chinese companies, which deliver quickly and have their risk mitigated by funding guarantees from the Chinese government, underpinned by oil-backed loans to Angola. Angola needs significant outside investment and there is relatively little competition. As a result, Chinese firms have found profitable deals, although they are now under increasing pressure to hire Angolans. Despite China's efforts to enter the oil sector, production is still dominated by Western companies.

For the Angolan government the relationship brings significant advantages to the country, helping to support economic growth. As a commodity-based economy emerging from twenty-seven years of conflict, Angola was in desperate need of new partners and a new source of FDI. China provides a new model of cooperation, based on credit lines, economy and commerce, which contrasts with Western efforts of cooperation based on aid attached to conditionality.

The influence of China in Angola is often overplayed, and there is a growing fatigue among Angolan officials about the West's fixation with it.[45] For the most part, Angolan officials are open about their cooperation with China and candid about not wanting to depend on any one development or commercial partner. President dos Santos in his 2008 New Year address to the diplomatic corps stressed that the Angolan government plans to reinforce its bilateral and commercial relationships with other countries: 'Globalisation naturally makes us see the need to diversify international relations and to accept the principle of competition, which has in a dynamic manner replaced the petrified concept of zones of influence that used to characterise the world.'[46]

This resonates well with Angola's stated desire to diversify its international and economic relations. India could be considered a natural partner in a multipolar world. In fact, however, India has been the greatest loser to date with Indian companies being flat-footed in competition with China for oil concessions and unable to compete directly in cash terms. The failure of Indian and others (including Chinese companies) to get a better foothold in Angola can be attributed to the dominance of Western oil companies, and the success of CSIH.

CSIH has prevented Chinese and Indian national oil companies from acquiring oil acreage in the past (see Marathon Block 32 above) but has its influence in Angola peaked? The awards to it in the pre-salt were limited and it looked as if a 25 per cent stake in Block 31 being relinquished by Exxon, could go to Indonesian state energy firm Pertamina although Pertamina said in November 2011 that Angolan companies would get a chance to buy into the block first and if that happened Pertamina would withdraw its $3.5 bn offer. Pertamina and China's CNOOC had considered a joint bid in May 2011 for the Exxon oil block stake but this failed and Pertamina bid alone. CNOOC and Pertamina have however 'declared interest' in a ten per cent stake held by the US's Marathon in Block 32, in Angola's deep offshore. In both cases, Angola's state oil company will have the right of first refusal – if China Sonangol or its affiliates benefit it will indicate that this JV vehicle continues to flourish as Angola's preferred oil partnership model with China. It is Angola's elite that decides who wins oil concessions, politics in the end often trumps over technical expertise and size of bonus payments. Indian and Chinese state oil companies have had to learn this the hard way.

References

1. This chapter is an update on a forthcoming chapter on 'China and its oil diplomacy' in Weimer and Vines, *Angola*. It also draws upon material from, 'Thirst for African Oil', report published by Chatham House in August 2009; Vines, et. al., 'Thirst for African Oil: Asian National Oil Companies in Nigeria and Angola', Chatham House Report, August 2009.
2. Chinese Imports of Iranian Petroleum Products Soar, 26 July 2011 (http://oilprice.com/Latest-Energy-News/World-News/Chinese-Imports-of-Iranian-Petroleum-Products-Soar.html - last accessed 01.08.11) .
3. Source: Global trade Atlas, FACTS Global Energy, EIA, in EIA 2011 (http://www.eia.gov/countries/cab.cfm?fips=AO – last accessed 28/11/11).
4. 'PR defende cooperação constutiva com a China', *Jornal de Angola*, 21 June 2006.

5. Source: BNA, in African Development Bank, Angola 2011-2015, Country Strategy Paper & 2010 Country portfolio Performance Review, January 2011, p. 5.
6. 'Angolan leader addresses OPEC summit in Saudi Arabia', *Angop*, 19 November 2007.
7. Visit by 'future leader of China' to Angola boosts bilateral relations, MacauHub, January 31st, 2011 (http://www.macauhub.com.mo/en/2011/01/31/visit-by-%E2%80%9Cfuture-leader-of-china%E2% 80%9D-to-angola-boosts-bilateral-relations/ last accessed: 10/08/11).
8. Foster, Vivien, et al., 'Building Bridges: China's Growing Role as Infrastructure Financier for Sub-Saharan Africa', World Bank and Public-Private Infrastructure Advisory Facility, July 2008.
9. EIU, Angola Monthly Report, April 2008.
10. Serge, Michel, 'When China met Africa', *Foreign Policy*, 166, May–June 2008.
11. 'CFB estende rota ao Zimbabwe', July 2011, Radio Nacional de Angola.
12. According to the Diário da República (State Gazette), No. 22, series 1, 21 February 2005, Oil Minister Desidério da Graça Veríssimo da Costa authorized the termination of the contract with Shell Development Angola BV for 50% participation in the exploration of Block 18, and the same type of contract for Sonangol EP and Sinopec International through SSI. SSI would be responsible for the timetable of amortisations, reporting of damages and accountability of recovery costs.
13. According to the Chinese version of the CSIH website, SSI is responsible for the part of the business related to oil blocks in Angola. (http://www.chinasonangol.com/chi/business.asp - last accessed, 19 August 2009).
14. This was over-subscribed as 40 banks replied.
15. Interview with BNP Paribas official, Paris, 10 March 2009.
16. 'Establishing new patterns of trade', *Trade Finance*, 1 December 2005.
17. 'The Angola-China Connection', *Africa Energy Intelligence*, 27 July 2005.
18. When Total's PSA expired on 30 June 2005 it was not renewed.
19. Manuel Vicente, President of Sonangol, signed the agreement in Beijing in mid-2005.

20. 'China's Sinopec wins bid for stakes in Angola oil blocks', *Shanghai Securities News*, 13 June 2006.
21. In Block 18(06), Brazil's Petrobas was awarded the operatorship of the block with a smaller share than its main equity partner on the block, SSI, which secured a 40% stake.
22. *Africa Energy Intelligence*, 18 June 2008.
23. http:www.streetinsider.com/Corporate+News/Marathon+Oil+(MRO)+to+Sell+Interest+in+Block+32+Offshore+ angola+for+$1.3+Bn/4800732.html, last accessed 30 July 2009.
24. 'China eyes more loans for cash-tight Angola', Reuters, 19 December 2008.
25. 'China, Angola discuss China's new credit line of over $1 bn', *Xinhua*, 12 March 2009.
26. 'Govt, China Development Bank Analyse Cooperation', *Angop*, 24 September 2008.
27. 'Mutual Growth Marks Sino-Angolan Partnership', *China Daily*, 22 January 2009. Gou Jiang is also vice-chair of the China Development Bank.
28. 'Head of State, Chinese Ambassador Discuss Cooperation', *Angop*, 17 February 2009.
29. The Angolan Vice-Minister for External Relations, Exalgina Gâmboa, and Chinese Vice-Minister for Commerce, Jiang Zengwei.
30. Interview with Chinese official, Luanda, 4 March 2009.
31. World Bank, International Development Association Interim Strategy Note for the Republic of Angola, Report No. 39394-AO, 26 April 2007, Annex 7: Non-concessional Borrowing by Government of Angola since 2004, p. 49. This reports that there were also three months' management commission at 0.3% and immobilization commission, also at 0.3%.
32. US Department of State, '2008 Investment Climate Statement – Angola', www.state.gov/e/eeb/ifd/2008/100819.htm
33. In AngolaPress, 23.09.2010 (http://www.minfin.gov.ao/NoticiaD.aspx? Codigo=10501 – last accessed, 01.08.11)
34. Interview, Luanda, 3 October 2007.
35. 'China's stock bubble can be traced to Angola', *Asia Times Online*, 27 March 2007.
36. SONIP is a 20% shareholder of newly formed Mota-Engil Angola (other shareholders include Mota-Engil 51%, Banco Privado Atlantico (BPA) 11%, and Finicapital Globalpactum 18%).
37. See www.sonangol.com and www.chinasonangol.com, which post an archive of 'CIF News'.

38. Vines et.al., 'Thirst for African Oil: Asian National Oil Companies in Nigeria and Angola', Chatham House Report, 2009.
39. 'Dan Yinmu speaks for the first time; Chinese embassy in Angola is not familiar with CIF background', *First Finance Daily*, 29 March 2007.
40. Zong Xinjian and Lu Yuan, 'Dan Yinmu shou du kai kou: Zhongguo zhu an shi guan bu liao jie Zhong ji bei jing' ('Dan Yinmu speaks for the first time; Chinese embassy in Angola is not familiar with CIF background'), *First Finance Daily* Newspaper, 29 March 2007 [USCC staff translation], http://finance.sina.com.cn/g/20070329/02383450690.shtml, in Levkowitz, McLellan Ross and Warner, The 88 Queensway Group, p. 23.
41. *Ibid.*
42. CIF maintains an Oil Department in Shanghai, where it holds regular training workshops.
43. http://www.minpet.gov.ao/PublicacoesD.aspx?Codigo=477 - last accessed 6 July 2009.
44. 'China approves Sinopec investments in Indonesia, Angola oil, gas fields' Singapore (Platts)—2Aug 2011/ 218 (http://www.platts.com/RSSFeed DetailedNews/RSSFeed/Oil/7099498 - last accessed 10/08/11).
45. Interview with José Pedro de Morais, Finance Minister, Luanda, 13 October 2007.
46. José Eduardo dos Santos, Presentation of New Year Greetings by Diplomatic Corps, Luanda, 10 January 2008.

SECTION 3

INDIA-AFRICA SECURITY ISSUES

7

Horizontal Africa and India's Security in this Millennium

Musambayi Katumanga

Introduction

The contemporary vertical Africa emerged courtesy to lateral pressures in Europe, Indian labour and military expeditionary force. This convergence of Mahan and Mackinder's naval and continental logics transformed Africa into a bridgehead for the securitisation of the British Raj. The reluctance of India and African Indian Ocean Littoral states to replicate a similar strategic construction for their own interests underpins their current and imagined future security threats. This paper recapitulates the foregoing, first by putting into context apparent security dilemmas anchored in energy denial imaginations. Second, it recapitulates on the Curzonian Raj-Africa security coupling. Third, it examines geopolitical dynamics and how they underpin the apparent security dilemma between India and China. Fourth, it imagines how construction anchored on dual security-enhancing energy and trade-driven horizontal infrastructure in the East and Horn of Africa can underpin security-based economic interdependence critical for stability in Africa, Asia and the Indian Ocean. The paper conceives the current insecurity, interdependence anchored in human and material lateral pressures in Africa and Indian sub-continent as dead capital that is likely to transform the Indian

Ocean and Africa into potential clash points to the extent to which they are not transformed into a platform for security-based intense economic interdependence.

Resource Access and Denial: Lateral Pressures and Construction of Threats

Critical in this millennium is the economic rise of resource-hungry and dependent India and China. The phenomenon of geographical continuity, similarity in demographic character and convergence in the same spatial realms in search for strategic resources underpins their apparent geopolitical tensions. Theirs is a classic case of how geography mediates political interactions among states. It affirms the link and causal relationship between political power and geographical space. Osterud's contention here is apt. Geopolitics provides the nexus and causal relationships between political power and geographical space. In concrete terms, the geopolitical tradition have some consistent concerns, like the geopolitical correlates of power in world politics, the identification of core areas, and the relationships between naval and terrestrial capabilities.[1]

Underpinning the identification of a geographical space as a pivotal area is what Angew calls geopolitical imagination,[2] or the constructed view of the world. Once constructed, geopolitical imaginations structure and explain the active specialisation, division, labelling, sorting out and the tendency to evolve a hierarchy of places of greater or lesser 'importance' by political geographers, academics and political leaders. This geographical framing provides rationale for action, outlines and justifies the use of certain means by political elite in the process of acting at one level, and the mobilisation of the critical mass support at another. Core to this process is the production of discourse that facilitates interpretation of threats and actions seeking to counter threats. Nazli Choucri and R. North names them 'lateral pressures'. In their contention, states facing high demands, for limited resources available within their territory seek the same outside their borders through trade or conquest. They attribute these lateral pressures to demographic and technological advancements. Such competition over resources may engender conflicts.[3] Scarcity can also be engendered by structural imbalances consequent to flawed distribution process.[4] Consumerism and demands for raw materials in both India and China is spawning the economisation of international affairs and contestations over resource ownership.[5]

China's growth has created a demand surge for African commodities, such as oil and gas at one level and fears about her trade, aid and investments policies in Africa at another. China's demand has animated interests in Africa and internal pressure on the part of African states to sell these resources for revenue generation. Its trade with Africa rose from a mere US$10 bn in 2005 to US$107 bn in 2008. India too has experienced a huge growth in its economy. India's trade with Africa on the other hand grew from US$3.39 bn in 2000 to US$30 bn in 2007 and is projected to hit US$150 bn by 2012.[6] By 2030, India is expected to be the third largest consumer of energy after the US and China.[7] Traits of this growth and competition are evident in their activities in Africa. For both states, space continues to evolve significance both continentally and also by necessity. This spatial salience is mediated by imaginations and anchored in discourses about resource access and fears of denial. The value of the said resources to the economy explains the emerging tendencies to label certain spaces as critical to national survival or vital and thus justifying their securitisation in terms of policy options evolved to securitise identified interests. States are likely to resort military actions if their interests are conceived to be core to their very survival or are in fact vital.

It is at the global level that states and other actors come together to engage in a number of activities (diplomacy, military action, aid, fiscal and monetary activities, legal regulations, etc.) with intentions of seeking to influence others and extend their power (political, economic and moral). The ability to engage here is a function of ability and the political will of states as actors. This is conditioned by the uneven distribution of human and non-human resources.[8] This factor explains the need to deny access to others of material resources deemed critical to their survival. This is the process Klare refers to as economisation of international relations.[9] Underpinning this is the declaration of certain resources to be critical for national survival necessitating the need to protect the sea-lines of operations (to and from) and the spaces from which the resources are obtained. This concern is best summed up as the subject matter of geo-politics. It calls for the appreciation of relative position among states and the consequent responses of statesmen to advantages and vulnerabilities that territorial and maritime space may bring to foreign affairs and national security.[10]

The Western states and India are concerned about China's responses to her lateral pressures. These are not limited to Chinese contestations of their engagements in Africa but also to the growing Chinese naval power especially the South China Sea and Spratly Islands at one level, and what is now famously referred to as a String of Pearls in the Indian Ocean. Gordon Faircelough notes that underlying this are China's commercial interests and the need to defend them. These are driving China to pursue her military might. Rapid economic growth in turn helps the Communist Party to hold onto power. Ni Lexiong, a fellow at Shanghai National Defence Institute seems to confirm these fears when he contends that, for China 'if commerce were cut off, the economy would plummet. We need a strong navy'.[11] This orientation accords with Klare's contention that resource scarcity and its strategies to assure the flow leads China to military deployment at exploitation points and securitisation of shipping lines. These Asian lateral pressures are equally animating two other pressures.

While in Africa imaginations about its export opportunities due to Asian demand engender resource nationalism and look-east policy restructurisation. In the West there have been efforts to intensify Euro-African summits, negative media focus on Chinese ventures and the setting up of African Military Command to anchor US and Western security and economic interests. What is apparent is the emerging securitisation of geo-economic interests led by both India and China (developing states) and the USA and Japan. Uncertainty, leading to limited trust, is feasting on an anarchic system prevailing in Africa and the Indian Ocean to enhance a security dilemma among the former. This attempt to ensure survival is causing the rush for spatial control. Space is becoming critical for physical control and future use, added by geopolitical imaginations and discourses about the spatial essence in the event a constructed actor deploys it to actions detrimental to their interests. What is emerging is a re-enactment of the 'great game'. The old game pitied the British Raj against the Tzar. While its key determinants were maritime superiority and a set of buffer states, the current one is made difficult by the fact that contenders are not only contiguous but that they are characterised by high levels of growth besides being resource hungry. This fact is forcing them to seek critical strategic resources in the same spaces using the same ocean as a medium of transport and hence the tensions. This is transforming spaces into pivotal areas vital to national interest, a factor that is leading to mutual military encirclement and a constant apparent risk of conflict.

Mahan and Mackinder in the New Great Game

A key variable in power configuration among states is the value they attach to sea and land. Both India and China take to heart Alfred Thayer Mahan and Alford Mackinder's theoretical underpinnings as their referential points on the sea and land mass in their power configurations and calculations. Mediating these are internal economic and political imperatives. As internal consolidation has grown, it has unleashed a demand and need to secure sea lines of communications. In *The Influence of Sea Power and History 1600–1783*, Mahan (1890) attributes world power to the control of the seas and the acquisition of colonies. Mahan's thesis revolves around the appreciation of the value derived from the control of the sea and how the said control translates into off-shore power to determine decisions. The domination of critical sea-lines and choke points enables forces afloat to exert direct pressure on those ashore through the use of blockades and interdiction missions. According to Mahan, it is sea power (that is, the command of the sea through naval superiority) and combination of maritime commerce, overseas possessions, privileged access to foreign markets which produces national wealth and power. Mahan's naval operations especially those directed against trade and logistic supplies or redeployments could be crucial to nations waging land wars:

> If navies exist for the protection of commerce, it inevitably follows that the stoppage of commerce compels peace. Wars are won by economic strangulation of the enemy from the sea (wars are lost by the failure to prevent such strangulation of one's own country).[12]

Control of the maritime commerce through the command of the sea is the primary function of navies. According to Mahan, the naval strategy and sea power of a state is conditioned by certain fundamental natural phenomenon. They include the nation's insular or continental situation, national policies related to the navies, merchant marine and overseas bases. These perspectives informed Mahan's geopolitical imaginations and the framing of spaces. Mahan forewarned the salience of Indian Ocean when he noted, 'whoever controls the Indian Ocean dominates Asia'. This ocean, he noted, is key to the seven Seas. In the 21st century, the destiny of the world will be decided on its waters. For the British, this postulation held absolute truth defining their strategy of transforming the Indian Ocean into a British Lake. Both China and India seem to be internalising the need to entrench their naval legs in a bid to guarantee their security. Chinese analysts rationalise their naval expansion by pointing to Admiral Zheng's fleet of 317 ships and 37,000 men between 1405 and 1433, which was said to have been larger than those under various commands in Europe at the time to affirm China's maritime status. It is notable that this armada sailed as far as the Indian Ocean with some being racked in Malindi (present day Kenya).[13] They attribute China's humiliation and annexation of its territory including Hong Kong by the British to the atrophy of its navy in 1800s. Indians, on the other hand, are increasing their naval activities not only in the Indian Ocean but also what China considers as infiltration in South China Sea through emerging links with Vietnam. China's sensitivity here is best grasped by what Karnad calls her 'soft belly.'[14]

Warnings about the end of this Columbian epoch emerged in 1904, with Halford Mackinder's thesis that industrial mechanisation; in particular, railways would redress the imbalance that had favoured sea over land.[15] Steam and internal combustion, he had argued, stood to equalise relative economy of water versus overland transport allowing land powers to dominate world affairs in the 20th century. Underlying this, he contended, the fact that steam and internal combustion would systematically enclose and integrate vast continents into individual autarchic units. What Mackinder did not anticipate was the converse situation where a continental state could (consequent to closing spaces) is forced by lateral pressures to indeed re-ignite a Columbian epoch as a way of securitising its lateral pressures or containing a neighbour's threat. The argument here is that, a State could actually consolidate on land and sea as a distance decay resolution measure that anchors its security. This is the emerging reality of the India-China Great Game. For Sir Halford Mackinder (1919: 150), the vital space was the Eurasian 'Heartland', which formed the 'pivot of history' whose consolidation would provide an insulated area within which 'you will be able to fling power from side to side'.[16] A heartland based attacker (the British read this to mean Russian consolidation over central Asia) will have flexible ability to hit China, Middle East and Europe while maintaining internal lines of supply and operations impervious to naval assault or constrictions. The net effect was the offsetting of balance of global power.

To Mackinder, the future belonged to Russia or a potentially eastward-looking Germany. Mackinder classified Europe, Asia and Africa as the world island, with the Eurasian 'heartland' at the centre. Accusing Mackinder of overrating the heartland, Nicholas J. Spykman (1944: 41–3) put emphasis on the inner crescent, which he called the Rimland.[17] This is conceptualised as the intermediate region between the heartland and the marginal seas. According to him, whoever controlled the Rimland ruled Eurasia, and whoever ruled Eurasia controlled the destinies of the world. In his article, 'The round world and the winning of peace', Mackinder (1943) once more emphasised not only the salience of the heartland, but also brought attention to what he called the outer/insular crescent of Africa. He pointed to the monsoon lands of Asia (China and India) and the tropical rainforests of Africa and South America as areas of salience. Mackinder converged with Spykman on the salience of the Rimland (China and India). To the former, 'were the Chinese to overthrow the Russian empire and conquer their territory, they might constitute the Yellow Peril to the world freedom just because they could add an oceanic frontage to the resources of the great continent'.[18]

Mackinder seemed to have charted out on paper options for securitising the British Raj like the Mughals who installed themselves in India by thrusting across the vast lands of the north and west, threats were conceived to stream from the north. For the British, naval supremacy is critical to blocking any effective seaborne challenge and buffer states such as Afghanistan, and Tibet assured the Raj. The main fear was the consolidation of Russia in Central Asia. Under their great game British policy of containment sought to prevent expansion of the Russian influence towards the Indian Ocean to maintain a 'geographical inter-space' between two systems of oceanic communication and Eurasian land power.[19] The loss of the colonies in the US placed value to trade and capital inherent in the control of the Raj. This calculation informed the decision by the British to seek effective securitisation by transforming Africa into a bridge head for the defence of the former through security coupling of the African land mass to India. Effective defence meant control of strategic spaces that would influence activities in the Indian Ocean. Critical for the British was the control of the Red Sea and the Persian Gulf. The former's control could only be affected through the control of Egypt and by inference the source of the Nile.

Converging Mahan with Mackinder, by bringing the latter on land through the construction of the strategic Uganda Railway facilitated penetration. It enabled the British to mobilise, redeploy and control in-depth. In the processes they were able to consolidate their power in East Africa, initiate land alienation and settlement of Asians along the railway. In effect the economic production saw the railway shift from being a security-related strategic asset located in the ministry of defence to a strategic economic asset now located in the treasury. The net effect was that the British succeeded in creating a naval and continental mass that prevented Russia from capturing the strategic Rim land (China having taken up Hong Kong and forced China to sign trade arrangements in her favour) and the world island (Africa). Mackinder and Spyman were right but they would need the convergence with Mahan, for the British to emerge as a world power. The realisation of this strategy was facilitated by the logic of value addition to dead capital. This involved the use of Indian labour to build a railway and the Indian Raj soldiers to help in military consolidation. Together with immigration of endangered labourers in South Africa, the British were able to close spaces while acquiring a strategic flexibility of mobility of forces on the African and Indian subcontinent, a factor that would come in handy during both First and Second World Wars. They were able to cement their transformation of the Indian Ocean into a British Lake by fact of control from the Gulf all the way to the Cape. The British logic was about extraction — their exit was driven by inherent strategic vulnerabilities that were now anchored in the arrival of airpower. The strategic imperatives of critical assets needed to defend both the Raj and Continental Europe transformed the idea of Indian independence as the best option for securitising British interests. This withdrawal saw the split of India (creating Pakistan and later Bangladesh), the reintegration of Tibet into China, the autarchy of Africa through fragmented independence. The result was the systematic dismantlement of the Raj Strategy.

Geopolitical Dynamics in Indian Ocean and Africa: Retrenchment and Re-entry of India

Covering an area of 28,330 square miles, Indian Ocean (IO) is framed by Australia, Africa, and Asia and extends to the Antarctic Ocean. Its eastern and western entrances are guarded by five strategic narrow stretches of water. These are Cape of Good Hope, the Suez Canal and the straits of Bal-el-Mandeb, Hormuz and Malacca. The Ocean has been at the core of maritime activities from ancient times facilitating trade between Africa littoral states, the Asian continent and Arabia. Indian Ocean played a critical role in the ascendance of the Chola Empire of South India in the 13th Century[20] and Eastern Africa Coastal city states. Their collapse and conquest was in a large measure their strategic blunder to atrophy their naval power.

The ocean was soon dominated by Arab merchants only to be succeeded by Europeans. The shift and ascendance of alternative powers is broadcasted by increase in power projection and pronouncements of their vital interests. The net consequences tended to be security threats for littoral states. The ocean is home to estimated 32 littoral states and 11 hinterland states. India constitutes the single largest coastline of 3,500 miles. Her maritime salience is underpinned by islands of Andaman and Nicobar in the east and Lakshadweep in the west effectively extending her communication lines by another 700 miles into the bay beyond and the Arabian Sea. The IO region is characterised by diversity in religion, culture and differentiated levels of development. Of salience are its endowments in energy and strategic mineral resources such as chromium, manganese and bauxite. Underdevelopment in most states in the zone implied that for many years, they remain sources of raw materials and destination of finished products. This logic anchored dependence dynamics, conflicts, poverty and polarisation.

A large part of tensions were driven by the salience of the IO and its resources to the external global powers such as USA and USSR. The largest form of militarisation since decolonisation and withdrawal of British (in 1968 from the East of the Suez) followed the Iranians revolution and the Soviet's invasion of Afghanistan. Zbigniew Brzezinski, the US National Security Advisor, captured the Jimmy Carter administration's perspective when he observed that, 'an area of crisis stretches along the shores of the Indian Ocean with fragile social and political structures in a region of vital importance to us threatened with fragmentation. The resulting political chaos could well be filled by elements hostile to our values and sympathetic to our adversaries.'[21]

Subsequently, Carter declared the Persian Gulf as an area vital to US national interest. Located in the Middle East, the Persian Gulf and the North-western Indian Ocean, these interests revolved around the need to access the resources of the area by the US and its allies to, most notably oil from the Persian Gulf states; strategic sea lines of Communication (SLOC's) that facilitate transportation of oil to North America, western Europe and Japan. Protection of these interests called for a greater military presence, a capability to surge additional forces into the region, access to facilities, sufficient to support both peace time and contingency operations. The US concluded agreements for use of support facilities in Oman, Somalia and Kenya and improvement of facilities in Diego Garcia.[22] The Soviet Union's response includes increased presence in the Indian Ocean and the strengthening of its anti-submarine defenses in a bid to neutralise the perceived threats the US submarines posed to its southern flank. Yet, while tensions in the ocean were largely animated by military overlays of global powers, India seemed to retrench her activities in the Indian Ocean and its neighbourhood in Africa.

Three elements seemed to influence Afro-Indian relations in this period. First, independence struggles. While some African leaders, such as Nkurumah, would adopt the non-violence strategy, but many others would be driven by the objective reality, and opt for armed resistance. India provided diplomatic and financial support to the non-aligned movements. African Fund for the support of liberation movements cost Rs. 500 m.[23] It was China's overt support for armed struggle that seemed to strike a rapport with African imagination on such sensitive issues such as apartheid.

The second was the question of the People of Indian Origin (PIO). Underlying this were Africanisation policies adopted and pursued in both Kenya and Uganda. Mainly geared towards facilitating regime consolidation through expansion of the realms of accumulation believed to be dominated by Asians, the Indian government's response did not endear it to either the regimes or victims. Indira Gandhi's government had sought to see PIOs as India's ambassadors instead of perceiving and encouraging them to see themselves as Africans of Indian Origin, who needed to seek integration. Such a perspective would have motivated India to direct support geared towards consolidating their integration. For instance, assistance in joint rural industrialisation would have supported their branching out from retailing, thus enabling job creation while undermining elite instrumentalisation of Asians.

The third was socio-economic. In the social realms, there were engagements characterised by provision of limited scholarships to African students and access of universities to self-sponsored students mainly in social sciences. India missed out on the opportunity to enhance her soft power credentials by expanding access in professional and research fields that would have laid a base for future cooperation while enhancing her economic penetration in the continent. In economic fields her main trade was with developed states.

Three mutually reinforcing dynamics in late 1990s changed India's perceptions on the Indian Ocean and Africa. First were security concerns within the sphere underpinned by Israeli-Palestinian conflict, poverty and crisis of governance. These converged to transform this realm into one of fundamentalist resistance manifested by terrorism, piracy and organised crime. Indeed both the first and last major conflicts in the last and current millennium have their roots here. The second factor was the dual economic growth of India and China; this spawned energy demands. With only 0.4 per cent of the world's oil reserves, India projects its demand by 2030 to transform her into the world's third largest consumer of energy ahead of Japan and Russia.[24] Her estimated average growth rate of five per cent over the next twenty-five years implies that her demands for energy are expected to grow from 2.65 mn barrels per day to 4 mn barrels by 2020.[25] Most of its energy needs are sustained by imports compared to China's dependence to be 40 per cent only. It spends an average $75 bn on imports. 75 per cent of India's energy needs are from the Persian Gulf region. It also has an estimated 3.7 mn Indians resident in the region that remit an average $8 bn annually. By 2010, India was transporting 95 per cent of her trade through the Indian Ocean. As a peninsular state, India has to guard a coastline of 7,515 km and EEZ of 2.02 mn sq kms. Unlike China, India has no contiguity with oil rich Central Asian states. These geographical and lateral dynamics transformed the ocean into a referent security object vital to the survival of India. This in turn anchored the third factor, the need to build the Indian Navy for purposes of securitising the sea lines of communications.

Soon, variables underpinning tensions in the ocean were now mainly rooted within its geography validating K.M. Pannikar's constructs that 'while to other countries the Indian Ocean is only one of the important oceanic areas, to India, it is a vital sea.' According to him India's lifeline was concentrated here, her freedom dependent on freedom of water surface. No industrial development, no commercial growth, no political stability is possible for her unless the shores are protected. Other geo-strategists like H. Kissinger seemed to see Indian's goals to be analogous to UK's East of the Suez in the 19th Century. This includes the desire to be the strongest state on the subcontinent; prevent emergence of major power in the IO or South East Asia. Kissinger's assumptions are that these geopolitical interests would converge with those of the USA leading to a point where India would agree to share burdens with US in this region. Neither Kissinger nor the Indians seem to recognise the importance of Africa to India's security. The need to diversify sources of energy, raw materials and markets apparently underlies her re-entry into the continent and indeed energy diplomacy. Crude oil accounted for 58.6 per cent of India's total imports from Africa in 2008-2009. This is likely to grow given the projections that India will run out of coal within the next forty years. Without such reliable energy supplies, the ability to sustain economic growth is likely to be undermined.

Nigeria ranked as India's fifth largest source of energy after Saudi Arabia, Iran, United Arab Emirates and Kuwait. It accounted for 9.4 per cent or US$8.65 m. State-owned Oil and Natural Gas Company (ONGC) has sought to secure India's energy needs on the African continent, focusing essentially on Nigeria, Sudan and Angola. In Nigeria, ONGC has sought to invest in an oil pipeline through a 25 per cent stake in the greater Nile Petroleum oil company project. ONGC sought to buy a 25 per cent stake in block 5B in addition to its shares in block 5A. It also invested US$1.2 bn in an oil refinery. An additional US$200 mn was invested in a multi-product export pipeline in Sudan. ONGC also entered into a US$ 6 bn joint venture with ARCELOR Mittal Steel for industrial development in Nigeria in exchange for oil exploration rights. ONGC's other investment division, Videsh Limited, has also been active in Cote d'Ivoire's offshore block C1-112, where it maintains a 23 per cent interest. It also has a 49 per cent participating interest in two offshore oil exploration blocks in

India and a concessional agreement to explore oil in Egypt's Ramadhan block in the north.

India also has oil companies operating in Cote d'Ivoire with an investment size of US$1 bn. Another company, National Thermal Power Corporation (NTPC) runs an investment of US41.7 bn liquefied natural gas in Nigeria. There is also Indian Oil Corporation with an investment of US$3.5 bn in an oil refinery and another proposed US$4 bn for liquefied natural gas plant and oil refinery. This drive is animated by geopolitical imaginations revolving around the notion of resource access and denial. The general impression is that China is pursuing a policy seeking to deny India access to vital oil resources as part of her military encirclement strategy; examples are the bids lost to Chinese companies in Angola and Nigeria. In Angola, Oil and Natural Gas Corporation (ONGC) was outbidded by China, which now draws 16 per cent of its oil needs. In Nigeria, China's National Offshore Oil Cor (CNOOC) Ltd took over the AKPO deepwater oil field after buying 45 per cent stake of South Atlantic petroleum. This followed the decision of the Indian government to block ONGC's $2.27 bn deal on the account of what it considered to be unacceptable risks. CNOOC also acquired an exploration licence in the Niger delta for 460 bn.[26]

India's response has been reactive in this case though it is generally driven by profit-motivated private-sector logic. The implications here are that financial considerations outweigh geo-economic and strategic security imperatives. This absence of a grand strategy integrating energy security with foreign and national security policy constrains the government's role and by inference the willingness to play big in terms of win-win projects between her and Africa. This contrasts China's model. Her security imperatives allow her to allocate large resources in exploration, infrastructure and extraction, risks notwithstanding. The net effect is the ability of China to evolve a long-term mutually reinforcing win–win situation that links her energy security with her maritime security strategy. China having gone from a net exporter of energy to the second largest consumer of energy in fifteen years has had to securitise energy.

These geo-economic threats are such that competition and power struggle and a new Great Game is becoming real possibility. This threat is acknowledged by Mani Shankar Aiyer, minister for petroleum and natural gas notes, 'it is clear to me that any imitation of the

'Great Game' between China and India is a danger to peace.[27] As the space linking India to vital resource spaces and a valve of transportation, Indian Ocean is thus becoming core to her national survival. With huge demographics likely to heat a billion people, high growth rates, huge agricultural potential, Africa will soon emerge to be a huge market and a source for food imports multiplying its value to both India and China. India is increasingly awakening to the reality of seeing Africa as a potential strategic trade partner. Her trade with the continent jumped from US$967 mn in 1991 to US$9.5 bn in 2005.[28] Between 2000 and 2005, India's imports from Africa increased from US$3 bn to US$4 bn respectively; and exports increased from US$2 bn to US$6 bn. In January 2009, the Associated Chambers of Commerce (ASSOCHAM) and Industry in India projected that India-Africa bilateral trade would grow to US$150 m by 2012.[29]

South Africa leads in imports from India, taking up 15.5 per cent of all exports to the continent in 2008-09. It was followed by Egypt at 11.2 per cent , Nigeria at 10.3 per cent, Kenya at 9.1 per cent, Tanzania at 7 per cent, Mauritius at 6.5 per cent and Algeria at 4.5 per cent. Nigeria dominated exports to India with its oil accounting for 35.8 per cent of total imports from Africa, followed by South Africa with 22.4 per cent, Egypt at 8.7 per cent, Angola at 5.6 per cent, and Algeria at 4 per cent and Morocco at 3.8 per cent.[30] Other strategic resources included gold (8.6 per cent), inorganic chemicals (8.3 per cent), metal ferrous ores and metal scrap (5.3 per cent), coal, coke and briquettes (4 per cent) and ion non-ferrous metals (28 per cent).[31]

India's engagements with Africa are essentially private-sector driven. Much of the investments have revolved around purchase of estate or some ongoing concerns. For instance in 2001, RITES secured a US$500 mn contract to manage Malawi railways. In 2004, RITES and the Indian Railways construction company limited secured a deal to revamp Sudanese rail network. RITES are also involved in a large-scale project that seeks to facilitate coal passage to the port of Beira for export across the Indian Ocean through rehabilitation of 600 km Beira railway system.[32] Tata has invested in steel and IT consultancies in South Africa, soda ash production in Kenya, transportation in Nigeria, Ghana, Mozambique and Senegal, and coffee in Uganda. The group employs over 700 persons in Africa. In Zambia, Tata invested US$800 mn in the renovation of Taj Pamodji hotel in

Lusaka, a vehicle assembly plant in Ndola. RITES and Ircon (Indian government owned infrastructure and engineering companies) have been making investments in rail and road investment sectors. Raite for instance, has been involved in leasing and refurbishment of locomotives in Sudan and Tanzania, while offering technical assistance in Kenya and Mozambique. Though on a small scale, Indian companies are also involved in communication and infrastructure development. They are involved in design and construction of roads in Uganda and Ethiopia. Ircon on the other hand, is involved in rail construction in Algeria and Mozambique, besides its active engagement in Nigeria, Sudan and Zambia.

Overseas infrastructure alliance, PVT limited signed a contract with the Ethiopian government to supply US$65 mn worth of electrical equipment. KEC international was awarded a contract for the construction of a 132 KV power project in Ethiopia worth US$40 mn. India's main vehicle for cooperation in Africa is the Indian Technical and Economic Cooperation Programme. In Liberia, Mittal Steel (ARCELOR Mittal) has invested US$1.5 bn for iron ore extraction. It also invested US$108 mn in hydrocarbon ferrocom plant at Richardsbay in Kwazulu Natal, South Africa. Recently, it invested US$ 12 million in an instant coffee processing plant in Uganda.

India has also begun to provide ***concessional*** lines of credit administered through the Exim Bank. It also uses the Export-Import Bank of India to facilitate trade and investment relations. Under Indian technical and economic cooperation programme, India provided US$ 1 bn worth of technical assistance and training of personnel. India has sought to provide short training programmes in small and medium scale industries such as food processing, textile and women entrepreneurship. There is also a special Commonwealth Assistance Programme and the Indian Council of Cultural Relations which promotes cultural interactions with Africa. Compared to China, India's grants are limited. In July 2002, the Indian cabinet approved a US$100 mn capital for Pan African E-network which was to be launched in July 2007. The objective of the scheme was to provide telecommunication, tele-medicine, and network video-conferencing for heads of state for all the fifty-three AU members. The network was also set to facilitate the connection of the fifty-three learning centres, ten super-specialty hospitals, and five universities, two of them in India.

An examination of these engagements points to several conclusions. Indian activities are mainly private-sector driven. They mainly concentrate in energy and trade realms. Their role in infrastructure development is low in impact and confined to specific states. There is no apparent grand strategy that can provide a framework for these engagements. This explains the apparent disjointed logic of Indian engagements in Africa, which contrasts with China's engagements. The latter are framed by a grand strategy. China is engaged in a political warfare supported by economic, political and military instruments in a bid to assure her national (security) interest. Her drive is for a multipolar international system driven by fact of demography (1.2 bn). The core here is the security inherent in the China policy achievable preferably through asphyxiation of Taiwan by way of resource and diplomatic denial. The push for the foregoing is animated by lateral pressures aiming at securing energy, metals and strategic minerals. China has the will and interest to couple her security with those of differentiated state systems without being encumbered with moral contradictions. Core here are the far-flung states in Africa endowed with oil and other minerals. They include Arab states with their hydro-carbons. As the second largest energy consumer, China has been importing 60 per cent of its needs from Middle East.[33] Estimates put its consumption to increase from 6 mn barrels in 2004 to 16-20 m barrels per day in 2020. This will bring its imports to 80 per cent of its total consumption and by inference increased vulnerabilities.[34] The implications here are that China has to become sensitive to sea line of communications especially the Indian Ocean and other vital spaces endowed with strategic resources and future markets such as Africa.

China's state-driven grand strategy has seen her engage in huge infrastructure constructions that have both state and region-centric impacts. These seek to address internal lateral pressures in both China and Africa including raw material for cash and infrastructure. The triangular logic of the copper belt infrastructure linking DRCs Matadi, Tazara and Benguela will complete the linkage with the South African built corridors of Maputo, Trans-Kaprivi corridor (which links Welvies Bay with landlocked Zambia by a 2500 km road and rail road system), DRC and Zimbabwe. It is also set to build 5,000 km railways network in Ethiopia effectively inter-connecting Eastern Africa and Horn of Africa. This will link up with a new rail link and port of Lamu, linking the seaboard to southern Sudan. China seeks to build oil pipeline from its newly acquired oil fields in Uganda to intersect with the proposed South Sudan pipeline. There are similar grand projects in Nigeria. The net effect will be reduction of distance decay, horizontalisation of Africa and the coupling of strategic interests of African states with those of China in a win-win logic. The end state is the connectivity of energy-rich states with Chinese sea board.

The Elephant's Response to the Dragon's String of Pearls

Despite the fact that there exist no established Chinese naval bases in the Indian Ocean, there is a strong perception that China is engaged in a grand strategic policy aiming at encircling and containing India. That this end state is being pursued through what Booz Allen conceived in 2003 as string of pearls strategy.[35] This string of pearls strategy sees China seeking to gain a strategic foothold in the Indian Ocean by establishing nodes of geopolitical influence. Indian Ocean is salient to China given the fact that it is not only the world's main hydrocarbon transport channel but also a link to South America, Arab and African continent platforms with their markets, investment spaces and minerals. In the Indian Ocean, China finds itself challenged by US and Indian military might, piracy and radicalism. Her main fear is the potential for a unified action by US-India to asphyxiate her from resources. China's energy threats are animated by geography, which situates her away from strategic sea-lines of communication thus making her extremely vulnerable to potential enemy lockout.

Accordingly, her string of 'pearls' include, Hainan island with upgraded military facilities, Woody island's upgraded airstrip located in the Paracel archipelago, a container shipping facility at Chittagoong (Bangladesh) and Sri Lanka's Hambantota, and a deep water port at Sittwe in Myanmar. It has helped build Kyankpyu Port, and has a planned trans-Burma gas pipeline that complements the Burma Road. It operates listening devices for Signal Intelligence (SIGINT) on Coco Islands transferred to Burma in 1950 by India and later leased to China in 1994. China is helping Pakistan develop the Gwader port with rail, road, pipelines that link it to western China. It has funded a rail line from Gwader to Dalbandin in Central Pakistan. This will be integrated to lines linking Pakistan to Iran. These pearls stretch from the mainland coastal China through South China Sea, straits of Malacca across the Indian Ocean into littoral of Arabian Sea and the Persian Gulf. The foregoing strategy supports the grand political strategy which seeks to ensure access to strategic resources considered critical to China's security. For China, access to these has involved the securitisation of these resources. The result is coinciding the interests of states where these resources are obtained with that of China. The implication has been China's will power to mobilise economic muscle to build infrastructure that ties her economic interests to those of newly-found allies.

Rather than seeking to encircle India, Ni Lexiong, a leading Chinese security expert close to the People's Liberation Army, interprets China's activities in defensive terms. Affirming the emerging salience of Sea to China he notes, '*In recent decades, as the overseas trade section in our national economy has grown bigger and bigger, the question of a lifeline at sea has become more and more important*'[36]. It is notable that China has gone as far as South America, Canada and the USA in search for survival resources. The drive is to assure sustainable access built around multiple sources of supply and conveyance arteries based on land and sea. China outbid India to capture PetroKazakhstan in shares with State Kaz-Munai-Gaz. This will allow oil to flow through 988 km pipeline constructed from Atasu, Kazakhstan to Alshankou, China, at a cost of US$ 700 mn. The pipeline is expected to transform a highly inhospitable environment.[37] It has also sought to build an oil pipeline to tap gas from Russia through two pipelines that will supply 60-80 bn cubic metres of gas a year. In a bid to avoid Malacca choke points, China offered to build a US$20 bn canal through Thailand's Kra Isthmus, a feat that would allow her ships to bypass the Malacca straights, built ports and railway link through Cambodia from China to the Sea.

The foregoing points to the fact that China would only likely opt for war if these are constricted. The imagination of it being held hostage in any strategic confrontation through resource asphyxiation achieved by naval interdiction calls for strategic reserves, alternative flexible options and development of a naval capability to negotiate it out of this. As Jacqueline Newmyer notes, '*Beijing aims to create a disposition of power so favourable that it will not actually have to use force to secure its interests.*'[38] Concern for energy vulnerability is such that China might go to war to defend her interests. According to Wu Lei and Shen Qinu, if confronted with serious threats to its energy security, China will mobilise all its economic, political and military resources to ensure a secure energy supply or to interfere in the energy supply chains of the United States and its allies like Japan in the key choke points such as South China Sea, the strait of Malacca or even the Taiwan strait.[39]

China is developing a symmetrical capability aimed at constricting freedom of operation of US navy in East China Sea. It has a design to acquire aircraft carriers, nuclear attack and ballistic submarines besides modernising its destroyer fleet. This confirms Admiral Zhao Nanqi's (Director of the Chinese Academy of Military Sciences) assertion that the People's Liberation Army-Navy would extend its operations beyond the south and east China seas to check India in the Indian Ocean. 'We can no longer accept the Indian Ocean as only an Ocean of Indians' (Nangi, 1993). China has shifted from coastal defence posture to offshore defence. One-third of its military defence budget now is going to the navy. By 2003, China was operating 60 Submarines, 62 surface combatants, 56 amphibious ships, 39 mine warfare ships, 368 coastal patrol craft and three replacement at-sea oilers.[40] As if implementing Mahan's thinking to the letter, Chinese Navy is expected to be the largest by 2020.[41] Its development of Anti-ship Cruise Missiles (ASCM), is beginning to worry the USA given the lack of countermeasures at the moment.[42]

In a classic security dilemma model, these Chinese actions are interpreted in India as a veritable threat that is evolving as a noose to constrict her. For India, the Indian Ocean basin is extremely vital. Notably, 'India wants to keep China out of the Indian Ocean. This has implied the strengthening of Indian Navy to bolster its bases in the region including its eastern command on the Nicobar Islands. It has to work with other navies to protect the sea lanes and enhance all maritime security in India's Economic Exclusive Zone (EEZ).'[43] India is seeking cooperation with littoral states in the Indian Ocean to secure critical choke points from Iran where straits of Hormuz are located to Singapore, Malysia and Indonesia where straits of Malacca are located; from Bab-el-Mandeb where Djibouti and Eritrea are crucial to Mozambique and South Africa (where the Cape of Good Hope is located). Cooperation is also sought with France, Israel and increasingly the USA and Japan.

To enhance her apparent naval encirclement of China, India has sought to project her power around Malacca Straight through development of Andaman and Nicobar Command as points of command structures since 2001. These will act as India's eastern maritime defence perimeter. For some Chinese analysts it is as a metal chain whose purpose is geared towards taking China out of the Indian Ocean. Her efforts equally include enlargement of airfields to take up Sukhois, Migs, and Mirages fighters. The decision to upgrade 108 Brigade based here to Division size while enhancing patrolling capacity is part of this efforts.[44] This strategic space allows India a reach into China coastal heartlands. Almost similar to China's continental reach achieved through control of Tibet and the development of horizontal infrastructure including rail (Lhasa to Golmund 2006), roads and airfields that swag the strategic balance in China's favour. This infrastructure can now facilitate supplies and missile deployment capable of striking India's heartland and centres of gravity such as New Delhi and Calcutta.[45] India's drive has been to acquire weapons that can allow her to project power. In 2004, India spent US$5.7 bn on weapon acquisition well above China and Saudi Arabia.[46] India is committed to equipping its navy and air force with nuclear capabilities. Under its new Indian maritime doctrine, India seeks to evolve a sea based leg for its nuclear posture, a factor affirmed by the naval service chief Admiral Arun Prakash in September 2005.[47]

In 2003, India purchased II-78 aerial tanker aircraft in a bid to facilitate support and deployment of fighter and transport aircraft to far-flung locations as far as South Africa and Alaska. It was not strange, therefore, that the air force performed non-stop flights of Su-30s from Pune, their operational base to Car Nicobar in the Bay of Bengal adjacent to Malacca Straits and China's populous heartland. In 2007, India acquired an additional force multiplier through the acquisition of three Phalcon airborne warning and control systems aircrafts (AWACS). This should give its air force a 360-degree surveillance capacity over 350 nautical miles allowing it to strike targets at greater distances with additional effectiveness. India also has Tu-142M and Il-38 maritime surveillance and anti-submarine warfare aircrafts. Its navy seeks to acquire P-3C Orions from the United States and Israeli built Heron-2 unmanned aerial vehicles for surveillance purposes.[48]

To improve its strategic strike capability, India plans to acquire 190 long range and air refuelable SU-30 fighters. It has also been upgrading its Jaguar fleet with modern navigation systems, electronic countermeasure gears and new armament pods.[49] India also plans to acquire an additional 126 multi-role aircraft from either low keyed Martin (F-16) or the Boeing/McDonnel Douglas F-18 hornet in addition to Mirage 2000-5 from Dassault aviation of France. This seems like a response to Indira Gandhi's warning, *'that the ocean has brought conquerors to India in the past, today we fight it churning with danger.'*[50] In addition to an aircraft carrier, there are three new and five older destroyers, four new and seven vintage frigates, three new Tank Landing Ships (LSTs), assorted covets and patrol crafts. There are planned two new aircraft carriers, six additional vintage destroyers, frigates, covets and patrol crafts. India is also set to acquire five new LSTs and a refurbished 17,000 ton former landing platform dock from the US.[51] With these aircraft carriers, India should be in a position to project power. The old Soviet aircraft carrier Admiral Gorshkov currently rechristened INS Vikramaditya is fitted with sixteen MIG 29s and eight KA-31 anti-submarine and airborne early warning helicopters. India has also acquired five German type 1500 and ten-kilo submarines produced in Russia.[52] India is also building a new naval station Kadamba, with an aerial capability at Karwar near Goa. It will be able to receive India's new aircraft carriers and to house her western naval command. It will also serve as the principal nuclear submarine base. At Cochin in Kerala, India has established a base for her unmanned aerial vehicles.[53] With these India seeks to compensate for deficiencies on land and hopefully maximise on its naval advantage to constrict China at the sea where it is vulnerable and sensitive using naval and aviation components. The assumption here is that land-based airpower could be used to sink naval vessels in all whether day and night. This is the argument Gen Paul Hester, Commander of Pacific Air Forces, 'the capability for airmen to rapidly respond anywhere in the Pacific to sink naval vessels in all whether day and night is crucial for Pacific command'.[54] Indeed while the two Asian powers are fixated on Mahan, it seems as if it is Mitchel and Admiral Julian Corbett who may eventually have the last laugh. The contention here is that without expanding existing assets, these competitors have the ability to take measures whose cost is sufficient to deter their adversaries.

Admiral Corbett de-emphasises the salience of decisive fleet battles in favour of interdicting commerce:

> it is obvious that if the object of Naval warfare is the control of communication, it must carry with it the right to forbid, if we can, the passage of both public and private property upon the Sea .... Such capture or destruction is the penalty which we impose upon our enemy for attempting to use the communications of which he does not control.[55]

For Corbett, the essence of naval strategy is not an end in itself but a means to an end; the need to evolve sufficient capacity to deter an enemy from starting a conflict and to prosecute it effectively if they do. Sea control becomes critical in the sense that enemies are asphyxiated from access to resources through constriction of sea lines of communications while your access is assured. Where the state's commerce and resources are dependent on the sea, lateral pressures on land transforms the sea into a Centre of Gravity. The intensity of state salience, economic growth and resource dependency is directly related to its sea-based activities as a survival variable. The higher the felt sense of survival interest the higher the felt sense of strategic vulnerability. This is the emerging reality for both India and China.

The net consequence of this phenomenon is the likely arms race in the Indian Ocean to the detriment of India. China is likely to drive her in such expensive ventures, allowing her to shoulder the securitisation logic of Indian Ocean allowing her to deploy critical resources elsewhere. In any case, any confrontation in the Indian Ocean or actions that leads to actions interdicting China's sea lines of communication is likely to backfire against India in Africa and South America.

Re-coupling India-Security on Africa: From the Horn to the Great Lakes Region

Security in the Indian Ocean and the need to access energy resources from Africa will continue to enhance the salience of these twin spaces transforming them to status of necessary and vital for India's national security. China's interest in these twin spaces will continue to spawn tensions between the two states to the extent that their engagements are exclusive. To secure each state's interest, enhanced maritime presence and collaboration with some African states depending on their perceived value return is inevitable. Acting as a multiplier factor in favour of these twin spaces with respect to India's energy considerations are both constraints and the successes if any in accessing the Iranian gas reserves at South pars field through proposed US$7 bn overland pipeline through Pakistan. For now, these plans have faced reluctance from Pakistan due to the Kashmir question and Afghanistan where Pakistan is concerned by what it sees as an increasing attempt of India to supplant her.

India's commitment is apparent with support it extended to Iran in modernising the Chabahar port, building rail linking the port with the National railway network. If it were to succeed, its objective would be to cover Iran and Afghanistan and securing itself, as was the case of the Raj security strategy before 1947. The necessity of extending this logic to the wider Indian Ocean would also be a given. Underlying this is the strategic value of the investments. The value of this triangle will increase further if her option of accessing Turkmenistan's Dauletabad gasfields estimated 1.4 trillion cubic metres succeeds. The $3.3 bn, 1600-km-long Turkmenistan to India pipeline via Afghanistan and Pakistan[56] is under discussion with Asian Development Bank. While the foregoing investments make realist sense for India, the current constraints incline her to Africa as the best option in the immediate term.

In effect, there exists a triple insecurity phenomenon tying Africa, India and China with a potential of forming a platform for security enhancing interdependence. Most salient is the East African and the Horn of African states. These states are characterised by mutual dependencies. These revolve around lack of infrastructure, ports, water and energy. None of the states have all these facilities, thus, making them dependent on each other. These states wallow in poverty despite their resource potential. Core in this is energy resource potential. The geopolitical imaginations of the British Raj about the importance of this region hold to date. The region hosts the Nile and is pivot to strategic oil energy resources in Uganda, Southern Sudan, gas and uranium in Tanzania. It is also proximate to the DRC with its vast mineral resources. The fact that the region is slated for integration increases its value as a potential market of more than 150 m once Southern Sudan joins the federation. Together with DRC, it has a potential of a population of more than 210 m people with an ocean front of 1200 miles. Its geostrategic flexibility would see it stretch from the Indian Ocean to the Atlantic Ocean. Its power projections in the Indian and Atlantic Ocean cannot be ignored given its access to the oil-rich Middle East and the Indian Ocean which controls 45 per cent of global trade transits. For both, China and India, this region cannot be ignored.

The interests of both the states are better served by a constructivist perspective that would see them invest in facilitating such integration efforts for their own national interest. Such ideas are security enhancing rather than emphasis on power politics. The assumptions of constructivists like Wendt are that fundamental structures of international politics are social rather than strictly material. If there is from the onset a focus on different ways of thinking geo-economics, it would assure security in the Indian Ocean and eventually Asia.

It is a given that states cannot be absolutely certain of the intentions of others, their core wish is to assure their survival. Yet, interests of states are constructed by the structure of the international system. Structures, as constructivists argue, are products of social relationships. They are anchored in shared knowledge, material resources and practices. They are in a large measure defined by shared appreciation and knowledge. The apparent security dilemma is a social structure, rooted in the inter-subjective imaginations that underpin threats of resource denial. It is characterised by two states that are distrustful to the extent of building discourses about worst case assumptions about each other's intentions, hence mutual encirclement and inclination towards self-help.

It is possible to anticipate a security community structure underpinned by shared knowledge, trust and built on economic resource mobilisation in Africa that transforms dead capital into security-enhancing live capital. This capital would have to build infrastructure and add value to energy and other natural resources while facilitating their access to these two states. Such a framework would see the emergence of security-enhancing intense but shared infrastructure on both the African continent and the Indian Ocean. The higher the dependence of both states on these the lesser the inclination to seek war. The argument here is that India does not have to seek to keep China out of the Indian Ocean, indeed her security at state-centric level, is inherent in the extent of vulnerability of SLOC China exposes herself to. Yet, the need to reduce these vulnerabilities would always increase the potential for work. The converse is the case where mutual dependencies are encouraged to emerge.

While this needs to be the long-term end state, in the interim period, India will need to restructure her strategy to the realities of the 21st Century. India's engagement in Africa will have to be constructed as core to her national interest thus, rationalising heavy investments. Its current private-sector-driven investments are limited in terms of responding to human and state security. Worse still, their reactive construction as opposed to China will not only fail but that they will also harm India's national interest as they push it towards power struggle in the Indian Ocean and Asia. Mani Shankar Aiyer points to dangers inherent in this option when he notes, 'any imitation of the "Great Game" between India and China is a threat to peace. We cannot endanger each other's security in our quest for energy security.'[57] Salience of energy to both is such that everywhere in the world that India goes in quest for energy, chances are that it will run into China engaged in a similar mission.[58]

The better option is one that seeks to build on state insecurity generating triple lateral pressures in Africa, India and China to produce a horizontal Africa as a bridgehead for securitisation. The foregoing security coupling can be realised by value addition on energy and trade-driven horizontal infrastructure in the East and Horn of Africa as a start. The end state here needs to be security-based economic interdependence that can stabilise Africa, Asia and the Indian Ocean.

In the initial stages, India will have to evolve a grand strategy that allows her to build on her soft power. This should allow her to maximise on state-supported investments in agriculture, technology, pharmaceuticals, education, to engender value addition critical to creating platforms for markets and investments. Some Indian companies are already showing the way with their geostrategically defined engagements in the realms of human security such as food production and pharmaceutical manufacturing. Shar Karuturi, for instance, has acquired 100,000 acres of land in Gambela, Ethiopia, that is likely to have far-reaching strategic implications in the region. This acquisition is set to engender food production in Ethiopia. Its main objective is to tap in on existing dead capital in food production and imports to address perennial food insecurity, while seeking to export within the continent. It is also set to transform Ethiopia into a net exporter of sugar. Karuturi seeks to enhance palm oil production in Ethiopia and to transform the Nile River into a key medium of exportation. The net impact of this will certainly be the development of lateral pressures within Ethiopia that are likely to push her towards regional economic integration. Positioning Africa as a food producer to feed itself and have the potential of export is likely to transform power relations in the world what with changing weather patterns worldwide.

Other Indian companies have sought to transform Ethiopia into a production point for pharmaceuticals. The aim is to use it as a source for export within the continent to respond to human insecurities. This realm will have far-reaching effects on the continent which continues to be crippled by human immunodeficiency virus (HIV) and malaria. Many in Africa are dependent on generics originating from India. HIV anti-retroviral medications from India cost one-tenth less. In Kenya alone there are 420,000 needy persons. Pressure from EU on India to effect patent rules is likely to cost Africa highly while negatively affecting India's standing on the continent.

Parallel to these are joint investments in larger energy exploration and infrastructure projects. This implies moving away from the current neo-liberal easy option of buying real estate assets, exploiting and later reselling them to other bidders, and instead going in for those that can reduce distance decay. The eastern Africa and the Horn of Africa regions are critical for starts. Key here is its geography and the strategic implications this poses first and foremost to India.

Geography allows the region to straddle a key sea-route and strategic energy resource. Most of the global oil supply passes through the Gulf of Aden to the Red Sea or the Indian Ocean.[59] Yet, the region is gripped by a wide range of security threats. These include state collapse and instability, terrorist networks, organised crime — human, arms and drug trafficking and piracy. In 2008, there were 293 incidents of piracy (an increase of 11 per cent) from 2007: forty-seven vessels were hijacked and 889 crew taken hostage, out of which 11 were killed and 21 reported missing.[60] Threats to security, stability and well-being posed by terrorism to states in the region and the globe[61] have increased consequent to increased US and Pakistan military pressure on Al Qaeda and Taliban in both Afghanistan and Pakistan. Al Qaeda's response has been to open up a new front in Yemen known as Al Qaeda in the Arab Peninsular.[62] India's role and support to these states has been lukewarm, yet security and stability in these states is very vital to India's Indian Ocean strategy.

India can help a great deal in supporting states building efforts from below by helping to state rebuild security-enhancing micro-economic infrastructure. These should help reduce political and social distance decay.[63] It can build up on its contribution to UN peacekeeping operations, using its 3,500 Indian troops in the DRC, in addition to 1,400 along Ethiopia-Eritrea border. All that needs to be done is sending in engineering and medical corps for infrastructure construction and medical treatment. These units would serve the role of penetrating Indian company production in east and central Africa while enhancing her soft power. Its military can also serve the dual role of securitising India and Africa by supporting the communities to constitute fishing industry while interdicting illegal fishing, trade, human, drugs and illegal trafficking of arms and contraband goods, dumping of waste is core.[64] India and China can help to enhance maritime security of states in this region at both bilateral and regional levels through contribution of assets, training facilities.

The entire IGAD, ICGLR and East African geography is characterised by potential and discoveries of energy sources from Tanzania to Somalia, to Southern Sudan (where India is already engaged) to Uganda where Tullow company is investing US$10 bn to extract and process oil, and Chinese Company (CNOOC) to develop the fields in the Albertins Rift Basin. Uganda alone has an estimated two bn barrels.[65]

References

1. Osterud, O., "The Uses and Abuses of Geopolitics", *Journal of Peace and Research*, Vol. 2, 1988, p.191.
2. Agnew, J., *Geo-politics: Re-visioning World Politics*, Routledge. New York, 2003, p. 7.
3. Hanns, W.M., *Raw Materials, Energy and Western Security*, Macmillan, Basingstoke, 1984.
4. Homer-Dixon, Thomas F., 'Environmental Scarcity and Mass Violence from Current History' 1996 in Tuathail, G.O., et al, (Ed), *The Geopolitics Reader,* Routledge, London, 1998.
5. Klare, Michael T., *Resource Wars: the Changing Landscape of Global Conflict*, Henry Holt, New York, 2001, p. 23.
6. http://economictimes. Indiatimes.com/news/economy/ForeignTrade in India and Africa to grow ninetimes by 2012 assocham/articles show/ 394875.
7. Madan, Tanvi, *Brooking Foreign Policy Studies Energy Security Series*, 2006.
8. Sprout, Harold, Margaret, 'Environmental Factors in the study of International Politics', in Rosenau, James (Ed), *International Politics and Foreign Policy*, 2nd edition, Free Press New York, 1969, pp. 41-56.
9. Klare, M., *Resource Wars: The New Landscape of Global Conflict*, Metropolitan/OW/Book, New York, 2002.

10. Kelly, P. 'Geopolitics of Paraguay: Pivotal Position within a model of Geo-politics', Historical Text Archives, 2002, p. 1.
11. Gordon, Fairclough, 'As China grows so does it long neglected navy: Warship buying spree prompts new worry to Washington and Tokyo', *The Wall Street Journal,* 18 July 2007.
12. Mahan, A., *The Influence of Sea Power Upon History* (1890); *The Interest of America in Sea Power, Present and Future* (1897), *Naval Strategy* (1911).
13. Excavations to recover remains of these ships and other links to Chinese presence on the East African Coast seeks to affirm a narrative that Chinese are merely returning where they have been before others. See also, *The Remarkable Ocean World, Zheng's Fleet*, http://www.Oceansonline.com/Zheng.htm
14. Karnad, B., 'India uses Pak, Vietnam Open to India', *Indian Express*, India, Oct. 2005.
15. Gray, Colin, 'Inescapable Geography' in Gray, Colin and Geoffrey Sloan (Ed), *Geopolitics: Geography and Strategy*, Frank Cass, London, 1999, p. 163.
16. *Ibid.,* 162.
17. Spykman, Nicholas, *The Geography of the Peace*, New York, 1944.
18. Mackinder, C., 'The Geographical Pivot of History', *Geographical Journal*, 23/4 1904, pp. 421-44.
19. Chapman, Graham P., *The Geopolitics of South Asia: From Early Empire to the Nuclear Age,* Aldershot, Hamshire, 2003.
20. Panikkar, K.M., *India and the Indian Ocean,* Allen and Urwin, London, 1995, pp. 33-34.
21. Brzezinski, Zbigniew, *Times*, 15 January 1979.
22. Namboodini, Anant and Sridher, *Intervention in the Indian Ocean,* ABC, New Delhi, 1982, pp. 159-60.
23. See The Indian National Congress, *India and the African Liberation Struggle*, 1976, New Delhi, pp. 92-96, cited in Beri, Ruchita, 'India's Africa Policy in the Post Cold War Era: An Assessment', *Strategic Analysis*, Vol. 27, No. 2, April-Jan 2003, p. 118.
24. Madan, Tanvi, 'India: Brookings Foreign Policy Studies', *Energy Security Series*, 2006.
25. See India's Ministry of Petroleum and Natural Gas. http://.petrolium.nic.in/; see also Tata Energy and Resource Institute-North America. http: //www.terina.org
26. Chellaney, Brahma, *Asian Juggernaut,* Harper Business, London, 2010, p. 108.

27. Aiyer, M., 'Asia's Quest for Energy Security', 13 January 2006, rep. *Frontline*, 11-24 Feb, 2006.
28. 'India and Africa: Its Old Friends, New Game and Rules', *The Nation*, 9 February 2007.
29. http://Economic Times.India Times.com//news/economy/foreign_trade/_India-Africa_trade_to_ grow_nine_times_by_2012_Assocham/articleshow/3948475.cms 2009
30. 'Trends in Indo-African Trade and Investment Relations'. *African Review,* Chamber of Commerce and Industries, p. 9.
31. *Ibid.*
32. Emma, Mawdsley and McCaine Gerard, 'The Elephants in the corner? Reviewing India African Relationships in the Millenium', *Geography Compass*, Journal Compilation, Blackwell, 2010, p. 86.
33. Ramachandran, Sudha, 'China's Pearl in Pakistan's Waters', *Asian Times,* 4 March 2005.
34. Ollard, Will, 'The Search for Sustainability : Consequences of China's Growing Energy Demand' in Line, David (Ed), *Asia Intelligence Special Report*, November 2004, p. 2.
35. Pentagon Report, cited in Gertz, Bill, 'China Builds up Strategic Sea Lanes', *Washington Times*, 18 January 2005, p. 1.
36. See Lexiong, Ni, 'Sea power and China's Development', *The Liberation Daily*, 17 April 2005, translated for the US-China Economic and Security Review Commission, http://////.uscc.gov/reseachpaper/translated_articles/2005/05_07_18__Sea power _ and China's _Development .htm
37. See Pala, Christopher, 'China Pays Dearly for Kazakhstan oil', *New York Times*, March 21, 2006.
38. Cited in Kaplan, R., 'The Geography of Chinese Power: How Far can Beijing Reach on Land and at Sea', *Foreign Affairs,* Vol. 9, No. 3, May /June 2010, p. 38.
39. Wu Lei and Shen Qinu, 'Will China go to War over oil?', *Far Eastern Economic Review*, Vol. 169, No. 3, April 2006, pp. 38-40.
40. Brown, Harold, Joseph Prueher and Adam Segal, *Chinese Military Power* (New York, NY: Council on Foreign Relations, 2003), p. 44.
41. See Kaneda, Hideaki (retired Vice Admiral), 'Japan's self Defense Forces, the Rise of Chinese Sea power', Project Syndicate. org/commentary /kaneda7.
42. Holmes and Yoshihara, *The Influence of Mahan upon China's Maritime Strategy*, p. 38.
43. MacDonald J.A., 2002.

44. See Mirg, Zhang, in Kaplan, Robert, 'Center Stage of the 21st Century, Power Plays in the IO', *Foreign Affairs,* March/April 2009.
45. See Buzan; also Singh, B., China Comes Closer, Peace and conflict, 9/6(2006), pp. 20-21.
46. See Karnad, Bharat, 'Shaping India's special forces into a strategic asset: Defense and Technology', 1 December 2004, p. 48.
47. Integrated Headquarters, Indian Maritime Doctrine, 'Second Strike N-Capability Should be devastating' Prakash, PTI, 1 September 2005.
48. Russia to upgrade T-142 warplanes, AGNTSTVO VOYENNYKH, Novostei, 21 October 2002; Singh, Bulbul, 'India US near to Completing P-Orion cell', *Aerospace Daily*, 28 August 2002.
49. See Singh, Pulkit, 'India Bolstering Jaguar Fleet: Phasing out some older MIGs', *Journal of Electronic Defense*, October 2002.
50. Gandhi, Indira, address to Commonwealth Heads of Government, Asia Pacific Region, New Delhi, September 1980, quoted in Tellis, Ashley, 'The Naval Balance in the Indian Subcontinent demanding Mission for the Indian Navy', *Asian Survey*, December 1985, pp. 1192.
51. India-US Ties in Focus, *Jane's Intelligence Digest*, 29 July 2005.
52. Karnad, Bharat, 'Putting Bang in the Bomb', *Indian Express,* 13 November 2002.
53. See Broez, Frank, Geo-strategy and Navy Ports in the IO since 1970, *Marine Policy*, 21, No. 4, 1997, p. 358.
54. See Pacific Air Force public Affairs, 'Resultant fury 05: What senior Leaders are saying' http: //www2.hicham .af.mil/PACAF/news/rf.htm
55. See Corbett, Julian, *Some Principles of Maritime Strategy,* Annapolis, MD: Naval Institute press, 1988, p. 8.
56. See Reuters report: 22 September 2005.
57. Aiyer, M., 'Asia's Quest for energy Security', 13 January 2006; rep. *Frontline*, 11-24 Feb, 2006.
58. *Ibid.*
59. 3,000 tankers or 12 per cent of global consumption into Europe and the US pass through here.
60. The most critical incidences included the capture of a Saudi Arabian oil tanker and Ukrainian ship carrying weapons apparently belonging to the GoK.
61. The convergence of internal vulnerabilities and presence of external high value interests according to Menkhaus makes states like Kenya high targets. See Menkhaus, K., *Somalia: State Collapse and the Threat of Terrorism*, Routledge, New York, 2006, p. 74.

62. 'The Threat in Yemen : Its perfect Territory for Al Qaeda, and a tough challenge for the West', *Time,* Jan 18, 2010, pp.12-16.
63. Social distance decay is the extent to which state economic, political and social structures are far removed from its citizens. The higher the distance decay, the higher the level of citizen alienation and ability of criminal elements to take advantage of time to organise and infiltrate into state spaces (terrain). Distance decay implies that the state lacks connectivity to society/citizens. It takes more time to reach citizens and get rid of criminal elements. Distance decay grants criminal elements initiative, time and organisational terrain.
64. These components are covered under organised crime.
65. *The Star*, Thursday, 17 March 2011, p. 16.

8

Indian Navy's African Odyssey

S. Utham Kumar Jamadhagni

Importance of Sea Power

By its very nature the sea is important to nations due to four attributes.[1] First, it is a resource often thought to be inexhaustible as it is a treasure house of living and non-living things much of which remains unexplored as yet. Next, it is perhaps been the most important means of transportation resulting in the movement of people and goods from one corner of the earth to the other since the early signs of civilisation. Interactions that resulted in cultural and trade exchanges that have come to shape the earth as we know it today has been one of the most positive effects of using the sea as a transport medium. This also resulted in making the sea a carrier of information and ideas that have spread religious beliefs, political ideologies, etc. The sea, finally, can be a weakness as well as strength with most regions of the world; the countries that came under foreign rule were helped by the sea through which the 'colonisers' entered these areas.

All these attributes today carry the same or in some cases added importance to nations that depend mainly on the seas for their economic growth and progress. This is the reason why nations wish to focus on their sea power to optimise their needs and minimise their vulnerabilities from the sea. The control and use of the sea to further national interest is sea power. It is not just the physical capability in the number of advanced ships and other vessels and equipment possessed by a navy but rather the effectiveness in employing or meaning to employ such instruments to achieve national interests.

Naval forces are among the most useful of diplomatic tools. Policy makers can send them to over two-thirds of the world's surface at any time without having to obtain advance basing rights or prior permission to conduct naval movements.

During peacetime in the present era, maritime forces are increasingly designed to influence non-national entities, such as criminal organisations and transnational groups. The role may be a supporting or enabling, contributing a supply of well-trained and equipped personnel who can adapt and sustain themselves. Peacetime operations generally mean a mix of security, humanitarian, and environmental components. They can be roughly thought of as the following:

1. *Presence and Deterrence*: Maritime forces can avoid confrontation and support political aims without necessarily violating national sovereignty. They can strengthen diplomatic efforts by 'showing the flag' (presence) in a benign fashion as a general indicator of interest and latent capability, thereby helping to prevent emerging conflicts. They can also be deployed as a deterrent against specific actions.
2. *Peace Operations:* There is a range of activities, including conflict prevention, peacemaking, peace keeping, peace enforcement, and peace building. Here maritime forces could be used to complement land forces and may involve a number of tasks like monitoring/observing ceasefires, interposition between the maritime forces of belligerents and establishing disengagement zones, providing a neutral venue for supervised negotiations, and preventing forces of the belligerent parties from violating agreements.
3. *Humanitarian Operations:* Maritime forces are well suited to support humanitarian aid efforts that relieve or reduce the suffering, loss of life, and damage to property caused by natural or man-made disasters. The speed with which the maritime forces can be moved and deployed make them particularly preferable. They may provide personnel, equipment, supplies, medical and dental care, security, limited construction and engineering, communication, and transportation support.

4. *Protection of Shipping and Freedom of Navigation*: In case of disputes over waters maritime forces can exercise freedom of navigation by traversing or exercising in the contested waters (in accordance with recognised international law). Navies may also protect merchant shipping with flag-state consent that could otherwise be threatened.
5. *Maritime Constabulary Tasks*: The expansion of EEZ has meant an increase in low-intensity constabulary functions. These functions may include: enforcement of fisheries regulations and EEZ arrangements; operations against piracy; counter-terrorism; interdiction of drugs and other contraband trade; interdiction of the slave trade or illegal migration; enforcement of environmental regulations and control of traffic separation schemes and other maritime traffic management tasks.
6. *Environmental Operations*: Oil spills and other environmental disasters on waters could also enlist the services of maritime forces. They possess specialised personnel and equipment for the purpose.
7. *Embargoes / Maritime Interdiction Operations (MIO)*: Maritime forces prove to be the most effective enforcer of embargoes and other sanctions. They could stop, inspect, seize, and divert suspect ships and aircraft and establish and enforce a maritime exclusion zone for the maritime vessels of one or more parties to a conflict.
8. *Noncombatant Evacuation Operations (NEO)*: Noncombatant evacuation operations are conducted to move personnel out of an area where deteriorating security conditions place lives at risk. They could accomplish this without assistance from other forces. If not, ships stationed at sea may provide lift capability and the close, secure staging areas for other forces. By evacuating the ships directly from a secure site to outside territorial seas a very low political profile can be maintained.

By Geoffrey Till's definition, sea power is the ability to possess control over a defined area and has the following constituents namely, not only the physical strength or number of ships possessed; the financial capability to maintain a force; maritime geography that factors in the topography of coasts, presence of harbours, access to open ocean; easy link between the other parts and these assets; maritime economy and doctrine or the conceptual component to put the limited resource to optimal use but more importantly the capacity to influence the behaviour of others by events at sea.[2] Thus, the sea and sea power continue to occupy a significant position in a country's strategic calculus. India, with all its advantages related to the sea, could be a strong sea power.

Indian Ocean

The significance of the Indian Ocean and its importance to India cannot be overemphasised. American naval strategist Alfred Thayer Mahan envisioned, 'In the 21st century the destination of the world will be decided upon its (Indian Ocean) waters.'[3] The Indian Ocean is one of the principal sea routes of the world. An estimated 40 per cent of the world's oil production comes from the Indian Ocean Region (IOR).[4] According to Robert Kaplan, the Indian Ocean currently accounts for half of the world's container traffic.[5] It is not only the economic component of the Indian Ocean that highlights its importance. The Indian Ocean region now houses more than half the world's armed conflicts. It is also witnessing strategic developments like the rise of China and India, American interventions and now withdrawal in Iraq and Afghanistan, Islamist terrorism, growing incidence of piracy in and around the Horn of Africa, and the problem of diminishing fishery resources. The Indian Peninsula juts into the Indian Ocean thus, providing us unhindered access to far-flung areas of not only Asia but Africa too.[6]

For India, the Indian Ocean is the lifeline of its economy, with nearly 90 per cent of trade sea-bound. Also its energy security is ensured through the transportation of oil from the Persian Gulf as India imports about 70 per cent of its oil through the Indian Ocean Region to its various ports. The safety of the sea lanes is thus paramount to India's economic strength. Controlling the piracy menace is another reason the Indian Ocean drives India's focus on it. The situation has even warranted joint multilateral action of navies around the world in patrolling and safeguarding commercial maritime routes across the Indian Ocean. India too has responded positively to this challenge by being active in averting piracy attacks and in some cases rescuing ships and crew that have been hijacked by pirates. India has for long, adopted a land-based approach to defending its territory. However, the long, porous and largely unguarded coasts now pose a grave threat. The non-state actors like terrorists could use the waters to reach the mainland comparatively easily or could exploit the remoteness of islands to use them as bases to launch attacks. India's influence is growing and this is being acknowledged even by external powers. In its 2010 Quadrennial Defence Review the US, for example, sees India as a 'net provider of security in the Indian Ocean and beyond'.[7]

India's Maritime Doctrine identifies the arc extending from the Persian Gulf to the Malacca Straits as being an area of interest. As a central power in the Indian Ocean region, India views the African coastline too as part of this sphere. In fact, India and Africa are neighbours separated by the all-weather Indian Ocean. The Indian Navy in its attempt to achieve blue water status would view the Indian Ocean as its principal area of vision and expansion. One of the tools that could fulfil India's aspirations to exert influence is the capacity building of the Indian Navy.[8]

India's potential of being a future superpower or great power rests on her ability to utilise the strategic value of the Indian Ocean and optimise the benefits. As Australia's ambassador to US[9] opines, 'In the long term the Indian Ocean is going to be massively more significant in global politics than it has ever been before....' India's future thus is intrinsically linked with the Indian Ocean as a naval power — overseeing and having a strategic role.[10]

Why Africa Matters?

Just as the Look East policy factored Southeast Asia in India's foreign policy and strategic framework, the rapid economic growth for India has meant seeking not only new markets for goods and services but also more importantly sourcing alternate points of raw material supply. As a resource rich continent, Africa holds the promise. African countries are also 'rising' from the internecine or tribal conflicts and other issues to realise their potential for economic growth. This has meant greater, closer trade ties between India and Africa which could serve as an excellent launch pad for extending the relations to other areas like capacity building, counterterrorism, anti-piracy and maritime security.

While greater engagement with the countries that lie to our east has been integrated into India's foreign policy parameters, regions to the west, especially Africa, despite much longer interactions has not received impetus. India has recently been rapidly enhancing trade ties and offering economic assistance by way of massive aid for infrastructure development and implementing new projects in fields like information technology. India-Africa relation has moved from a period of high political, emotional and moral solidarity to a more material, concrete and pragmatic approach.

Not only economic but security issues also affect Africa. Piracy along the Somali coast has now been acknowledged to be a global concern. The sea lanes cross African waters which have become a security nightmare with Somali pirates hijacking many ships and now holding hostages for ransom. The problem has heightened to such magnitudes that it has warranted an international response. As one of the closest neighbours, India has much at stake to keep the waters safe. India's maritime economy and energy dependence make Sea Lines of Communication (SLOC) safety a crying need. The Indian Navy has played a very active role in curtailing and at times preventing possible piracy attempts and also succeeded in rescuing hijacked ships. The movement of the pirates further east towards India's western shores only means need for more vigil and investment of men and machines. The Indian Navy and Coast Guard launched 'Operation Island Watch' in December 2010 designed to man the uninhabited island territories of India to prevent them from becoming havens for pirates. The task force consists primarily of three to four ships that are based along the western seaboard along with land based Dornier DO 228 aircrafts for long-range reconnaissance.[11]

Next reason is the Chinese foray which has increased by leaps and bounds to cover anything from outright military aid to even building presidential palaces. China's engagement has moved a long way from the anti-colonial solidarity to that of a major force on the continent. India's trade with Africa is only a fraction of Chinese.

Strength of the Indian Navy

The geostrategic centricity of India in the Indian Ocean Region has not guided its defence policy, which is characterised by sea-blindness or the tendency not to accord the primacy that the sea should acquire in a nation's security and general outlook. India has been a maritime economy since days of yore and the apparent neglect to strengthen its naval power in the interim has been cited by various historians as one of the principal reasons for colonisation. However, the dawn of Independence too did not restore the primacy to her maritime power. This was highlighted by K.M. Pannikkar through the historical trace of India's rise or rather fall as a power due to the apparent neglect of the power that the sea could have bestowed on a nation of this size.[12] Keshav Vaidya opined that developing an invincible navy would help defend her distant ocean frontiers that are spread far and wide.[13] It is slowly being replaced by sea awareness. While the first ever maritime doctrine published in 2004 outlines India's ambition to be a naval power to be reckoned with, it still has to match it with adequate political will and appropriate support structure.

India began its naval ship account with one British aircraft carrier, two old cruisers and eight new frigates in 1961. However, gradually, it developed or acquired replenishment ships, diesel submarines, and a maritime reconnaissance element was progressively added. An indigenous warship-building capability was created laying the foundation for a balanced blue-water navy.[14] India possesses some 135 ships including aircraft carriers, nuclear submarines and is en route to naval modernisation in a big way. The Gorshkov aircraft carrier rechristened INS Vikramaditya will join the Indian Navy as its flagship soon. INS Arihant inducted opens India's account as a nuke sub. The ATV project and the slew of acquisitions on the pipeline will surely augment the physical attributes of a sea power. India's geostrategic position right at the heart of the Indian Ocean with access to both flanks, a long coastline and a huge increase in the number of port facilities that are being developed mean that its maritime geographic element is more than favourable. The infrastructure development factors in greater connectivity between the ports and other areas of commercial and trade interest. Taking these calibrations, India is termed a medium regional force projection navy. This would amount to a limited sea control, not a coercive power projection, with adequate ability to perform national security and constabulary operations, and offer humanitarian assistance.

Naval Forays

India's strategic and economic interests require increased naval presence and engagement. India had earlier begun deepening its ties with the countries along the east coast of Africa. This has spanned a variety of activities, like establishment of listening, providing the countries with aircraft, boats and other equipment for security.

Currently, India has employed a variety of measures to not only face the present situation but also prepare for the future. The

India-Brazil-South Africa maritime exercise or IBSAMAR was born out of the sentiment in 2007 expressed by Vice Admiral J. Mudimu and Admiral Suresh Mehta, chiefs of the South African and Indian Navies, who felt there was a need to 'formulate a system of regional cooperation in the Indian Ocean Region to combat threats emanating from non-state actors, particularly those related to terrorism, armed robbery and piracy'.[15] The inaugural exercises were held between 5 and 16 May 2008. The exercise proposed to enhance interoperability and coordination; achieve participative unit compatibility; increase combined operation readiness and fulfil mutual objectives. All IBSAMAR exercises will be hosted by South Africa due to its geographical location. The second set was held in September 2010. India and South Africa have also pledged to conduct joint naval exercises when the leaders of the two countries met on the sidelines of the BRICS summit in April 2011.[16]

The Indian Ocean Naval Symposium (IONS) that began in 2008 is an informal exchange of views at the highest level of the naval fraternity. It is to serve as a consultative forum to discuss maritime-related issues and concerns in order to chart out an agreed course of action on transnational issues. Comoros, Djibouti, Egypt, Eritrea, Kenya, Madagascar, Mauritius, Mozambique, Seychelles, South Africa, Sudan and Tanzania are the African countries that are members of IONS. The second edition was held at Abu Dhabi in May 2010.[17]

Training is also yet another area of interaction between India and the African countries in the naval realm. Capacity building for African countries in the form of providing equipment as well as training has been a long-term commitment for India. Under the Indian Technical and Economic programme (ITEC), out of 1,350 training slots allotted each year for defence personnel, 800 went to Africa.[18] This covers training to personnel belonging to all the three wings of defence services, viz. army, air force and navy, nominated by the ITEC partner countries in prestigious institutions like National Defence College, Defence Services Staff College, etc. The training field covers security and strategic studies, defence management, marine and aeronautical engineering, logistics and management, etc.[19]

Apart from being trained under the ITEC scheme, many African naval personnel are being trained in submarine warfare, counter-piracy operations, and maritime surveillance. For example, the South African naval officers obtained training on Type-29 submarines at INS Satavahana, the submarine training school of the Indian Navy.[20]

Flagship Countries

Indian Navy is already holding joint exercises with South Africa, donated aircraft for maritime surveillance, undertaken hydrographic survey of islands of Mauritius, set up a listening post, possibly lease the island of Agalega and provide training to naval personnel. There is growing concern that African island nations, like Seychelles, Mauritius, could become bases for terrorist activities. India gifted the ship INS Amar to Mauritius as early as 1974, an interceptor patrol boat named INS Observer in 2001 and a Dornier maritime surveillance aircraft 2008. It gave a Dhruv helicopter in 2009; and a coastal surveillance radar installation too. In addition, India has aggressively expanded its naval presence reportedly to include the establishment of listening posts in the Seychelles, and Mauritius.

Some other interactions include hydrographic surveys undertaken in Mauritius since 2005. These surveys help to chart navigational routes that would help the trade, add weightage to continental claims, conduct surveys to help establish new industries and loan surveillance equipment for anti-piracy. On 25 October 2005, the Mauritian Prime Minister Navin Chandra Ramgoolam and Indian Prime Minister Manmohan Singh signed an agreement on the hydrographic work to be undertaken by India's Navy. Ever since, Indian navy has completed hydrographic surveys of Mauritian capital Port Louis harbour, Port Mathurin in Rodrigues Island, Carajos Cargados Shoals and Agalega Island.[21] India is also helping Mauritius in its attempt to become world's database hub by setting up sea water based air-cooling system.[22] It has also repaired the propulsion system of the Mauritian warship MCGS Vigilant.

The Mauritian-held twin islands of Agalega in the Indian Ocean are much closer to India than the parent country. Seen as an ideal tourist destination these islands could be given to India either on long-lease or by perpetual ceding of control. However, the Creoles who form part of a diverse community make-up have objections to such a deal.[23] Training in anti-piracy and diving operations were provided by Indian naval commandos to Mauritius. Special heli-borne operations training, VBSS (Visit, board, search and seizure) procedure familiarisation and even fresher training underwater welding, cutting, video-graphy and salvage were given.[24] Mauritius also had expressed interest in acquiring the Indian-made Advanced Light Helicopter and buying fast boats from Indian shipyards. Mauritius also sought to buy

Dornier aircrafts and Indian Offshore Patrol Vessels for maritime surveillance.[25]

In 2005, India gave a fast attack craft INS Tarmugli to Seychelles. It has also given helicopters and Indian ships visit the archipelago regularly.[26] Earlier, INS Savitri, the Offshore Patrol Vessel, helped the Seychelles Coast Guard to carry out surveillance of its exclusive economic zone.[27] Maritime relations with Seychelles have strengthened. Following the visit by Indian defence minister A.K. Antony in July 2010 to this island nation, maritime security cooperation assumed special impetus. A Dornier aircraft and two Chetak helicopters were provided to Seychelles for anti-piracy duties.[28]

The island nations of Mauritius and Seychelles have thus had extensive relations with India in the maritime security realm.

Other Efforts

India has its first listening post and monitoring station in foreign soil in Madagascar. India also inked an MoU in defence cooperation with Mozambique in 2006 to mount periodical maritime patrolling off its vast coast. Other than joint maritime patrolling of the Mozambican coast, the activities include mutual training in military institutes, supply of defence equipment/ services and establishment of partnership and transfer of know-how and technology foı assembling and repair of vehicles, aircraft and ships as well as rehabilitation of military infrastructure.[29] This was reiterated in a visit in June 2011 by Mozambique's defence minister Filipe Jacinto Nyussi to India. Earlier in 2003, the Indian Navy provided seaward protection for the African Union summit at Mozambique.[30] In March 2011, Indian Navy captured sixty-one pirates aboard the Mozambican fishing vessel 'Vega 5' that was hijacked in December 2010.[31] Tanzania is another African country that has sought assistance from Indian Navy to combat piracy.[32]

The anti-piracy operations of the Indian Navy in the Horn of Africa in 2008 deal with a pressing international problem. The menace of piracy which has, in the words of Prime Minister Manmohan Singh moved 'much beyond the infested areas of Gulf of Aden, pose a serious threat to us by putting at risk a large number of Indian seafarers and ships as well as our seaborne trade',[33] has to be effectively dealt with. The navy's tasks include escorting foreign and Indian commercial vessels through the Internationally Recommended Transit Corridor (IRTC) along the southern coast of Yemen.[34] Now the involvement has increased to rescuing ships that have been hijacked by pirates or prevent pirates from taking ships and in some cases arrest them. Indian Navy has averted attempts to hijack ships like MV Full City a Chinese bulk carrier in May this year off Karwar in the Arabian Sea and even sank several mother ships.[35] The Indian Navy has escorted a total of 1,700 commercial ships including foreign-flag vessels and thwarted thirty-nine hijacking attempts since 2008.[36]

Caveat Sinea

China's interest in Africa has of late raised global attention. China has entered Africa in a big way in the form of investments and to tap the abundant raw materials that the continent contains. To sustain its economic growth, China badly needs all the resources it can lay hands on. Energy and trade relations with African countries have increased at a massive pace. Despite earlier allegations that China was helping Sudan to continue to fight in Darfur through the oil economy, China later changed its policy and was acknowledged to have played a vital role in Sudan agreeing to allow UN-African Union peacekeeping in the troubled region.[37] China offered Seychelles $4.5 mn in grants in 2006 and built its new National Assembly.[38] China has wooed Africa with economic and military relationship. Africa is now China's second largest supplier of oil. China, an energy dependent and deficient economy, requires this. Its rapid economic growth also means look out for raw materials and that is why the African foray. The trade has soared in recent years.

The African countries are also benefitting from the China involvement. They are able to increase their bargaining power with other countries including India to extract a better price for their much-valued resources. The infrastructure and other support that China is offering has been delivered at a much faster pace winning friends in the region.[39] China is also selling or giving arms often to repressive regimes for which it has come under much criticism from around the world.[40] Beijing is now among the top conventional arms suppliers to African nations.[41] Trade has already crossed the $100 bn mark in 2010. The oil imports and other raw material imports from Africa to China need to be safeguarded. Such deep economic interaction entails possible political and even strategic engagements. For instance, the stakes of naval engagement are quite high simply at least to guard commercial ships in the piracy-ridden waters off Africa. China is showing a more active role in counter piracy. It is deploying destroyers and assault ships like the amphibious Kunlunshan in the vicinity. She is prepared to use fire of stun grenades and heavy machine guns against the pirates.[42] Her involvement will only increase in the coming years. India needs to look at China's African foray with caution and concern.

Conclusion

The region of Africa is a fast-growing economic and energy source. It also holds strategic significance. It has now figured, though after much delay, in India's security framework. The journey of Indian Navy's engagement of African countries in keeping with its stated maritime doctrine of expansion of influence has just begun. The Indian Navy has active interaction not only with island countries like Mauritius, Seychelles and Madagascar but other East African countries like Mozambique, South Africa, Tanzania, Djibouti and Eritrea. Djibouti, for instance, due to its proximity to the Arabian Peninsula and the piracy-ridden Somali coast, continues to gain India's attention. India has demonstrated its naval presence since 1967 and also by sending ships on counter-piracy operations. One of India's missile frigates INS Beas was sent to Djibouti in 2009.[43] The interaction with these countries is in the form of training of naval personnel of the respective countries in relevant areas like anti-piracy and search and rescue. Surveillance aircraft have also been given. Defence personnel from several African countries enrol in courses at specialised Indian institutions. Not only are the African nations benefitting but the Indian Navy is also deriving certain advantages like obtaining areas for lease to erect monitoring stations, gaining additional, valuable experience in dealing with the menace of piracy that has affected the African coasts too by active involvement in continuous vigil and patrolling the waters of the Indian Ocean. The foothold India could possess due to the Indian Navy's activities along the African coast could provide much required leverage in the competition with China, which is making great strides in occupying African economic space now and strategic edge in the near future. While the journey has begun on a positive note there is need to hasten the pace of involvement lest the African Odyssey could turn into an unfinished one.

References

1. For a detailed discussion of the four attributes and the subsequent elaboration on peace-time operations see, Till, Geoffrey, *Seapower: A guide for the twenty-first century*, Frank Cass.

2. *Ibid.*, p. 4.
3. http://www.apri.ac.nz/maritime.html
4. Bateman, Sam and Anthony Bergin, *Our Western Front: Australia and the Indian Ocean*, Australian Strategic Policy Institute, March 2010, p. 11.
5. Mungai, Christine, 'Africa: Scrambling for sea power in the Indian Ocean', *The East African*, January 10, 2011 as cited in The Norwegian Council for Africa website http://www.afrika.no/Detailed/20204.html
6. Cdrs Venugopal, A., Surendra Ahuja and Surendra Singh, Indian Navy's role as an instrument of India's Foreign Policy, http://indiannavy.nic.in/nott_winner_2001.pdf
7. Quadrennial Defense Review Report, February 2010, US Department of Defense p.60 http://www.defense.gov/qdr/QDR%20as%20of%2026JAN10% 200700.pdf
8. Jacob, P.J., 'India and Regional Maritime Cooperation', Seminar proceedings of Securing the Ocean: An Indian Ocean Perspective, 04 June 2005, National Maritime Foundation, p. 39.
9. DeSilva-Ranasinghe, Sergei, 'Why the Indian Ocean Matters', *The Diplomat,* March 02, 2011, http://the-diplomat.com/2011/03/02/why-the-indian-ocean-matters/?all=true
10. Rao, Radhakrishna, 'India's Geopolitical Future: How Critical Is Naval Power? – Analysis, *IPCS*, March 29, 2011. http://www.eurasiareview.com/29032011-indias-geopolitical-future-how-critical-is-naval-power-analysis/
11. Abhimanyu, S., Anti Piracy Operations of the Indian Navy, *South Asia Defence and Strategic Review*, 23 March 2011, http://www.defstrat.com/exec/frmArticleDetails.aspx?DID=284
12. For a detailed discussion of Panikkar's thought see, Holmes, James, James R. Holmes, Andrew C. Winner, Toshi Yoshihara, *Indian Naval Strategy in the Twenty-first Century*, Taylor & Francis, 2009, pp. 6-35.
13. Vaidya, Kesav, *The Naval Defence of India*, Thacker, Bombay, 1949 p. 9 as cited in Scott, David, 'India's Grand Strategy for the Indian Ocean : Mahanian Visions', *Asia-Pacific Review*, Vol. 13, No. 6, November 2006, p. 100. http://www.thescotties.pwp. blueyonder.co.uk/india-mahanian-visions.pdf
14. Prakash, Adm Arun. 'The Rationale and Implications of India's Growing Maritime Power', in Kugelman, Michael, *India's Contemporary Security Challenges*, Woodrow Wilson International

Centre for Scholars, Wash. D.C., 2011, p 78 http://www.wilsoncenter.org/sites/default/files/ASIA_100423_ IndiaSecurityFINAL.pdf

15. Sakhuja, Vijay, 'IBSA Navies: Strengthening Maritime Multilateralism', *South Asia Defence and Strategic Review*, 18 August, 2009 http://www.defstrat.com/exec/frmArticleDetails.aspx?DID=191
16. http://stratsisincite.wordpress.com/2011/04/14/south-africa-and-india-to-conduct-joint-naval-military-exercises/
17. http://indiannavy.nic.in/ions/welcome_to_ions_website_new.htm
18. http://www.modernghana.com/news/148874/1/itec-day-marked-in-accra.html
19. http://itec.mea.gov.in/
20. http://pib.nic.in/newsite/erelease.aspx?relid=12639
21. Bhatia, Rajiv, 'Horn of Africa: Why India should care more', *The Hindu*, 17 December 2010 http://www.thehindu.com/opinion/lead/article 959202.ece
22. http://southasia.oneworld.net/todaysheadlines/mauritius-to-become-global-database-hub
23. http://www.defence.pk/forums/india-defence/76561-mauritius-could-hand-over-2-islands-india.html
24. Navy trains Mauritius CG in anti-piracy ops, *Stratpost*, June 8, 2010 http://www.stratpost.com/navy-trains-mauritius-cg-in-anti-piracy-ops
25. India, Mauritius Plan More Defense Cooperation http://www.india-defence.com/reports-750
26. Ramachandran, Sudha, 'India's Quiet Sea Power', *Asia Times*, Aug 2, 2007, http://www.atimes.com/atimes/South_Asia/IH02Df01.html
27. Indian Navy: INS Savitri to Assist Coast Guards of Seychelles and Mauritius, http://www.marinebuzz.com/2009/11/23/indian-navy-ins-savitri-to-assist-coast-guards-of-seychelles-and-mauritius/
28. Indian Navy deploys surveillance aircraft in Seychelles, *The Times of India*, February 24, 2011. http://timesofindia.indiatimes.com/india/Indian-Navy-deploys-surveillance-aircraft-in-Seychelles/articleshow/7564087.cms
29. India, Mozambique Agree to Cooperate on Maritime Security, July 1, 2011 http://maritimesecurity.asia/free-2/maritime-security-asia/india-mozambique-agree-to-cooperate-on-maritime-security/
30. Indian Navy Activates Listening Post, Monitoring Station in Madagascar, Indian Ocean http://www.india-defence.com/reports-3453
31. Indian navy captures 61 pirates on Mozambican ship 'Vega 5', March 14, 2011 http://www. clubofmozambique.com/solutions1/sectionnews.php? secao=international&id=21177&tipo=one

32. Tanzania seeks support from Indian naval ships deployed in the Gulf of Aden, May 28, 2011 http://frontierindia.net/tanzania-seeks-support-from-indian-naval-ships-deployed-in-the-gulf-of-aden
33. 'Manmohan for reinforcing maritime security', *The Hindu*, October 2, 2011.
34. Pai, Nitin, 'Policing the Indian Ocean', *Business Standard*, November 15, 2010 http://www.business-standard.com/india/news/nitin-pai-policingindian-ocean/414797/ Nitin Pai: Policing the Indian Ocean
35. Indian Navy Warship Protect Chinese Ships from Pirate Attacks, 6 May 2010 http://www.india-defence.com/reports-5094
36. 'Indian Navy Foil Attacks, Captures Pirates', *The Journal of Commerce Online*, September 27, 2011 http://www.joc.com/security/indian-navy-foil-attacks-captures-pirates
37. Downs, Erica, 'The Fact and Fiction of Sino-African Energy Relations', *China Security*, Vol. 3, No. 3, Summer 2007, p. 61.
38. Agnihotri, Kamlesh Kumar, 'Chinese Quest for a Naval Base in The Indian Ocean - Possible Options for China' http://www.maritimeindia.org/pdfs/Chinese%20naval%20base%20KKA-12%20Feb.pdf
39. For a fuller discussion see Freemantle, Simon, 'China in Africa: Is the continent being re-colonised?', http://www.africagoodnews.com/africa/newsletters/item/953-china-in-africa-is-the-continent-being-re-colonised?.html
40. Volman, Daniel, 'The Military Dimensions of Africa's New Status in Global Geopolitics', September 2008 http://concernedafrica scholars.org/african-security-research-project/?p=49
41. http://www.gimmiethescoop.com/china-and-india-battle-for-influence-in-africa-part-1, 2, 3, 4
42. https://stratsisincite.wordpress.com/tag/pla-navy/
43. Mohammed, Khalid, 'India and Djibouti in the Indian Ocean Geopolitics', *Research Journal of Social Sciences*, Vol. 18, No.1, 2010, pp. 35-44. http://www.scribd.com/doc/63315981/India-and-Djibouti-in-the-Indian-Ocean-Geopolitics

9

India - Africa Expanding Ties: Strategic Interests and Concerns

Nivedita Ray

Introduction

India's interest and intense engagement with Africa is not new; it is age-old and rests on firm historical foundations of shared colonial past and similarity of post-independence development experience. The relationship has evolved over the years. From an ideologically-driven relationship, based on shared commitments to anti-colonialism, anti-racialism, non-aligned movement (NAM) and Afro-Asian solidarity, it has moved into a more pragmatic engagement with focus on economic and geo-strategic issues. Particularly after the 2008 India-Africa Summit there has been a perceptible shift in the relations with renewed initiatives taken by India. The 2008 India-Africa Forum Summit institutionalised India's engagement with Africa and elevated it to a partnership at the Pan-African level. The partnership is aimed at sharing each other's experiences, knowledge and resources for mutual benefit. The strategic relevance of both regions for each other and common interests drives this partnership, which in the true spirit of South–South cooperation is set to grow stronger in the days to come. In this partnership model of engagement India's approach has been development-centric with focus on empowerment, sustainable development and nurturing of human resource of the continent.

This paper focuses on the expanding ties of India and Africa in the current times; explore the factors that are shaping the relationship; and notice the emerging areas of strategic interests and the challenges. The first section dwells on the historical perspective of India-Africa ties; the second section focuses on strategic significance of Africa to India; the third section looks into India's significance to Africa and its developmental needs; and the last section on challenges.

India-Africa Ties: Historical Perspective

India-Africa relations can be traced back to ancient times when Indian merchants from western seaboard traded along the eastern littorals of Africa.[1] With varying degrees of importance, Africa has been part of India's foreign policy since Independence in 1947. It is in Africa that for the first time an Indian leader, Mahatma Gandhi, raised the issue of discrimination and became personally involved in the anti-colonial movement in South Africa. The experience of discrimination of Mahatma Gandhi in South Africa left an abiding influence in identification of India with the freedom-loving peoples of Africa. His philosophy, which he successfully put into practice to achieve India's independence, inspired a generation of African leaders-including Kwame Nkrumah of Ghana, Obafemi Awolowo of Nigeria, Julius Nyerere of Tanzania, and Kenneth Kaunda of Zambia – in their own national liberation campaigns.[2] While Mahatma Gandhi was the common icon for Indo-African relations, it was Jawaharlal Nehru who gave the relationship its political structure.[3] Jawaharlal Nehru, India's prime minister until 1964, referred to Africa as a 'sister continent'.[4] Under him India took definite diplomatic stands on many African issues. First, he supported the decolonisation of African states. Second, he took a firm stand against racial discrimination in South Africa and broke off India's diplomatic and trade relations from the racist regime. India's engagement with Africa, its diplomacy and interactions in non-aligned movement, United Nations, Commonwealth, Afro-Asian organisations were mainly on the lines of anti-colonialism and anti-racialism. He was one of the founding fathers of the 1955 Bandung Conference, which in turn paved the way first for the non-aligned movement and later for the Group of 77. In the late 1960s, India as a beacon of decolonisation in Africa, as one of the founders of non-aligned movement and a leader of Afro-Asian resurgence had been let down during Indo-Chinese

War of 1962. In the early 70s South-South cooperation was high on the agenda with focus on economic cooperation and both, India and Africa, countries played important roles. The oil crisis of the 70s split the South, and South-South cooperation came to exist in name but not in substance. This situation was mirrored in India's relations with Africa. However, with India's liberalisation beginning in 1991, focus has been more on attracting investment, expanding trade and upgrading infrastructure to fuel growth and development. Indian companies are venturing into new markets and investment possibilities outside India, including in regions with large Indian diasporas, such as eastern and southern Africa. India's present engagement with Africa has been fuelled by pragmatic concerns, namely expanding economic interdependence and meeting the resource needs. The interaction centres on trade, energy security, capacity building, agriculture, science and technology. Bilateral trade has grown rapidly, from $967 m per year in the mid-1960s to $62 bn in 2010-11, and India now intends to increase it to $90 bn by 2015.[5]

Strategic Significance of Africa to India

Africa, no more is a marginalised player in the global affairs. The resource-rich continent has become the new chessboard for powers that shape global geopolitics.[6] Significantly, it is Africa that is setting the direction and pace of external power engagement. India, as one of the powers, is leading a new push into Africa. New imperatives and winds of change in both the territories add a fresh momentum to the engagement. There has been a rise in the significance of Africa for India from economic, political and security perspective. The positive changes seen in Africa, both politically and economically, add to the continent's significance for India. The indicators of such changes are very much evident. Unlike the 1990s, Africa no more remains ravaged by frequent wars. Most of the conflicts have come to an end with peace and stability being established. Military coups and counter-coups, once a norm are giving way to democratic governments, which though often fragile and far from perfect, are nonetheless indicative of the change for the better. Today more than 80 per cent of all African countries have embraced multi-party democracy. Regular elections have become a common feature in the continent.[7] Governance and transparency issues, as well those of corruption, are being taken up in a serious manner. There is a greater consciousness now to put their own house in order and confidence to find solutions for their problems. At the international level it is now playing an enhanced role. Economically, it is growing fast. During this decade Sub-Saharan Africa has had an average growth rate of more than five per cent per year. Not only was the growth widespread across countries, with about 40 per cent of them growing at five per cent or above, it was also broad-based, with many sectors contributing resources, finance, retail, agriculture, transportation and telecommunications. Some countries have registered spectacularly higher rates. Across the sub-regions growth was strongest in West Africa (6.5 per cent) powered by Nigeria's robust growth (7.9 per cent) and supported by Ghana's (7.7 per cent) gains in the year. GDP growth in East Africa is almost as strong, with Ethiopia (7 per cent), Rwanda (7.5 per cent), Tanzania (7 per cent) and Kenya (5.6 per cent) all recording robust gains.[8]

For India, from an economic perspective, Africa, unlike in the past has become a major trading destination. Trade and investment is one of the major drivers of current engagement. The Indian private sector with its 'outward-looking' attitude tempted by the easy availability of capital and driven by the search for new markets, have been targeting those regions in Africa, in which they had shown little interest earlier. The economic boom in India and the success of both home-grown and NRI/PIO (Non-Resident Indian/Person of Indian Origin) companies in Europe and parts of South America have provided Indian businesses the confidence to venture into Africa. Moreover, there is a growing recognition that African economies are at a stage of development where India could offer the most appropriate technologies and products at competitive prices. The success of India-Africa project partnership conclaves since 2005 indicates the growing interest of Indian industry in Africa. The recent robust trends in Indo-African trade relations, wherein bilateral trade has increased almost five-fold in the last five years, from USD7.1 bn in 2003-04 to USD62 bn in 2010-11 makes it evident how Africa is turning out to be an attractive destination for Indian private companies. Africa's share of India's global trade has also increased from 5.8 per cent in 2002-03 to eight per cent in 2006-07.[9] Increased activities of Indian companies in Africa have spurred the government to link its economic diplomacy in the continent more explicitly to its economic requirements.

From a geo-strategic perspective, Africa's abundant energy resources have attracted India's attention. Today it is one of the key drivers of India's relations with Africa. India's growing energy needs have forced it to diversify its oil imports and look towards Africa, in a way to decrease its dependency on West Asian countries for its oil imports, which accounts for two-third of the oil imports.[10] In recent years, India is increasingly engaging with African oil-producing countries, namely Nigeria, Sudan, Côte d'Ivoire, Equatorial Guinea, Ghana, and Angola. Consequently, Africa accounts for about 20 per cent of India's total import of mineral fuels. Other key African partners include South Africa, Egypt, Morocco, Tanzania, and Tunisia. Indian companies like ONGC, Indian Oil and Reliance have been active in seeking prospects for exploration indirectly. Other mineral resources like coal, diamond and uranium in Africa are also strategic to India's requirements. Coal and diamond firms from India are investing across Africa. New embassies in Niger and Malawi have been opened to assist firms in securing uranium for India's fast-growing nuclear power industry.[11]

From India's security and strategic point of view there is a growing recognition that the eastern coast of Africa from South Africa to Somalia – fall under India's maritime strategic neighbourhood. Insecurity in the Indian Ocean region is on the rise, owing to the threat of terrorism, trans-national crimes such as trafficking in drugs, arms and humans, and piracy. Alarming increase in incidents of piracy in Somali waters, in particular, threatens the security of the Sea Lanes of Communications (SLOCs) and impacts global maritime trade, a large part of which passes through the Gulf of Aden. The Indian Navy, particularly its Coast Guards, has been active in its diplomacy in the Indian Ocean, providing maritime security cover. But despite all the measures that have been taken to curtail this menace the situation, as termed by India, is still 'worrisome'. While significant gains have been made in the last one year by the African Union Mission in Somalia (AMISOM) and Kenyan and Ethiopian forces in securing Mogadishu and other areas in south and central Somalia, terror group Al Shabaab with its recent affiliation to Al Qaeda remains a serious threat to peace and stability not only in Somalia but the region as a whole. India, which made an uncaveated $2 m contribution in 2011 to the African Union and UN Trust Funds for AMISOM, is ready to provide further support to AMISOM.[12] Peace and stability of the region is of utmost importance to the region and in India's interest too.

Politically India has acknowledged the importance of African countries in global governance. In the context of UN reforms Africa is significant as it is rich in votes at the UN General Assembly. As India intensifies its efforts to bring about UN reform and secure for itself a permanent seat in the Security Council, the fifty-three votes from Africa in the General Assembly will play a crucial role.

Significance of India in Africa's Development

For Africa India holds immense significance from the perspective of its development and growth. India is held in high esteem - in particular, on account of resilience of its democratic institutions and the manner and speed of its economic growth. As a democratic developing country, it serves as a role model for these African countries and is a source of support in various sectors, especially agriculture, services and small- and medium-scale manufacturing. Above all, it is the image of India – that of a leader in the information technology industry and computer software, biotechnology and telecommunications - that attracts Africa to India.

The question is, how has India been responding to Africa's developmental needs? The development cooperation initiatives taken up by India are claimed to be relevant to Africa's needs and requirements, although the cooperation has been, and still is, minuscule compared with both China and the big traditional donors.[13] It comprises several different programmes which are of mutual benefit. They range from capacity-building measures, which include training, skill development and scholarships, to Lines of Credit (LOC), grants and humanitarian assistance. Historically, the most important development assistance programme has been the Indian Technical and Economic Cooperation (ITEC), which was initiated in 1964 and is still running. According to the Ministry of External Affairs (MEA), India currently transfers Rs. 500 m (US$10.3 m) a year via this programme.[14] The MEA has also increased its slots to a number of African countries. ITEC has a sister programme called the Special Commonwealth Assistance for Africa Programme (SCAAP). Basically, this programme makes use of the same aid modalities as ITEC but, unlike ITEC, only targets African countries in the Commonwealth (nineteen in all). However, not all African Commonwealth countries are targeted with the same degree of eagerness and offered the same conditions. Rather, the extent of help varies with the perceived importance of the recipient country for India. Hence, countries like Mauritius, South Africa and Uganda (with large Indian diasporas and/or economic importance) receive a relatively larger proportion while countries with hardly any Indian diaspora, no natural resources and no economic influence receive a smaller share.

India also offers scholarships to overseas students (university courses at various levels, professional courses and courses linked to Indian music, dance and art) via the Indian Council for Cultural Relations (ICCR) scholarship scheme. During 2009-10, some 15 per cent of the slots have gone to African countries. Like the ITEC and the SCAAP, India uses this scheme geo-politically. Hence, countries like Mauritius (40), South Africa (25) and Kenya (20) are allocated far more scholarships than Cameroon (1), Guinea (1) and Togo (1).[15]

India also provides development assistance to Africa in financial terms, though it is not significant yet. To note that it has been boosted massively over the last few years. It is totally linked to India's own capabilities and interests in Africa. Since it is framed as a partnership between equal partners, which can enhance developmental aspect, it has the potential to create a new platform for South-South dialogue. Since 2003, numerous development schemes with a particular focus on Africa have been launched, totalling Rs. 26.7 bn (US$547 m) in 2008.

Among the most important new initiatives is the Focus Africa Programme (2002-07) totalling US$550 m, administered by the Export Import Bank of India. Essentially, it seeks to enhance commercial links between India and African countries by offering export subsidies to Indian companies trading with African nations and extending lines of credit to African governments and regional entities. The lines of credit is may be seen as a form of development assistance. Indian government needs to find a comfortable space between the rhetoric of South–South coordination and articulating India's national interests and the extension of lines of credit to sub-Saharan African countries could be a route to finding this. It is generally accepted that this helps to promote Indian exports and improve political relations. Likewise, the Techno Economic Approach for Africa India Movement (TEAM-9) is important. Just as the other Indian aid programmes, the focus of TEAM-9 also reflects India's political-economic interests. Hence, the TEAM-9 countries overlap with countries courted by Indian oil companies, and much of the assistance provided by India is tied to purchases of products and services from India. In addition, India has offered NEPAD, a US$200 m credit line and has funded the Pan-African e-Network with US$100 m. Besides the LOC, India has offered bilateral debt relief (by 2008, India had written off debt totalling US$24 m), UN peace-keeping operations and humanitarian assistance to several African countries.

These initiatives seem to bear fruits for the Indian private sector. This is evident from the growing trade with Africa, which amounts to US$62 bn as stated earlier. This picture is also mirrored by Indian investments in Africa, which come in all shapes and sizes (and ownership patterns), ranging from small family firms to large multinational enterprises in the manufacturing, construction and telecommunication sectors. The developmental partnership has also witnessed an increase in African exports to India, and in this regard, the Duty Free Tariff Preference Scheme announced by India for the least developed countries appears to have been fruitful.

As development of infrastructure is a priority for Africa, India has been contributing to this end through the concessional lines of credit. Africa places strong emphasis on augmentation of regional connectivity. In this context, India is contributing towards establishing a new Ethio-Djibouti rail network through a line of credit worth US$300 m. The role of the private sector in the operationalisation of some of the lines of credit needs no emphasis. This has acquired prominence through the announcement of lines of credit to Africa at the two Forum Summits. The prime minister announced US$5.4 bn as line of credit in the First India Africa Forum Summit and an additional US$5 bn in this regard during the Second Africa India Forum Summit in Addis Ababa in 2011.

Besides the LOC, which is allocated for undertaking different development projects in Africa, Indian prime minister Manmohan Singh has pledged, US$700 m for eighty new institutions and training programmes. Under the rubric IAFS-I and II, India would be establishing more than a hundred capacity-building institutions in Africa encompassing wide variety of fields. There is also a provision for 22,000 scholarships for African students in various academic courses and training programmes including special scholarships focusing on agriculture sciences and fellowships for science and technology.

What is clear in this development-oriented partnership is that the focus is on South–South cooperation with particular attention being given to interaction between equal partners. It has been consultative, responsive and focused on capacity building, infrastructure and human resource development. The initiatives taken up by India for Africa's development and growth are laudable but they definitely are not wholly altruistic.[16] India has to balance them with its own economic and political interests, and also security concerns.

Challenges Ahead

Balancing initiatives for Africa's developmental needs with its own self-interest remains an onerous challenge for India. India's interaction is primarily economic, led by private sector. Government-to-government, as well as academic and civil society, interaction is much less. A private-sector led India's economic engagement, generates concerns as to whether the economic relations will be able to distinguish qualitatively from the North-South relations.[17] If it would not do so it might create problems for India's role in Africa and its goodwill. India has immense goodwill and it needs to preserve it, particularly now when competition for Africa's goodwill and resources has intensified among various powers that are trying to increase their foothold in Africa. It becomes imperative for India to be relevant to Africa's priorities, needs and expectations for their development and growth.

The challenge for India is also to ensure that its development aid initiatives are effective. It needs to evaluate whether its strategies and methods so far adopted are really making a gainful difference on the ground and if they are really unique, as is claimed? India's development assistance initiatives constitutes a combination of tied project aid and scholarships, mainly targeting African countries that are rich in resources or rich in Indian diasporas; to a large extent this mirrors the actions of China, though on a much smaller scale. China also uses aid to facilitate other financial flows and the modalities are somewhat similar, i.e., comprising technical assistance, grants, export credits, debt relief and unilateral zero-tariff access for African products. India needs to ensure, as it claims, that its engagement with Africa focused on aid and capacity building is effective and qualitatively different from that of others. Africans should be satisfied that their developmental concerns are being considered.

As far as economic engagement is concerned so far it is observed that India's trade with Africa has not progressed smoothly. It is still confined to a dozen countries only, and India's import and export basket still follows a colonial pattern of buying and selling finished goods. Even Indian industry focuses on handful of relatively more advanced economies. The rest of Africa is yet to feel the industrial strength of India. This is an area that needs attention.[18] It is time to shift from conventional trade to more creative ways of economic cooperation like shifting some of the manufacturing to the African countries, which could cut transport costs and more importantly provide employment to the Africans. Some pharmaceutical companies like Ranbaxy have already started this trend and there is a need for more of this.

There is a felt need for greater engagement between India and Africa on issues of a geo-strategic nature. India has always been keen to cooperate with Africa on issues of global security. Owing to their rising global politico-economic profile, both India and Africa are justifiably expected to highlight the concerns of the developing world at various international fora. This shared responsibility calls for a greater understanding of each other and synchronisation of their views and response to a variety of global issues that may have a direct bearing on the development prospects of the peoples of both regions.

Conclusion

India should be able to harmonise its South–South coordination policy and its economic self-interest in order to have a sustainable long-term partnership. Business and governments need to strike deals that not only generate wealth but help eradicate poverty by investing in Africa's peoples. The strategic partnership between India and Africa should bring tangible solutions for various issues which are included in the African Programme, namely NEPAD (The New Partnership for Africa's Development). The expansion of development of infrastructure facilities will facilitate intra-Africa trade, economic cooperation and provide improved market access for their own products. As far as visibility in terms of development deliverables of India in Africa are concerned still much needs to be done. India needs to expand its presence and pay greater attention to implementation of the projects.

At the same time these initiatives throw up a challenge in terms of enhancing capacities within India – diplomatic, academic and professionals. Within India's Ministry of External Affairs there is a need to strengthen the team of officials working on Africa. As India's dialogue with Africa increases, it is quite natural that there will be demand for professionals and scholars with expertise in African affairs. It is time that these issues are given priority. Finally, the Addis Ababa Summit has revealed that 'Brand India' in Africa is a model that stresses on partnership in enhancing skills and capacity building within the continent. India will have to tap on the goodwill that exists within the continent to make this partnership work.

References

1. Alex Vines, India's Africa Engagement: Prospects for the 2011 India Africa Forum, Program paper, AFP, 201 1/01, Chatham House, UK.
2. Gupta, Anirudha, 'India and Africa, South of the Sahara', in Bimla Prasad, (Ed.) *India's Foreign Policy,* New Delhi, 1979, p. 269.
3. Dubey, Ajay, India-Africa Relations: Historical Connections and Recent Trends, in Ajay Dubey (ed) *Trends in Indo-Africa Relations*, Manas Publications, New Delhi, 2010.
4. Sharma, A., 'India and Africa: Partnership in the 21st Century', *South African Journal of International Affairs,* Vol. 14, No. 2, 2007, p. 20.
5. 'India Africa Set Trade Target to $90 bn in 2015', *The Economic Times*, 17 March 2012.
6. Eze, Osita C., 'Principal Interests of EU and India in Sub-Saharan Africa', in Dilip Lahiri, Jorg Schultz (ed), *Engaging with a Resurgent Africa*, Macmillan Publishers, Delhi, 2009.
7. *Ibid.*
8. Global Economic Prospects 2011: Regional Annex, Sub Saharan Africa ,http://siteresources.worldbank.org/INTGEP/Resources/335315-13074 71336123/7983902-1307479336019/AFR-Annex.pdf, accessed on 5 June 2011.
9. Bajpaee, C., 'The Indian elephant returns to Africa', *Online Asia Times,* 25 April 2008, http://www.atimes.com/atimes.
10. Sharma, D. and D. Mahajan, 'Energising Ties: The Politics of Oil', *South African Journal of International Affairs,* Vol. 14, No. 2, Winter/ Spring 2007, pp. 37–53.

11. Alex Vines, India-Africa engagement: Prospects for the 2011, India-Africa forum, Chatham House, December 2010.

12. 'Increase of Piracy Attacks off Somalia coast Worrisome: India', *The Hindu,* 7 March 2012.

13. Kragelund, Peter, India's Africa Engagement, ARI, 10/2010, 19 January 2010.

14. *Ibid.*

15. *Ibid.*

16. Sudha Ramchandran, India Deepens Africa Role, Asia Times Online, 2 June 2011, http://www.atimes.com/atimes/South_Asia/MF02Df01.html, accessed on 3 June 2011

17. Dubey, Ajay, 'India-Africa Relations: Historical Connections and Recent Trends', in Ajay Dubey (ed), *Trends in Indo-Africa Relations*, Manas Publications, New Delhi, 2010.

18. Mansingh, Lalit, 'Engaging a Resurgent Africa: India's Choices' in Dilip Lahiri and Jorg Schultz (ed), *Engaging with a Resurgent Africa*, Macmillan Publishers, Delhi, 2009.

10

India's Involvement in Africa since 1990s: Increasing Institutionalisation of State-Business Relations

Shaji S.

Introduction

In the current period of globalisation, state-business relations at international level have assumed paramount significance. State-business relations, which usually refer to the linkages between the state and capital in the internal economy of the state, can also include how a state handles foreign direct investment (FDI). In the last two decades states from across the developing world have begun to economically engage with the outside world by striking economic alliances and linkages in an unprecedented manner. Under this trend, the states in the African continent are increasingly facilitating such alliances and linkages by incorporating FDI, especially through multinational corporations (MNCs) from different countries across the world, in different sectors. In the meantime, Asian countries have increasingly begun to look for natural resources, such as oil and gas, to strengthen their energy security and also for new markets for their finished goods. The presence of new Asian powers, such as India and China, can be seen in the all-pervasive operations of their companies – both private and public – in the continent of Africa. Against this setting, the current paper while throwing light on the involvement of Indian companies in African states in general, analyses the impact of such an involvement in addressing India's concerns and the needs of African countries. The first part of the paper analyses general setting of foreign policy of India; the second part discusses the involvement of Indian companies in various countries; and the final part concludes the paper.

Rise in India's Involvement in Africa: Emerging Realities in India's Foreign Policy

In the current architecture of global power politics, shaped by the emerging geopolitical/economic landscape, growing economies/powers make earnest effort to place themselves in a vantage position vis-à-vis other economies. Such efforts to attain position of advantage prominently figure in their foreign policy formulations. Since early 1990s, the process of globalisation of markets and marketisation of economies in the period of the ascendancy of neo-liberal globalisation, under auspices of United States, gained vigour all around the world. Owing to supranational integration of production through multinational and transnational corporations, knowledge has moved the farthest in the economic arena. The operation of capital markets, money and foreign private investment has rendered the entire globe virtually borderless.[1] Furthermore, the collapse of the socialist bloc at the international level and the apparent triumph of capitalism following the demise of the Cold War and decline of socialist model of development strategies has redefined and reshaped foreign policies of nation states across the world.

At the domestic level, in India, weaknesses of planned economy, under-performance of public sector units, corruption, fiscal deficit crisis and lack of sufficient foreign reserves had shaken the very foundation of planned economy in the beginning of 1990s. The inward-looking economic policy and the strategy did not bring desired results in terms of power, either economic or political, in international arena. Countless problems began to weaken the state of the economy in India. Primarily, the problem of resource mobilisation from outside became more pressing by the late 1980s. Despite better sophistication in debt management, the Government of India found it increasingly difficult to raise money in the late 1980s on favourable terms. The state of the economy worsened and became more chaotic in the 1990s. Postponement of 1991-92 budget presentations, balance of payment crisis and an alarming fiscal deficit were some indicators of the worsening economic situation in the country. These systemic and domestic factors became a major catalyst to launch New Economic Policy (NEP). The policy envisaged vast scope for markets in the economic activities of the nation, along with the public sector. The new economic policy launched during the Narasimha Rao government (1991-96) began to reshape the foreign policy of the country in an implicit fashion. India was ushered into market economy by opening up its economy in a big way in the early 1990s which, in turn, has made the state to recede from the commanding heights it occupied previously. Thus, India entered into the phase of globalisation by opening its door to foreign direct investment (FDI), relaxing the licensing and privatising of certain services through disinvestment, hitherto reserved for the public sector and so on. Regulatory reforms initiated by the government brought in large number of private entities in hitherto government-controlled sectors, such as telecom, power, port, petroleum and so on.

In addition to this, after the end of Cold War, at the international level, there originated an increasing power struggle between developed states of the first world and developing states, such as India and China, especially over FDI including technology through direct and indirect ways. Its reflections can be seen in the formation of a hegemonic alliance/ order of transnational capitalist classes, concentrated in the developed states. In general, hegemonic order is the one where consent rather than coercion primarily characterises the relations between the state and the civil society. In order to cope with these realities at international and domestic level, India has reformed its foreign policy premises, such as non-alignment, by shedding political emphasis to give thrust to economic aspects. India has forged new alliances, reinvigorated traditional relations and gave new dynamism to regional groupings while breaking new pathways.[2] As stated earlier, economic reforms initiated by India have subsumed forms of trade and investment liberalisation, which could gradually facilitate India's integration with the world economy. According to some scholars, the link between India's domestic policy and external relations has to be constantly reworked, with the reforms underway. Consequently, India had to engage with several states to survive in the changing international order. This process was warranted because of India's need for technology, finance and capital to meet domestic demands. In tune with economic restructuring at the domestic front,

India redefined the major premises of its foreign policy substantially in the 1990s, in order to cope with evolving global scenario.[3] Such newly-defined premises of India's foreign policy included de-emphasis on the practice of non-alignment, multi-directional engagement with major powers, and increased vigour in regionalism and so on.

Against this setting, at operational level, a dominant regional and middle-level power, such as India, has to play a more proactive role in persuading other like-minded developing states through diverse networks of development cooperation, which include transfer of technology. In this context, the continent of Africa with its immense mineral wealth, market and geo-strategic location is incontestably an important area where India could effectively launch projects of development cooperation, including technology transfer through multifarious cooperation.[4] To take advantage of such possibilities, India began to build linkages with African states in a dynamic manner wherein public- and private-sector companies from India struck alliances with their counterparts in Africa. The private sector in India had started to dominate the business and economy.

India in Africa since 1990s

India needs a huge amount of hydrocarbon in order to sustain its domestic economy. The Asian requirement of oil is expected to increase from 30 m barrels per day currently to 130 m barrels per day in 2020. The bulk of this projected increase is expected to be consumed by China and India, together accounting for 35 per cent of the world's incremental consumption of energy.[5] In 2010-11, India's consumption of crude oil stood at 206.15 MMT, out of which 163.59 MMT was imported.[6] In other words, internal production was only 37.7 MMT (approximately 18 per cent of the total consumption in corresponding year, according to statistics of Ministry of Petroleum, GOI). This clearly shows a glaring gap between the total demand for oil and the domestic production (supply). Against this context, in the realm of search for oil and attaining energy security, Africa assumes significance for all major growing Asian economies including India. In addition, the volatile political situation prevailing in West Asian region is another reason that makes Africa attractive for Asian countries. The new developments in countries, such as Syria and Yemen, further complicate the situation. In this context, the continent of Africa, which has enormous natural resources and a fledgling market, along with its geo-strategic location, provides huge opportunity to states to launch development cooperation including transfer of technology. Such cooperative ventures need to be carved out imaginatively by being sensitive to changing political and economic situation in Africa and the world. It is only through such a policy, pursued on a durable basis, that economies such as China and India can eventually succeed in building coalitions of developing states to encounter the challenges of the globalising world effectively.[7] Thus, it can be contended that India and China began forming alliances and linkages with developing states, such as South Africa, Sudan from Africa and Brazil from Latin America, to name a few, in order to meet the challenges posed by globalisation.

Africa is in the centre stage of global attention with the race for its oil reserves. Africa owns 13 per cent of the world's known oil reserves with Angola, Nigeria, Libya, and Equatorial Guinea as the regions' leading oil producers. It is estimated that 70 per cent of Africa's oil production is concentrated in West Africa's Gulf of Guinea, which stretches from Ivory Coast to Angola. China has oil interest in Algeria, Angola, Chad and Sudan, while India has stake in Sudan, Nigeria, Gabon, Egypt and Algeria. Due to the enormous business potential, foreign direct investment has increased substantially from US$6 bn in 1995 to US$36 bn in 2006 (WID, 2008). It further rose to US$88 bn in 2008 despite the global financial and economic crisis. This increased the FDI stock in the region to US$511 bn. Primary commodities have been the major source of investment attraction in the region. In 2008, of the total flows, southern Africa attracted a third of the total FDI inflows while West Africa recorded the largest percentage increase (63 per cent), while North Africa registered a decline. Developed countries were the leading source of FDI in Africa, although their share in the region's FDI stock has fallen over time. However, this has been compensated largely due to increased investments from Asian countries, such as China, India, Singapore, Malaysia, South Korea and Japan.

Indian Involvement in Africa: Emergence of Tangible Ties

Since 1990s, India's involvement in African energy sector began by striking a deal with Sudan (undivided), a nation from North Africa. Along with Sudan, the countries around the Gulf of Guinea, such as Nigeria and Angola, too emerge as the major producers of hydrocarbons. India has developed a successful collaboration with Sudan wherein they also contributed to the development of local infrastructure and educational and medical facilities in the areas of its cooperation. China, India and Malaysia control 90 per cent of the Sudanese oil industry, which exported US$6 bn worth of oil into these countries in the year 2009. The referendum conducted in Sudan in 2011 decided to have a new state for the people of South Sudan which owns 90 per cent of oil resources of undivided Sudan. This scenario can have some implication for oil business of Asian powers in the country. However, Sudanese model of oil cooperation involving other Asian powers has been replicated by India in other African states, such as South Africa, Nigeria and Angola. Similarly, OVL has oil blocks in Gabon, Nigeria and Egypt.

In addition to the involvement in oil sector, public- and private-sector companies from India began to invest in infrastructural sectors. Bharat Petroleum Company Limited's (BPCL) subsidiary and Videocon have ten per cent stake in Rovuma basin in Mozambique. Essar Energy has a 50 per cent stake in Kenya Petroleum Refineries. In the mineral extraction sector, Sterlite, an Indian company has acquired zinc assets from Anglo American Skorpion mine in Namibia, and 74 per cent stake in Black Mountain Mining. Similarly, Jindal Steel and Power operates a coal mine in South Africa.[8] Tata Steel's JV with Riverdale Mining has 35 per cent stake in two coal tenements in Mozambique.[9] In the pharmaceutical sector, Ranbaxy and Lupin have made forays into South Africa. In telecom sector, Bharti Airtel, India's major private telecom entity has begun to operate in sixteen countries by acquiring Zain's telecom assets in the continent.

India's involvement in Africa has increased substantially if one looks at the statistics. India is one of Africa's most important trading partners, with total trade worth $35 bn in 2008, substantially higher than the $967 m recorded in 1991. Total trade is expected to triple to $100 bn by the year 2012. India imports from Africa double of what it exports to Africa; its biggest imports being fuel and metals, mainly from Algeria, Morocco, Nigeria and South Africa. Indian FDI in Africa stood at $2.5 bn in 2008, 2.8 per cent of total FDI into Africa (China has invested $8 bn by way of FDI, nine per cent of the total). Similarly, UNCTAD's statistical report 2010 points to a gradual decline of American and European investment in Africa. India's investment has increased considerably due to major energy construction and mineral extract projects. India's approved overseas direct investment in Africa increased by US$5.7 bn between 1996 and 2007, out of which Mauritius (US$3.5 bn) and Sudan (US$1.1 bn) received substantial portions.[10]

In the African continent a wide array of private investors from India operate: Angelique International (agriculture), Apollo Group of Hospitals (health care), Kirloskar Brothers Limited (KBL, agriculture equipments), ESSAR Group (infrastructure/ telecommunications), Fortis Escorts Hospitals (health care), Infrastructure Alliance (infrastructure), WAPCOS (water resources, power and infrastructure), Larsen and Toubro Limited (engineering), Mahindra and Mahindra Limited (agricultural equipment), NIIT (information technology), Shapoorji Pallonji and Company Limited (construction), Tata Group (automobiles, chemicals and others). Tata group was one of the first Indian companies that entered Africa almost six decades ago and Tata Motors was a well-known brand in the truck segment way back in the 1960s. Today, through its affiliate TATA-Africa, the company has significant investments and has a presence in eleven African countries.[11] Bharati Airtel has acquired Zain's telecom operations in Nigeria, Sudan, Kenya, Tanzania, Uganda, Madagascar, Congo, Gabon and Ghana. Essar Reliance has telecom licenses in Uganda.

The Government of India (GOI) enterprises that have a presence in Africa are: Telecommunications Consultants India Ltd (TCIL), Indian Telecom Industries (ITI) Ltd, Rail India Technical and Economic Services (RITES), Konkan Railways, IRCON International Limited, Oil and Natural Gas Corporations (ONGC) Videsh Limited (OVL), Bharat Heavy Electricals Ltd (BHEL) amongst others. More recently a laudable initiative by the Ministry of External Affairs (GOI) has been the US$500 bn worth investment in the Pan African e-network, the distance telemedicine programme launched in February 2009 as a part of its 'Aid to Africa' programme. To put it tersely, Africans have a basket of options from which they can choose their investors, with respect to oil fields, mines, agriculture, manufacturing, infrastructure and health. Thus, it is imperative that India has to present itself to garner attention of the African states as far as investment in these sectors are concerned.

Institutionalisation of Involvement

In an era, when geo-economics is shaping international politics, this relationship is also no exception, and programmes like-Focus

Africa Programme, TEAM-9 Initiative and NEPAD are the key areas of institutionalised relationships which figure in India-Africa ties. Agriculture has emerged as an area of cooperation in some of these initiatives because India has made rapid strides in agricultural technology, which tackled issues of India's food security. Therefore, a continent with huge population, land and natural resources like Africa look towards India in the area of agriculture, as is evident from the fact that more than eighty Indian companies have invested about £1.5 bn in buying huge plantations in Ethiopia, Kenya, Madagascar, Senegal and Mozambique to grow grains for the domestic market.[12] New Delhi has also cut import duties for food produced in Ethiopia. The largest company which invested in Ethiopia is Karuturi Global, one of the world's largest producers of cut roses. It has signed deals for 350,000 hectares to create the world's largest agricultural land-bank. The Bangalore-based company, which has bought farm land in Kenya, is growing sugar cane, palm oil, rice and vegetables.

Similarly, India is in the process of helping African countries to set up small and medium enterprises. In addition, India provided a line of credit of $200 m for African Union under New Partnership for African Development (NEPAD), a Pan African strategic framework for socio-economic development of African States. The Focus Africa programme of India had initially given emphasis on cooperation with seven countries in the African continent - Ethiopia, Nigeria, South Africa, Mauritius, Kenya, Tanzania and Ghana, which accounts for 69 per cent of India's bilateral trade with the Sub-Saharan Africa.[13] Similarly, in order to enhance bilateral and multi-lateral ties in the realm of trade in West Africa, India initiated Techno-Economic Approach for Africa India movement (Team-9 Initiative, the countries covered are Burkino Faso, Chad, Congo, Côte d'Ivoire, Guinea-Bissau, Ghana, Senegal, Mali and India). Team-9 Initiative, among other things such as institutionalisation of cooperation through public sector, also envisages role for private investment and participation in the economies of these African states. India has also joined India-SADC Forum to strengthen its relations with SADC in different sectors. India's trade to SADC countries increased from $1.5 bn in 1997 to $4 bn in 2007. There are regular consultation processes going on to increase the trade. Another initiative called PAN African E-Network project, linking all countries of African countries has been undertaken by India since 2002. Indian Ocean Rim-Association for Regional

Cooperation (IOR-ARC), a transcontinental alliance which came into existence in 1997, is an initiative on the part of India to link with southern African countries, along with other countries from West Asia.

Similarly, Federation of Indian Chamber of Commerce and Industry (FICCI) have set up FICCI Africa Desk to deepen India-Africa ties. In addition to this, FICCI has entered into alliance with its counterpart, Apex Chambers in African States through an institutionalised mechanism called Joint Business Council (JBC). JCBs offer an array of business facilitation services by closely working with government and business promotion organisation in India and their respective partner countries.[14] CII has constituted CII-Africa Committee to prioritise business and economic linkages with African States. These kinds of linkages are likely to take India-Africa trade to $70 bn by 2015.[15]

Business Involvement and Contending Criticisms

There are several shades of criticism levelled against the involvement of Asian states in the continent of Africa. Sanusha Naidu characterises Asian involvement in the contemporary period as 'second scramble for African resources'.[16] Another layer of criticism points to the fact that multinational corporations (MNCs) from petroleum industry are increasingly trying to influence/ disrupt the democratic movement in Africa. There are widespread criticisms against the involvement of petroleum giants, who are apparently, hand in glove with several dictatorial regimes who sabotage the establishment of democratic practices in several countries in the continent, such as Nigeria, Sudan and several others.[17] Some charge that democratic movements were stifled in Africa in the hot pursuit for oil by citing the instance of Ken Saro Wiva and other Ogoni leaders in Nigeria in 1995. They further highlight the admission of Shell Company in the killing of Nigerian leaders and the subsequent agreement on compensation.[18] After being implicated in the execution, and on 8 June, after being sued in US courts by the families of those executed, the firm agreed to pay $15:5 m in out-of-court settlement. In other words, such atrocities continue to happen. The significance of this instance is that such complaints are often heard from countries such as Sudan, Algeria, Angola and so on where there is the involvement of a large number of MNCs, especially from Asian countries in oil excavation and drilling. It has to be noted that *Freedom House* dropped three African countries from its list of 'electoral democracies' 2010, and reported decline in political freedom in ten others. The reason attributed to this decline is the rise of China in African horizon, which provides cheap loans and investment to resource-rich countries while asking no hard questions about human rights, thus strengthening the hold of Authoritarian governments.[19] The underlying thread in these criticisms is that there lie tendencies of neo-colonialism in the involvement of Asian powers in the continent. Such a criticism is a pointer to happenings in Africa which India has to be cautious of.

Institutionalisation of State-Business Ties in Indo-African Relations: Some Emerging Trends

There are certain emerging trends in Indo-African relation in the present times. First, cooperation between Africa, India and other growing economies, like Brazil and China, is of strategic importance to the continent and is ushering in a new phase of tangible South-South cooperation. Second, Indian investments in Africa have been private-sector driven and they are encouraged to partner in Africa's development, especially in sectors such as infrastructure, agriculture, science and technology and so on. This is an interesting aspect of Indian involvement in Africa, compared to China whose investment in Africa is mostly through its public-sector companies.

Third, India and Africa share a strategic relationship with each other which is aimed at sharing each other's development experiences and resources for mutual benefit. Fourth, since India and Africa are relatively at similar levels of development compared to more advanced regions of the world, the two regions are well placed to enter into a symbiotic relationship with each other. The new wave of South-South cooperation is different from the North-South cooperation which emerged after the Washington consensus. While the North-South cooperation was based on transfer of aid from developed to developing countries, the South-South cooperation is more of a genuine partnership between the developing countries. Fifth, India can make use of the fact that products from India are cost effective and more suited to African geographical and physical conditions. Sixth, unlike China, Indian involvement in Africa has received fewer criticisms, especially on the political front.

Concluding Remarks

India began to engage with Africa in the realm of business and economy since 1990s in an unprecedented manner. The search for energy sources, primarily petroleum, has prompted India to look for new destinations, such as Africa, which in turn has led to better business and economic ties primarily in private sector, though there is substantial presence of Indian public-sector entities. A new trend emerging from Indo-African ties is a higher degree of institutionalisation of business and economic tie-ups, which further deepen the trade, as is evident from statistics. The paper essentially argues that Indian public and private entities has to balance the needs of Africa while searching for market and natural resources such as oil, in order to have sustainable ties with African states/communities.

References

1. Shaji, S., 'India and China in Contemporary Africa', *Indian Journal of Politics and International Relations*, 2(2), (2010), pp. 361-75.
2. Mohan, Raja C., *Crossing the Rubicon: The Shaping of India's New Foreign Policy*, Viking Books, New Delhi, 2003.
3. Shaji, S., 'Foreign Economic Policy of India in 1990s : A case of Counter Hegemonic Strategies through India-South Africa Ties', *Insight on Africa*, 1(2), 2009, pp. 157-72.
4. Harshe, Rajen and K.M. Seethi (eds.), *Engaging with the World: Critical Reflections on India's Foreign Policy*, Orient Longman, New Delhi, 2005.
5. At present, China's consumption has been increasing at the rate of five per cent per annum. China, which was self-sufficient in hydrocarbon till 1993, will be importing 40 per cent of its requirements in the near future. In the year 2020, the consumption of oil in China will be 9.5 m barrels per day with import dependence being well over 60 per cent. Today, China is the world's second largest energy consumer.
6. Government of India, Ministry of Petroleum and Natural Gas, *Basic Statistics on Indian Petroleum and Natural Gas* 2010-2011 (2011), http://www.petroleum.nic.in/, accessed on 15 March 2012.
7. Harshe, Rajen and K.M. Seethi (eds.), *Engaging with the World: Critical Reflections on India's Foreign Policy*, Orient Longman, New Delhi, 2005.
8. 'India Inc's African Safari', *Business Standard*, 16 June 2011..
9. *Ibid.*

10. *African Review*, a publication of India-African Chamber of Commerce and Industries, 2010, pp. 13-20.
11. Indo-Asian News Service (IANS), 19 September 2008.
12. *Economic Times*, 9 June 2009.
13. Kumar, Suresh, 'African Agriculture: An abiding investment venue for India', *African Review*, a publication of India-African Chamber of Commerce and Industries, 2010, pp. 13-20.
14. Information from FICCI website accessed on 24 March 2012, http://www.ficci.com/global-africa.asp
15. Speech of Mr. Anand Sharma, Minister for Commerce and Industry at the inauguration of the 7th CII-EXIM Bank Conclave on India-Africa Project Partnership, 'Creating Possibilities: Delivering Value', organised jointly by Confederation of Indian Industry (CII) and Exim Bank with the support of Ministry of Commerce and Industry and Ministry of External Affairs on 28 March 2011, information appeared in CII website, accessed on 24 March 2012, http://www.cii.in/
16. Naidu, Sanushain and Henning Melber (eds.) 'China–African Relations in the 21st Century: A "Win–Win" Relationship',*Current African Issues*, no. 3, Upsala: Nordiska African Institute, 2007, pp 41-46.
17. Bond, Patrick and Khadija Sharife, 'Shell Oil: Guilty in World Court of Public Opinion', *Economic and Political Weekly*, 18 July 2009.
18. *Ibid.*
19. Mclure, Jason, 'Africa's failing Democracies', *Newsweek*, 12 July 2010.

SECTION 4

INDIA-AFRICA RELATIONS: EXPANDING TIES

11

India-Africa Trade: A Review

Manendra Sahu

India-Africa share vibrant trade relations for centuries, however, in the last two decades, astounding growth took place in trade between them. India-Africa bilateral trade in 1991 was less than $1 billion, which has now reached to around $ 40 billion. The Government of India expects that by 2015, this trade would reach $70 billion. Above all, in comparison to other regions, trade with Africa has been grown much faster. In the period between 2000-01 to 2009-2010 the export to the European Union and to North America has increased by around three times but for export to Africa it is much more. In the same period, trade with southern Africa increased by more than eight times, with east Africa by six times and with west and central Africa by around five times.[1] In terms of growth in export from India very few regions of the world could match this growth. The unprecedented growth in India-Africa trade has attracted attention of scholars from all over the world.

The paper aims to map the astounding growth in India-Africa growth. It is divided into three sections. The first section discusses about attraction of African markets for Indian businessmen. It is followed by sections on top trading commodities as well as top trading partners. The statistics of trade in the India's top commodity and top trading nation is dominated by petroleum oil which India imports from many African countries. Its volume is so high that many products India exports to Africa do not get desired attention. Thus, import of oil overshadows India's manufacturing strength which is reflected in its exports. This problem can be overcome with focusing only on export statistic. It is undertaken in the section on India's top exports. The concluding parts comprises of discussions on problems associated with India-Africa trade.

The Attraction of African Market

The African economies are witnessing upswing in the recent time and it has long-term repercussions. These economies have witnessed unprecedented growth since the end of 1990s, the average economic growth has been around five per cent which is more than twice the growth in 1980s and 1990s. In the years between 2000 to 2010, six of the fastest growing economies of the world were from sub-Sahara Africa. The resilience can also be seen the way it weathered global recession much better than the most regions of the world and its performance was second only to that of Asian economies. It is noteworthy that the growth is observed in both, oil and non-oil economies. If oil producing Angola is one of the fastest growing economies than Rwanda, Uganda, Ghana and Tanzania too are growing at a fast pace. In fact, growth in oil economies created few jobs but in non-oil economy job creation was better.[2] The cumulative effect of economic boom was the growth in personal income and many Africans could afford to buy more than just the daily necessities. Above all there is fast formation of African middle class, which is estimated to be one in every ten African. This is a class of 'solvent customers' which can afford the latest smartphones, the newest computer and want to lead life like their global peers. This recently acquired purchasing power is attracting attention from across the world. A lot of foreign direct investment is following African middle class. Walmart, a global leader in retail outlets proposed Africa plan is a good example. It has bid for major South African company Massmart which owns 265 wholesale and retail stores in South Africa and 13 more in other African countries.[3]

The future prospect for growth in Africa has equally strong appeal. The growth in African economies are likely to be supported by increased demand for commodities like oil, natural gas, minerals and food. There would also be greater flow of international capital into Africa and greater interaction with the international trade. This will see rapid increase in spending power in Africa. In 2008, continent's household spent $ 860 billion, which is more than combined household expenditure in India or Russia. This is likely to reach $ 1.4 trillion over the next decade if the real GDP continue to grow at its current. In 2008 around 85 million household in Africa had income of $ 5000 or more. This is the level above people start spending roughly half their on items other than food. In the next ten year this number to jump to 128 million. There would be rapid urbanisation in Africa, in 1980, only 28 per cent of Africa lived in cities and today 40 per cent of population live in cities, a proportion close to China and larger than India. The top cities in Africa Alexandra, Cairo and Cape Town ostensibly will each have more than $ 25 billion a year household spending power comparable to size of Mumbai and New Delhi. In addition, more than a dozen cities will have consumer market worth more than $ 10 billion each per year. By 2030, the top 18 cities could have combined spending power of $ 1.3 trillion.[4]

The four growth areas for Africa would be resources, agriculture, infrastructure related industries and consumer facing industries such as telecommunication, retail and banking. It is estimated that together these industries will be worth $ 2.6 trillion by 2020. Agriculture, out of above mentioned industries, could play crucial role as it is directly related to larger section of African society. Africa still has vast tract of land available for agricultural use, in fact it has 60 per cent of world's uncultivated arable land. Agriculture in Africa suffers from low crop yield. There are many barriers in improving crop yield like lack of advanced seeds, inadequate infrastructure and lack of technical assistance etc. If these hurdles are overcome then Africa could experience a 'green revolution'. This could enhance agricultural output from $ 280 billion per year today to around $880 billion by 2030. Additionally, $ 275 could be added for demand it would create for various agricultural input, Africa, thus holds promise for trade at present as well as in the decades to come.[5] This opportunity cannot be overlooked. The companies which take lead in going to Africa will enjoy 'first movers advantage' like to create market for itself, establish brands, shape industry structure, influence customer presence and establish long-term relations with African consumers.

India's Top Trading Commodities

India's top export commodities include refined petroleum product, pharmaceuticals, motor vehicle, electric machinery and plastics (see Exhibit-1), while top import commodities from Africa are crude oil, edible fruits (pulses, oil seeds), mineral ones, organic and inorganic material and iron and steel (see Exhibit-2). It is clear that petroleum oil is the most important commodity in India-Africa trade relation and dwarfs all other commodities. The oil trade, however, is intricate; there is mutual dependence on each other. On the one hand, India imports crude oil from Africa as the domestic sources of oil is insufficient to meet demand on the other hand Africa imports refined petroleum oil from India because of unavailability of sufficient refined products in Africa. As mentioned above, India is an oil deficit country, its domestic source of supply provides roughly one-third of India's total demand. As a result, India imports two-third of its demand from across the world. In addition, the fast growing Indian economy is observing increase in demand in oil. The Planning Commission of India expects the demand to double by 2030.[6] India is devoid of any large discovery of oil resources even after aggressive exploration policy. It is clear that in India's dependence on imported oil is not going to reduce in the decade to come and will have to continue to look for sourcing of oil from across the world.

In India's import of crude oil, Africa is increasingly playing crucial role. Africa has large reserves of oil resources. It has 9.6 per cent of global crude deposit and 11 per cent of global oil production.[7] The total consumption of oil in Africa is around 30 per cent of its production and rest is available for exports. These oil reserves are located largely in north and western Africa. The major oil exporters are Nigeria, Algeria, Libya, Angola, Egypt and Sudan. There are small oil exporters like Equatorial Guinea, Gabon and Chad. This oil trade and investment offers several advantages for India and Africa. For India, African oil helps not only in meeting immediate oil demand but also in diversifying source of oil import. India consciously takes step to reduce its dependence on the Middle East oil especially in the light of experience of the Gulf War in 1991. For Africans oil trade offers opportunity to come out of Euro-centric trade. Many oil producing countries in Africa want to diversify both trade and investment away from traditional Euro-dominance and Indian oil trade and investment helps them to meet their objective.

In the case of crude oil, India is dependent on African oil, reverse is true in the case of refined petroleum. Africa refineries are not able to meet local demand of gasoline. This deficit is seen not only in non-oil producing countries but also in many oil producing countries too. The average oil consumption in Africa is about 2.8 million barrels per day and actual capacity of refineries in Africa is about 3.3 million barrels per day, but their output is much lower. They suffer multiple problems like diseconomy of scale, inefficient, poorly maintained and technologically not upgraded.[8] Africa, to meet local demand imports refined products from abroad and India plays an important role. India has vibrant downstream oil sector, in fact India is emerging as refineries of the world. It has the largest refineries in the world. There are 17 refineries in public sector and 2 refineries in the private sector. India's total refining output is expected to reach 235 met by 2012 and will have surplus capacity of 86 met.[9] Refined oil is mainly exported to eastern Africa touching the Indian Ocean. The exporting volume is significantly high for countries like Kenya, Tanzania, South Africa and Mauritius. Apart from the Indian Ocean, Indian refined petroleum product also reaches the Atlantic Ocean. Angola is a good example where India regularly exports refined petroleum oil. Indian oil companies have also invested in oil refineries and oil retail sector in Africa.

The second leading export product is pharmaceuticals. There exists medical exigency in Africa. The health profile of African countries is deteriorating. Africa has been facing many tropical diseases. The diseases like Malaria and Tuberculosis are resurfacing with alarming pace. On top of it, Africa is severely affected by diseases like HIV/AIDS and Ebola Haemorragic fever for which there is no proper treatment/cure or vaccine available. HIV/AIDS has become the greatest health threat. Sub-Saharan Africa has just over ten per cent of the world's population, but is home to more than 60 per cent of all people living with HIV/Aids. Ironically, on the one hand Africa is facing several difficulties to meet falling health profile, on the other hand it has limited pharmaceutical manufacturing capability.[10] In Africa, there is a pharmaceutical exigency and can only be met by outside supply.

Africa has a special position in India's pharmaceutical exports, because it is just in continuation of domestic market due to similar tropical diseases. Indian pharmaceutical industry for Africa is also a source for affordable generic medicines. The Indian pharmaceutical sector, as mentioned earlier, was at a nascent stage at the time of independence. The industry was rudimentary with small and medium plants which were producing elementary products like quinine, aspirin and anti-dysentery drugs. Over the years, it has grown in all directions, now, it has vibrant bulk drug industry, sophisticated pharmaceutical machinery industry and above all competitive pharmaceutical manufacturing industry.[11] Today India has become fourth largest pharmaceutical producer in the world and accounts for eight per cent of the total production in the world. The industry plays a crucial role in generic drug segment where it has become the global hub of production. The most important contribution of Indian generic drug to Africa is in bringing down cost of Anti-Retroviral Drugs (ARV) used in treatment of HIV/AIDS. It has brought down cost from $10000 a year to less than $ 100, a boon for HIV/AIDS patients.

Motor vehicles are the next big export commodity. Indian automobile sector has reached coveted position and joined the group of nations which have capabilities from designing to manufacturing a vehicle. India's technological capability in automobiles along with the low cost of production has attracted all leading vehicle makers of the world. India today has emerged as car manufacturing hub of the world.[12] These companies produce cars for domestic market as well as for exports. Africa is big market for Indian automobile industries. Tata Motors, Mahindra and Mahindra and Ashok Leyland have wide presence in Africa. However, it is not restricted to one segment, three wheeler by Bajaj Auto and two wheeler by TVS, Hero Honda and Bajaj Auto enjoy similar popularity.

It is noteworthy that Indian automobile company, Tata Motors have invested in Africa. It is the leading Indian company in export of cars, light commercial vehicles and heavy vehicles like bus and trucks. In Senegal the company has set up assembly plant for its vehicles. In some cases Indian manufacturers have design vehicles specially designed for African needs. Ashok Leyland, a leading vehicle manufacturer in India designed special buses for Angola. It has designed to meet the demand of rural traders who visit cities to sell the products. The bus is designed to accommodate large boxes which local traders carry to the cities along with passengers. There are other companies like Mahindra and Mahindra which sell certain range of products in Africa which they do not sell in India at all.

India's Top Trading Partners

India's largest trade partners in Africa are Nigeria followed by South Africa, Angola, Egypt and Algeria (see Exhibit-3). As seen in the table it is largely dominated by oil exporting states in Africa. Nigeria is India's largest trade partner. Oil import from Nigeria plays crucial role in trade relations. Nigeria is the largest crude supplier to India in Africa and in the time to come it expected that Nigeria would supply as much as twenty per cent of India's energy need. Keeping oil sector in mind, India tried oil diplomacy in Nigeria. Prime Minister Manmohan Singh visited Nigeria in October 2007 'to talk oil'. This was a second visit by Indian Prime Minister after Pundits Jawaharlal Nehru who visited Nigeria in September 1962.

Several Indian companies have taken keen interest in Nigeria oil sector but the result of bidding for Nigeria oil companies have shown mixed result. The ONGC Videsh (OVL) bid for stake in Nigeria's offshore oil and gas field in 2005, was successful in winning the bid. However, the Government of India declined to go ahead in the process claiming it an unviable investment. In December 2006, the same block was successfully overtaken by the ONGC Mittal Energy Limited (OEML). Indian companies also have shown interest in downstream oil sector in Nigeria. The OEML has invested in building up oil refinery with a capacity of 200,000 barrels per day. The other Indian companies like Essar group, Mittal Investment, Global Oil and Energy have shown interest in acquiring Port Harcourt refinery. The Nigerian government expects that the Indian company should not only stop at energy sector but also set up fertilizer plants, power plants and transport infrastructure in return of oil investment in Nigeria.[13]

In addition to oil investment, Nigeria also happens to be lucrative market for India. Pharmaceuticals from India have been a fast growing business. In fact, it is widely reported that in order to utilise the market created by the hard work of Indian pharmaceutical companies, China has been selling pharmaceutical product with 'Made in India' label in the Nigeria market. This is also done to malign reputation of Indian pharmaceutical companies by providing sub-standard products. Motor vehicle is thriving exports for Indian vehicle manufacturers. Trucks and busses made by Tata Motors as well as by Ashok Leyland are seen on the roads. Cars by Maruti and three wheeler by Bajaj Auto too seen in Nigeria. Two wheeler by TVS company as well as by Hero Honda is popular in the country. Indian tractor manufacturer Mahindra and Mahindra has supplied tractors to Nigeria. Information and communication technology (ICT) sector is attracting Indian companies to Nigeria. Several training companies like Aptech, SIS and others have opened institutes in Nigeria.

South Africa is the second largest trading partner. India's trade with South Africa is discussed in the subsequent section. Angola is the third largest trading partner for India in Africa. Angola is one of the fastest growing economies not only in Africa but also in the world. Angola has suffered civil war for nearly three decades. It came to an end in 2002 and after establishing peace in the country, Angola economy has experienced fast growth. Angola has large resources of oil and diamond, two most sought after commodities. India imports crude oil in significant quantity from Angola. Indian oil companies have tried to invest in Angola oil assets but they have not been able to get equity in oil blocks in Angola. In 2004, the Oil and Natural Gas Commission (ONGC) made a bid to buy Anglo-Dutch energy giant Shell's 50 per cent shares in Block 18. It was a lucrative deal and would have yielded about five million of crude oil daily. The ONGC was sure to get the block, but last minute Chinese intervention spoiled the deal. Chinese offered an aid package of US$ 2 billion for projects in Angola which dwarfed India's offer of $ 200 million for developing railway. Angola's state owned oil company, Sonangol exercised its pre exemption rights and blocked the ONGC deal in favour of Chinese company.[14]

However, undeterred by such experience, Indian companies still kept option open to buy oil assets in Angola. In January 2009, the Confederation of Indian Industries (CII) led a delegation from Indian oil and gas sector to explore cooperation in the field which included executives for leading Indian companies. On the front of exports from India results are encouraging. There is an exponential growth in trade between two countries. In the year 2000-2001 bilateral trade was mere US$ 15.15 million which has jumped to US$ 1.29 billion registering a growth of 800 per cent in the last seven years. The main items of India's export are tractor and transport vehicle agriculture machinery, pharmaceutical food and meat products, tea, spirit and beverages.

Egypt is the fourth largest trading partner with a long trading history. Both the nations offer the most favoured nation status to each other through the India-Egypt Bilateral Trade Agreement which is operational since 1978. India has been among the top five importer of Egyptian goods. India imports crude petroleum, LNG, coke and semi-coke and cotton products from Egypt. It exports light oil and its preparation, meat, cotton yarn and synthetic filaments as its top commodities. There is large investment is done by companies from both the sides. The Egypt government identified India as a key target country for attracting investment in 2007. Both the countries have signed the Bilateral Investment Protection Agreement between the two countries which entered into force in November 2000.

India has invested around $ 3 billion in about 45 projects in Egypt. Dabour India has production facilities. Another consumer product company Marico has acquired two hair care company. The OVL has stake in Egyptian oil block. In 2007, the OVL with its Egyptian partnering company IPR Red Sea Inc. discovered a large oil deposit in North Ramadan field in April 2007. They announced second discovery in 2008. The Gujarat State Petroleum Corporation Ltd. has acquired five oil exploration blocks. The Gas Authority of India Limited (GAIL) has invested in gas distribution companies and operates in cities of Cairo, Fayoum. In the motor vehicle sector, Ashok Leyland, Tata Motors, Maruti Suzuki, Mahindra and Mahindra and Bajaj Auto has been marketing their vehicles in Egypt. In the ICT sector Satyam Computers and Wipro have set up global delivery centre in Cairo. Ranbaxy runs pharmaceutical manufacturing facility. Kirloskar Brothers have assembly unit for its engine and pump set.[15]

India's Top Export Destinations

In terms of India's major export destinations South Africa is the largest destination in Africa. The volume of export to South Africa is around one-third more than export to Kenya which is the second largest export destination for India. It is followed Nigeria, Egypt and Tanzania (see Exhibit-4). In India's top ten export destinations majority of nations are the Indian Ocean littoral states and geographically closer to India. Eastern Africa attracts the largest volume of Indian goods followed by southern Africa. However, west Africa is not far behind. Only central Africa has far less export volume which is almost one-tenth of other African regions. Thus, it is clear that geographical proximity and transportation link play crucial importance in India's export to Africa.

It can be further seen that, these top export destinations of India are relatively large states in Africa. They also have large population and thus a large market for Indian products. These states also work as gateway to Indian products for neighbouring small states. Thus, significant export to small African countries remain invisible as it is routed through these large states. The dominance of large market in attracting Indian goods is also felt when we study destinations of least export receiving country from India. These countries are Cape Verde followed by Sao Tome e' Principe, Central African Republic and Chad (see Exhibit-5). These are mainly small states with less population.

South Africa, as mentioned earlier, is India's top export market. India had thriving trade relations with South Africa for centuries. However, in the last century, the trade relations with South Africa suffered a lot because of the apartheid government. India cut not only trade relation but also diplomatic, sports and cultural relation. India, in 1949 was the first to lodge protest in the United Nations about the racial behaviour of the white minority government. It further decided to cut its all trade relations inspite of the then existing trade was significantly large and severing it meant loss to India. The trade was restored only when apartheid government was removed from South Africa. Both the government took active interest in establishing diplomatic and trade offices in major cities in 1993.The India-South Africa business council was established. The keenness to establish business relation can be gauged seen when Mr. Ratan Tata, a leading Indian business man was appointed on the International Investment Council set up by the President of South Africa.[16]

Indo-South African trade relation is thriving today. There is significant investment is done in each others country. South African investment in India is spread across sector. The Airport Company of South Africa, a parastatal in South Africa is helping Indian companies in airport modernisation. The South African Breweries have invested in Mysore Breweries and acquired a majority stake. However, the joint collaboration between SASOL, a South African parastatal and Indian oil companies is still under negotiations for coal-to-oil plant with investment of around $6 billion. This is an area where South Africa has vast expertise and India would gain significantly. The pharmaceutical sector in India-South Africa relation is a success story. In this sector Specpham, a South African company has entered into

Similarly, Pharmadynamics and Wokhardt Pharmaceuticals have established joint venture. Aurobindo, a major bulk drug manufacturer in India announced plan to set up a manufacturing plant in South Africa. The other Indian company Ranbaxy has joint venture with Community Investment Holding. This joint venture, known as Sonke Pharmacy, is the second largest supplier of anti-retroviral (ARV) medication in South Africa. Cipla, another Indian pharmaceutical company has joint venture, Cipla Medpro.[17]

Indian companies have invested in other sectors too in South Africa. Tata group from India has investment in sectors such as auto, steel and telecom. Other companies in vehicle segment are Mahindra and Mahindra, Ashok Leyland and Apollo Tyres. There around 35 Indian companies have invested in South Africa and number is still growing. It is expected that investment from India would reach around $ 500 millions in South Africa. In terms of exports to Africa, refined petroleum products occupy the top position followed by Motor vehicles and Pharmaceuticals. Electric machinery as well as other machinery is another key item of export to South Africa.

Kenya is the second largest export destination for India. Trade between Kenya and India exist for the last several centuries and spirit is maintained till date. The presence of large Indian diaspora is added advantage for India. A large portion of diaspora traditionally involved in business in Kenya which makes easier for Indian manufacturers to reach customers in Kenya. Both the two countries have signed the India-Kenya Trade Agreement in 1981 which accorded Most Favoured Nation Status to each other. This was followed by the India-Kenya Joint Trade Committee in 1983. The bilateral trade is further promoted through trade organisations. The Kenya National Chamber of Commerce and Industry (KNCCI) set up a Joint Business Council with the Federation of Indian Chambers of Commerce and Industry in 1985. The Confederation of Indian Industry (CII) signed agreement with the KNCCI in 1996.

As a result of trade facilitation bilateral trade has increased from $ 140.93 million in 2000-01 to $ 1452 million in 2009-10. India's main exports to Kenya is refined petroleum products, pharmaceutical, steel products, machinery and motor vehicles. India's main imports from Kenya are soda ash, tea, leather and metal scrap. Kenya has attracted a lot of investment from India. Tata group has invested in Malady Soda Company since 2005. Reliance Industries have invested in petroleum retail. Essar group has invested refineries and telecom. Agriculture firm, Karuturi Global Limited has invested in cut roses production facility. Many leading companies like Kalpataru Power Transmission, Kirloskar Brothers, Thermax, Cipla have business presence in Kenya. Two Indian banks, the Bank of India and the Bank of Baroda have branches in Kenya.[18]

Conclusions

The unprecedented growth in India-Africa trade can be attributed to the attraction of African market on the one hand and emergence of India as manufacturing hub of the world on the other. The growth in African economies in the last decade has created huge demand in Africa. The growth in economy has also created 'African middle class' which aspires to lead life like their global peers. These factors have turned Africa into lucrative market for Indian businessmen. The additional attraction is the growth potential of African markets. It is likely to emerge as key global market. India is well poised to serve this market. With the growth of technological ability, India has emerged as a competitive manufacturing location. It has ability to manufacture from items of day to day use to large machineries. This strength is seen across the industries, in oil refineries, pharmaceuticals, automobiles, plastics, machineries and many more. There is additional reason for flourishing India-Africa Trade. They are highly complementary to each other. If India is oil deficit country, Africa has oil resources which can help India to meet energy demand. Similarly, if Africa has demand for refined petroleum oil, India has excess refining capacity to supply it to Africa. It is because of such complementarities, petroleum products are the most important commodity in India-Africa trade. Similar complementarities can be seen in other top commodities like pharmaceuticals, automobiles etc. Thus, the attraction of African market and competitive Indian manufacturing has generated an unprecedented momentum in India-Africa trade. This momentum is likely to last long and with it $ 70 billion of trade with Africa by 2015, the target set by Government of India is achievable.

Exhibit 1

India's Top Export Commodities

Rank	*Name*	*Value in Rs. Lakhs*
1	Petroleum Products (Refined)	1234,405
2	Pharmaceutical	566,094

(Contd.)

(Contd. Table 1)

Rank	*Name*	*Value in Rs. Lakhs*
3	Motor Vehicle	343,233
4	Electric Machiner	335,873
5	Plastic	162,533

Exhibit 2
India's Top Import Commodities

Rank	*Name*	*Value in Rs. Lakhs*
1	Petroleum Products (crude)	6667,436
2	Edible Fruits	275,994
3	Mineral Ores	252,050
4	Organic and Inorganic Material	199,449
5	Iron and Steel	127,289

Exhibit 3
India's Top TradingPartners

Ranking	*Name*	*Value in Rs. Lakhs*
1	Nigeria	4,105,834
2	South Africa	3,665,148
3	Angola	2,302,343
4	Egypt	1,467,406
5	Algeria	738,272

Exhibit 4
India's Top Exports Destinations

Ranking	*Name*	*Value in Rs. Lakhs*
1	South Africa	975,125
2	Kenya	689,241
3	Nigeria	668,124
4	Egypt	663,818
5	Tanzania	436,964

Exhibit 5

India's Least Trade Countries

Ranking	*Name*	*Value in Rs. Lakhs*
1	Cape Verde	3.85
2	Sao Tomee' Principle	6.04
3	Central African Republic	27.27
4	Burundi	55.94
5	Chad	65.94

References

1. The import and export data from India is for the financial year 2009-10, taken from yearly data provided by Directorate General of Commercial Intelligence and Statistics, Government of India, Kolkata.
2. Andre-Michel Essoungou, Foreign investors eye African consumer, *Africa Renewal,* April 2011.
3. Walmart in South Africa: the beast in the bush, *The Economist*, February 17th, 2011.
4. Charles Roxburgh et.al., *Lions on the move: The progress and potential of African Economies*, McKinsey Global Institute, June 2010.
5. *Ibid.*
6. Government of India, *Integrated Energy Policy: Report of the Expert Committee*, Planning Commission, New Delhi, August 2006.
7. British Petroleum, *BP Statistical Review of World Energy June 2010* (London: British Petroleum p.l.c., 2010).
8. African Union, *Fuelling Africa's Sustainable Development: The Oil and Gas Perspectives*, AU/EXP/OG/5 (I), Report of First African Union Conference of Ministers responsible for Hydrocarbon, Cairo, December 11-15, 2006.
9. The Ministry of Petroleum and Natural Gas has detailed information on refineries in India on its website, http://petroleum.nic.in/refinery.pdf
10. Manendra Sahu, A healthy Africa: In pursuit of cure, *Africa Quarterly,* Vol. 47, No. 4, November 2007-January 2008.
11. Kohli, J.P.S., Sen A.G., *Pharmaceutical Exports* (New Delhi: Business Horizon, 1997) also see Narayana P.L., *The Indian Pharmaceutical Industry: Problem and Prospects* (New Delhi: NACER, 1984).

12. Ministry of Heavy Industries and Public Enterprises, Government of India, *Draft Automotive Mission Plan 2006-2016: Documentation of inputs for Ten Year Mission Plan for development of Indian automotive industry into a global hub* (New Delhi: September 2006).
13. Parvathi Vasudevan, *Changing Nature of Nigeria-India Relations*, Programme Paper: AFP 2010/02, Chatham House, London, December 2010.
14. Sushant K. Singh, *India and West Africa: A burgeoning relationship*, Chatham House Africa Programme, AFP BP 07/02, April 2007.
15. The country profile available on the Ministry of External Affairs, Government of India's website http://meaindia.nic.in
16. Additional information on the President, Government of South Africa website, www. The presidency.gov.za/docs/reports/annual/2009/section_b3.pdf
17. Elizabeth Sidiropoulos, *India and South Africa as Partners for Development in Africa?* Chatham House briefing paper, Asia Programme and Africa Programme, ASP/AFP BP 2011/01, March 2011.
18. Author has given a comprehensive data on India's investment in Kenya, however he is critical of investment and sees competition from other players in Kenya. Gerald McCann, Ties that bind or binds that tie? India's Africa engagements and the Political Economy of Kenya, *Review of African Political Economy*, Vol. 37, No. 136, December 2010.

12

India's Relations with Francophone Africa

Vidhan Pathak

Introduction

In the decade of 1990s, with the collapse of the Soviet Union a unipolar world emerged and since then international economic, political as well as strategic environment has undergone dramatic changes. Globalisation has become a force, which no country can ignore. In this fast globalising world, India displayed the first signs of strategic assertiveness and a willingness to acquire national power and military power and not be apologetic about it. Important events - India's nuclear weaponisation, i.e. Pokharan II, India's Nuclear Doctrine and India's response to Pakistan's adventure in Kargil - indicate India's growing strength and importance. Further, India's economic liberalisation and its willingness for integration into the global economy reinforce this image.

The economic liberalisation that started in 1991 opened up the Indian economy to foreign economic competition. India launched itself on a definite path of economic reforms, liberalisation and greater integration with the global economy. Also, it brought about a significant shift in India's priorities in world affairs and diplomacy The focus has shifted from its active role in political developments in favour of a higher priority for promoting international economic cooperation and consequently economic diplomacy.[1] Economic development has become the primary concern of India's foreign policy, which is more realistic and conforms to the national interest. It is based on the recognition that India's place in the community of nations is determined by its economic and military strength.

Economic diplomacy becoming a key component of India's foreign policy, an Investment Publicity Unit (IPU) was specifically set up in 1990 with a view to disseminating economic information and coordinating the economic and commercial activities of Indian missions abroad. Annual reports of the Ministry of External Affairs reiterated that, 'in the future, new relationships based on concrete economic, technological and educational cooperation will assume enhanced significance'. The foreign policy has been increasingly driven towards finding export markets, attracting foreign capital and know-how. As a result, India gives more importance to developed countries - US and other Western countries. Also, the countries in the neighbourhood are given importance, e.g. South-South Cooperation.

Francophone Africa fits well into Indian foreign policy priorities. The abundance of natural resources and minerals in the area provides economic opportunities for India. African countries have embarked upon economic reforms and political liberalisation, and many of them have shown a healthy rate of growth. India is conscious that a new Africa is coming into being - free, economically vibrant and politically representative. Reform-oriented African leaders have crafted the 'New Partnership for Africa's Development' (NEPAD); they see India as a reliable partner in pursuing this vision. The prospects offered by this partnership and the vast potential for sustainable progress inherent in African initiative show that there is room for countries like India, to share and be part of this new dynamism. Technology transfer from India to Africa can be very useful.

India and Francophone Africa[2]

The increasing cooperation between India and African countries is partly due to India's historical affinities with the aspirations of the people of Africa. India has welcomed the opportunities emerging from the wide-ranging political and economic changes taking place throughout the Francophone Africa; which, when viewed in conjunction with India's own changing profile, provide a functional framework to exploit for mutual benefit the complementarities of their skills and resources. India attaches priority to sustaining and rejuvenating its close and privileged relations with these countries. Building on almost five decades of close political support and provision of technical assistance, India is now moving towards closer economic and trade relations with the countries of Francophone Africa in true spirit of South-South Cooperation. The goodwill and credibility of India among these countries has its foundation in the historical role India played in the freedom struggle in the continent of Africa besides its growing economic strength in the 1990s.

Historical Perspective

Historically, India has identified with Francophone African countries in their anti-colonial struggles. Independent India's pursuit of the goal of freedom and self-government for all countries in Africa, as well as Asia, brought the French-dominated territories of Africa within the general ambit of India's Africa policy. India consistently and constantly championed the cause of the political advancement of the African colonies of France in the UN Trusteeship Council and the UN committee on non self-governing territories.[3] However, India's anti-colonial pronouncements on the French imperialism were generally muted. This was partly because of the peculiar juridical status and constitutional evolution of the African colonies of France and partly because India was engaged in negotiations with France for the transfer of sovereignty in respect of former French settlements in India.[4] However, the confidence of the Francophone African countries on India stems from the fact that India had always been in the forefront of all motions, actions and movements that pressed and aimed at the decolonisation of the African countries and doing away with 'settler colonialism'. India had initiated and chaired UN committees on decolonisation. The declaration of independence by the then French territories in August-September 1960, led by Ivory Coast was greeted by India with caution, probably as their juridical status was still uncertain. By August 1961, when the Francophone African states were celebrating the first anniversary of their independence, India was represented in almost every capital by a special envoy, though in most cases it was the head of the Indian mission in a neighbouring Anglophone country. India has had cordial relations with these countries since their independence. However, with the independence of these countries, the rallying point between the two regions, i.e. support to liberation struggles, came to an end.

The foreign policy of independent India had political goals to achieve, which meant that economic issues got a back seat in the decades after Independence in 1947. Thus, the driving force for Indian economic initiatives in Africa during mid-60s was political. India acknowledged their developmental concerns and extended support and assistance to these countries. Thus, with its ideological commitment to NAM and Afro-Asian resurgence and based on its relative economic strength, India kept on pursuing her economic goals in this region. In the 1960s, the call for South-South Cooperation could not become popular in Francophone Africa, because of the prevalent belief that massive injection of capital from France and other developed countries to this region would lead to their economic development. Even during the 1970s, the Indian government's talk of South-South Cooperation could not get encouraging response from this region. This happened as their hope for France-aided development had not completely shattered. France had close socio-economic and military ties with Francophone African states and more than half of France's foreign aid flowed to these states. Under cold war conditions, political issues again took precedence over economic ones and Indian government's emphasis on South-South Cooperation in trade, technical education and such like matters did not yield required dividends. By the 1990s, they had realised that development of South lies in the hands of South. In today's globalised world this is the framework in which developing countries like India and Francophone African states could pursue their journey of growth and development to its logical end.

Present Perspective

There has been comprehensive shift and changes in the foreign policy of India in the 1990s from the earlier decades post-Independence. With rise of economic thrust in Indian foreign policy, it is increasingly driven towards finding export markets, attracting foreign capital and know-how. As a result, Indian foreign policy gives much importance to US, Western countries and developed nations. Despite the westward orientation the importance of Francophone Africa in the foreign policy of India is increasing over the years. There has been a significant change in India's Francophone Africa policy; the big leap in Indian thinking occurred in the 1990s when it stopped seeing these countries in terms of the old third world agenda of decolonisation and non-alignment. The recent Indian efforts were about plugging a huge gap in India's strategy of intensifying political and economic contact with these countries. India has adopted several means of economic interaction with these countries, which include bilateral agreements, granting of credits and loans, etc. High-level visits from India, study-cum-business tours organised by institutions, like the ASSOCHAM, CII, FICCI, FIEO, etc., and government representatives have opened up new vistas of cooperation in the trade and industrial ventures. India has taken a large number of initiatives by way of visits by senior experts, policymakers and diplomats to some of the important Francophone African countries. Development cooperation is an integral part of Indian foreign policy and has been used as a means to facilitate trade and investment and to get more international political leverage. Indian foreign policy has taken several development initiatives recognising its importance as an instrument to gain political and economic influence in Francophone Africa. Under ITEC, the Indian government has sent technical assistance worth US$ 2 bl to Africa. The launching of IOR-ARC, India-Africa Interest Group, TEAM-9, Focus Africa, etc., shows that the Indian foreign policy in context of Africa is on an upward move. More precisely, to gain their strategic support in various international organisations, like UN and WTO, and the vast untapped economic potential of these countries have driven Indian foreign-policy strategists to emphasise stronger relations with these countries.

Priorities of the Indian Foreign Policy[5]

As an emerging power, India is ready to play a growing role in Francophone Africa as it provides India with its growing need for markets and new sources of raw materials. For a variety of reasons, these countries are important for Indian foreign policy consideration. First, India needs to gain support in various international fora for policies vital to its national interest. Second, Francophone Africa economically provides vast scope for mutually beneficial trade and commercial linkages in the spirit of South-South Cooperation. The imperatives of India's liberalised and globalised economy make it necessary that the developing countries and their markets are more seriously explored. The need for expanded export market and the challenge of the developed and industrialised economies should induce India to develop closer ties with these countries. Third, India has a stake in NAM, G-77, G-15 and also Africa. It has also interest in

WTO and restructuring UN, which needs partnership and cooperation with these countries. Thus, the quality and depth of Indo-Francophone Africa bilateral relations assume even greater significance and a broader canvas of empathy and support.

Some of the Indian foreign policy priorities are listed here:

1. *Reform Process of the Institutions of Global Governance:* High on Indian agenda is the reform process of the institutions of global governance, like UN, and international financial institutions, like IMF and the World Bank. From Indian point of view these institutions were established in conformity with influence and interests of developed countries while developing countries, to which India belongs, do not have their adequate representation. Taking into account its population, the constantly growing economy and the economic and political influence in the world, India demands changing of these institutions so as to get better representation in them. Francophone African countries. India has staked its claim to a permanent membership in the UN Security Council for which it needs the support.
2. *Preservation of Strategic Autonomy:* One of the important Indian foreign policy priorities is creating conditions for the Indian development out of the sphere of influence of any world or regional power. In accordance with this priority, that has been present since India gained its independence, India was one of the founders of the Non-Aligned Movement, whose members did not want to be a part of the world bloc division. India is determined to retain its strategic autonomy. Today, the implementation of this priority implies the promotion of cooperation with developing countries i.e., South-South Co-operation.
3. *Global Order:* The international order is in a state of flux. The global environment is today marked by the rise of new power centres and relative decline of the West. India is one of the rising powers of the world. In order to leverage its strengths and mitigate its weaknesses, India needs to think strategically to navigate the turbulent global order. India is committed to multi-pluralism. It is not in favour of unipolarity and therefore the kind of global order, which India envisage and is working for, is not one merely of technical equality in the United Nations but greater balance among nations of the world. India is trying to coordinate activities with other developing countries in order

to be able to deal with the enormity of the inequality, which exists in the world today and create an environment, which is more equitable.

4. *Energy Security*[6]: The Indian economy has been growing at 7 to 8 per cent annually in the last few years. Maintaining a high rate of economic growth brings about the increase in the Indian energy needs, and it is estimated that these needs would be doubled every five years for the period of next twenty-five years. Thus, the immensely important direction in the Indian foreign policy will involve efforts to find stable energy sources, especially in developing countries. The quest for African energy resource and the vast untapped economic potential of these countries has driven Indian foreign policy strategists to emphasise stronger relations with these countries.
5. *Maritime Security*[7]: India needs a secure maritime environment to achieve sustained national development. This is not restricted to just guarding the coastline and island territories but also extends to safeguarding interests in the exclusive economic zone as well as protecting the trade. To advance its security and economic interests in the Indian Ocean region, Indian diplomatic initiatives are aimed at gaining strong partners and are focused on several Francophone Western Indian Ocean African states.
6. Issues in the security area and in all the arrangements internationally, which govern nuclear weapons, missiles, high technology, etc., also needs partnership with Francophone African countries. India has been consistently of the view that the countries of the world should not be divided into two separate categories; the same rules should be applicable to all.

The implementation of these priorities implies the promotion of cooperation with Francophone African countries. Indian foreign policy has taken several initiatives to rope them in its new drive for economic and strategic cooperation to achieve the developmental goals.

Indian Initiatives in Francophone West Africa

India has made efforts to strengthen political understanding and expand economic cooperation with the countries of Francophone West Africa.[8] The bilateral relations with countries like Senegal, Cote d'Ivoire, Burkina Faso, Mali and Togo, is progressing well.[9] A wide-ranging political dialogue with several key countries in the region also displays a considerable degree of understanding of India's security interests.[10] This region has become an important source of hydrocarbons for the world in the recent years. In the coming decades, India along with China is going to become the largest consumer and importer of petroleum products. American oil companies are making beeline to the region and Chinese oil companies are already in Africa. India does not want to be left behind. India's ONGC Videsh has also invested in Ivory Coast. Energy diplomacy, therefore, is an important component of Indian foreign policy towards this region. Considering the potential that this region offers and insignificant Indian presence in that market, India launched 'Team-9 initiative' in March 2004.

In terms of multilateral diplomacy, these countries have always been important but were rather overlooked or ignored. They form a very important voting bloc in global forums. India is seeking their support in its candidature for permanent membership of UN Security Council, in WTO and other international organisations. Given their membership of several multilateral fora, such as G-77, NAM, and their common endeavour to set up a just and equitable global order, the renewed contact at the highest political level underlines the need for strategic consultations between them. The Indian foreign policy has shifted to forge beneficial economic relations with Francophone West Africa. In fact, Indian foreign policymakers are looking forward to identify common areas of understanding and mutual benefits in the fields of economy, politics and strategy with these countries. They are conscious that friendship with this large bloc of African countries will be of considerable value in the future. With the focus on Francophone West African region, the Ministry of External Affairs, Government of India, appointed a joint secretary for West African region in the 1990s. These countries are now receiving greater attention in India's foreign policy consideration with the establishment of a high-level inter-ministerial coordination board for the sub-region.[11]

Some of India's development initiatives in this region are:

- *Techno-Economic Approach for Africa-India Movement (TEAM-9):* Considering the potential that West Africa region offers and insignificant presence of India in that market, the 'TEAM-9 initiative' was launched by India on 1 March 2004. The endeavour was to put these countries and India together in an economic cooperation framework. It provides eight West African countries with credit lines worth US$500 million. The Government of India also offered access to training resources in India and facilitate deputation of Indian scientists, technologists and other experts. The 'TEAM-9 initiative' is expected to diversify sources of India's energy security. Thus, India's TEAM-9 initiative point to a renewed focus on the region, which offers a huge strategic potential.

- *Line of Credit:* India is trying to counter the commercial competition from countries like China and European nations by offering lines of credit to African firms. The Government of India has provided concessional credit facilities (LoC) for financial assistance for various projects and schemes.
- *Agricultural Development Projects and Food Security Programme:* Several development programmes in Francophone Africa are supported by India. The most important among them is the food security promotion programme, which India supports financially and by providing its technology. Agricultural Development Projects were undertaken by India in countries like Senegal, Burkina Faso and Mali.
- *Increasing level of bilateral interactions, visits and agreements:* There is increase in bilateral interactions, visits and agreements between both the regions in recent years. India has taken a large number of initiatives by way of visits by senior experts, policymakers and diplomats to some of the important Francophone African countries.
- *Equity in West African Development Bank (BOAD):* Exim Bank has taken up equity in West African Development Bank (BOAD) to the tune of $1 million, and given $10 million credit.
- *Private Initiatives:* In the 1990s organisations, like the CII (Confederation of Indian Industries), ASSOCHAM (Associated Chambers of Commerce and Industry), the FICCI (Federation of Indian Chambers of Commerce and Industry) and the FIEO (Federation of Indian Exporters Organisation), identified the region as a thrust area and launched programmes to promote economic and business cooperation. They also organised study-cum-business tours to this region. In fact India Inc. has been on a roll in Africa in recent years. The Africans expect them to bring new technology and substantial investment in socio-economic development which, in turn, will present attractive

business opportunities. The Indian presence in Africa of leading members – India Inc, the TATAs, the Mahindras, Ranbaxy, NIIT, and the Bharti; public sector undertakings, OVL, RITES, IRCON and NSIC; of banks, the State Bank of India, the Bank of Baroda, the Bank of India and ICICI; and contribution by top national business chambers to wide-ranging business promotion – has imparted content to India's economic representation.

- *Francophone Western Indian Ocean African States:* India is seeking to increase its profile almost in all direction from its shores to advance its security and economic interests, including the security of the various gates to the Indian Ocean. Indian strategic and diplomatic initiatives are aimed at gaining partners in the Indian Ocean region and are focused on several Francophone Western Indian Ocean African states. India has key connections with some of the states like Mauritius, Madagascar and Seychelles in the region. Since the early 1990s, India has demonstrated its keenness to engage the littoral states, regional powers as well as the great powers in its security strategy for the Indian Ocean region. The wave of globalisation in the 1990s compelled India to revise its policy for the Indian Ocean region. The readiness to shed the ambiguities of the non-alignment era and willingness to enter into strategic dialogues with those interested in India has set the stage for cooperation in the Indian Ocean region. Now engagement is the key word of India's Indian Ocean policy in contrast to the cold war policy of isolation. This engagement has been beneficial in terms of deepening India's economic and security links with the Francophone Western Indian Ocean region. It has helped to remove widespread doubts and apprehensions about India's political motivations in the region.
- *Defence and Maritime Cooperation:* The Indian initiatives in the Francophone Western Indian Ocean region include signing of MoU on defence cooperation with Seychelles (in 2003) and negotiations on a 'comprehensive economic cooperation and partnership' agreement with Mauritius. Indian activities in the region include naval surveillance and patrol of territorial waters of Mauritius and Seychelles, hydrographic surveys, training of police and military personnel, donation of a patrol vessel and

helicopters to help with coastal defence of both island states. India has its own designs in the Western Indian Ocean region and has been reaching out to the littorals in the region from Africa through joint naval exercises with some countries and by patrolling sea lanes. India is trying to forge a web of partnerships with certain littoral states and major external powers in the region to increase her influence and to acquire more strategic space and strategic autonomy.[12]

- *Initiative to Rope in Indian Diaspora:* People of Indian origin are extremely important sources of support for the Indian government in the execution of its policies through the influence and respect they command in the countries in which they live. It is an important factor in its relations with Francophone Western Indian Ocean states like Mauritius, Madagascar and Seychelles. India's diaspora policy has demonstrated a change during the 1990s – there has been a proactive interest of Indian government in the overseas Indians. The government has undertaken initiatives like celebration of Pravasi Bharatiya Diwas; and the creation of a separate Ministry for Overseas Indians in the light of the recommendations of the L.M. Singhvi Committee Report. The Indian government now seeks active and overt association of the PIOs for foreign policy objectives of India.

In continuation of its broader Africa policy, India has also taken several development initiatives which cover the entire African continent including Francophone Africa. These are:

ITEC Programme: One of the important programmes is the Indian Technical and Economic Cooperation (ITEC), which has been in effect since 1964. According to the Ministry of External Affairs, India currently transfers Rs. 500 million (US$10.3 million) annually via this programme. Basically, ITEC uses a slots system to allocate aid. Slots may then be exchanged into five different aid modalities, namely: (1) training of personnel in India, (2) project aid, (3) technical assistance, (4) study trips and (5) humanitarian assistance. The slots are adjusted annually and recently a number of African countries, to a large degree coinciding with the TEAM-9 countries have had their ITEC slots increased.

- *Focus Africa:* Among the most important new initiatives is the Focus Africa Programme totalling US$550 million (2002-07). It was launched in the year 2002-03 to enhance trade with Africa and administered by the Export Import Bank of India. Essentially, it seeks to enhance commercial links between India and African countries by offering export subsidies to Indian companies trading with African nations and tied lines of credit to African governments and regional entities. The initiatives taken under this programme have received encouraging response from the Indian exporting community. It is likely to boost bilateral trade with African countries in the coming years.[13]
- *Pan-African e-network Project:* India had started Pan-African e-network project that helps African countries to avail services of tele-education and telemedicine. It provides for the integration of African companies, health and education institutions by the Internet and other connections with companies and institutions in India. India is also investing a huge amount of money in capacity building of the local self-government and the supply systems in African states.
- In addition, India has offered NEPAD a US$200 million credit line apart from funding the Pan-African e-Network with US$100 million. India has also offered bilateral debt relief, UN peace-keeping operations and humanitarian assistance to several African countries. India is the third-biggest contributor of UN peacekeepers to the continent of Africa and India's navy is also engaged in chasing Somali pirates.
- *India-Africa Forum Summit:* The most important step towards the promotion of the partnership between India and Africa, and the greatest diplomatic success of India since it gained Independence was made at the first India-Africa Forum summit in April 2008 at Delhi. At the second India-Africa Forum summit held at Addis Ababa in 2011 the Indian prime minister declared astonishing packages for African countries – 500 crore [in million dollars?] dollar debts allocation for the development of African countries; ten thousand scholarships to African students; 30 crore dollar for railway station construction between Ethiopia and Djibouti; forming of food clusters for the sake of exports in Africa; forming of clusters for textile industry development; to set up a university for African students; to give chance to

African airlines to provide services in India; to provide satellite services and to provide help in disaster management; and to set up coaching centres for vocational courses.

India has announced several financial development pledges including a US$5.4 billion credit line over the next five years, grants worth US$500 m over the next five years and a unilateral opening of India's economy for exports from all LDCs (34 African countries). The India-Africa Forum Summit is conceived as a way to reinvent and rejuvenate an old relationship between India and Africa (with focus on South–South Cooperation) and thereby influence the global political and economic agenda.

India's diplomatic vision extends to embrace the interests of Africa as a whole, particularly in the priority area of economic progress and development. Such an economic congruence is facilitated by a broad agreement between India and the countries of Africa on their vision of a new world order characterised by peace, justice and equity, and fully responsive to the needs and interests of the developing world.[14] India's engagement with Africa has clearly become multilayered. It runs at three levels, at the Pan-African level through growing ties with the African Union; at the regional level through Regional Economic Communities; and with all countries at the bilateral level.

Conclusion

India didn't have a definite and clear-cut policy towards the Francophone African countries prior to liberalisation of 1991. They were broadly covered under the broader policy framework towards African continent as a whole. The reforms in India and the fast globalising world brought in changes in India's foreign policy initiatives; it led to a new drive for economic and strategic cooperation to achieve their developmental goals. The quest for energy, the vast untapped economic potential of Francophone African countries and to gain their strategic support in various world forums like UN and WTO has driven Indian foreign policy strategists to emphasise stronger relations with these countries. As a result initiatives like Team-9, Focus Africa, Agricultural Development Projects, Lines of Credit (LoC) facilities and investments in energy sector by OVL are already in place. Doubtlessly Indian foreign policy is paying serious attention to the Francophone Africa countries.

Commensurate with national interests and security, the improvement of bilateral relations is an important component of any foreign policy and India has succeeded in establishing a network of mutually beneficial relations with the Francophone African countries. As the US, Europe and China have stepped up their diplomatic activism in these countries; India cannot afford to stay away from a friendly and an inviting economic space, which is also critically important for its defence and trade in the Francophone African countries. India needs to develop a more sustained political and economic effort if it wants to stay at the front in an area of great strategic significance. A sense of common cause and a shared future is an unbreakable link between India and Francophone African countries which will extend to facing the new and emerging challenges confronting them in the new millennium.

References

1. Rajan, M.S., 'Introduction', in Kokila Krishan Gopal and Krishan Gopal, eds., *India's Foreign Policy and Relations: A Documentary Survey: 1972-92*, Shipra Publications, Delhi, 1999, pp. 3-4.
2. Francophone African countries (25): Benin, Burkina Faso, Cote D' Ivoire, Guinea, Mauritania, Mali, Niger, Senegal, Togo, Burundi, Chad, Cameroon, Congo P. Republic, Central African Republic, Zaire (Democratic Republic of Congo), Gabon, Rwanda, Madagascar, Algeria, Morocco, Tunisia, Djibouti, Comoros, Mauritius and Seychelles.
3. Taliyarkhan, Homi J.H., 'India and African Liberation Movements and Economic Growth', in R.R. Ramchandani, ed., *India and Africa*, Radiant Publishers, New Delhi, 1980, p. 71.
4. Ramamurthi, T.G., 'India's Relations with Francophone African States', *Africa Quarterly*, New Delhi, Vol. 34, No. 1, 1994, p. 40.
5. Pathak, Vidhan, 'India's Francophone Africa Policy: Leniency to Partnership', *The Indian Journal of Political Science*, Vol. LXVIII, No. 2, April-June, 2007, Meerut, IPSA, pp. 293-310.
6. Pathak, Vidhan, 'India's Energy Diplomacy in Francophone Africa: Competitive-Cooperation with China', *India Quarterly*, Vol. LXIII, No. 2, ICWA, New Delhi, April-June 2007.
7. Pathak, Vidhan, 'China and Francophone Western Indian Ocean Region: Implications for Indian Interests', *Journal of Defence Studies*, Vol. 3, No. 4, 2009.

8. Government of India, Ministry of External Affairs, *Annual Report*, 1998-99, New Delhi, 1999, p. 52.
9. Government of India, Ministry of External Affairs, *Annual Report*, 1999-2000, New Delhi, 2000, p. 47.
10. Government of India, Ministry of External Affairs, *Annual Report*, 1995-96, New Delhi, 1996, p. 57.
11. Government of India, Ministry of External Affairs, *Annual Report*, 1996-97, New Delhi, 1997, p. 53.
12. Pathak, Vidhan, 'France and Francophone Western Indian Ocean Region: Implications for Indian Interests', *Journal of Indian Ocean Studies*, Vol.14, No. 2, SIOS, New Delhi, August 2006, pp. 186-203.
13. *The Hindustan Times*, New Delhi, 2 March 2004.
14. Government of India, Ministry of External Affairs, *Annual Report*, 1984-85, New Delhi, 1985, p. 22.

13

India Engaging with Africa for Development

Jamal M. Moosa

There is an increase in the number of players with significant global imprint. This is resulting in contemporary global landscape undergoing tremendous transformation. There is also a move away from the overlapping of social, political and economic and more importantly the strategic or military hierarchies into a more complex mosaic of interconnection and engagement between many new players.

Africa as a continent has had long and chequered relationship with India. In the last decade or so dramatic and significant transformation has taken place within these two regions. These internal changes have had a critical and crucial bearing on the emerging engagement. However, to understand the dynamics, it is essential to factor the larger international context and role of various powers especially former colonial powers. US war on terror has resulted in its trying to expand its presence in the continent. Similarly, the traditional French military and economic presence and the growing Chinese interest in the region too need to be taken into account. It is also essential to study the context of transformation of Africa for an effective understanding of future trend in the engagement especially in the context of developmental challenges.

These relations took a major positive turn as a consequence of Indian ambition to play a more proactive global role. The holding of the India-Africa Forum Summits in 2008 and 2011 is a pointer to the growing Indian interest in the continent. There are some critical questions: how is Africa engaging with the rest of the world? Are they continuing the old pattern of interaction? What are their developmental agenda and goals? More importantly, what do they expect from us in return? This paper will look at some of the developmental challenges that the continent faces and the possible role India can play.

Developmental Challenges in Africa

The heads of state and governments of the African Union (AU) have stated that the 'continued prevalence of armed conflicts in Africa and the fact that no single internal factor has contributed more to socio-economic decline of the continent and the suffering of the civilian population than the scourge of conflicts within and between states.[1] This was followed by the enactment of Protocol relating to the Establishment of the Peace and Security Council of the AU in July 2002. AU is envisaged to play a central role in bringing peace, security and stability on the continent.

Parallel to these efforts the continent also engaged with the world to become a partner in its efforts to attain sustainable peace and development. The New Partnership for Africa's Development (NEPAD), which was announced at Abuja, Nigeria, in October 2001, was the culmination of a long process towards this end. It is reflective of the African leaders desire to extricate themselves from the malaise of underdevelopment and exclusion. They felt an historic opportunity was present to end this scourge. Abundant resources were available, all that was needed was to mobilise and effectively use them. But more importantly it also proclaimed that Africans will determine their own destiny and called on the rest of the world to complement their efforts.

A vicious cycle of economic decline, reduced capacity and poor governance reinforced each other and confined Africa to the periphery. Peace, security, democracy, good governance, human rights and economic management are considered as essential conditions for sustainable development. Thus, to promote these principles various actions were envisaged. This paper will now analyse whether over the last decade or so this intent of the African leadership has resulted in significant changes and transformation on the ground.

Africans have consistently emphasised the importance of trade and made commitments to reduce supply-side constraints, trade barriers and deepen regional integration. Moving towards this goal, there has been increased investments in infrastructure projects, such as the North-South Corridor and productive capacity building. The ambitious project of a Free Trade Area between COMESA, EAC and SADC has the potential to integrate about half of Africa.

Before the global economic crisis, Africa benefited from the rapid growth in world trade. Africa's share of world merchandise trade increased to 3.2 per cent in 2008 from 2.8 per cent in 2007. In value terms total African merchandise trade crossed the trillion-dollar mark in 2008. Against a backdrop of a steep contraction in world trade in 2009, Africa's share remained stable at 3.1 per cent.[2] However, this conceals sharp falls in volume and more importantly in value. The adverse impact of the crisis on Africa's terms of trade is linked to poor diversification of both content and destination of exports. Oil, minerals and primary agricultural goods constitute 80% of Africa's exports. The EU and the US continue to account for about one-third of Africa's exports. However, trade with emerging economies, such as India, has grown significantly to about one-fifth. Intra-African merchandise trade remains low at about ten per cent of total African exports. However, it is more than 20 per cent in manufactured and agricultural products. India can engage in a significant way by enhancing value addition of primary commodities and the requisite skill development within the continent.

The next set initiatives by the African governments included measures for agricultural development. It had committed to raise the share of their national budget for agriculture to ten per cent and through the Comprehensive African Agricultural Development Programme (CAADP) Framework[3] they have called for annual agricultural growth rates of six per cent. Similarly they committed to increase agricultural trade within Africa, harmonise policies and reduce costs of procurement. In 2009 AU acknowledged CAADP as the overarching framework for agricultural development and investment and made food security and agriculture the first priority of its mandate.

Recent data[4] from forty-five countries shows that only ten countries have met their commitments in 2008. The aggregate agricultural spending has made little progress, ranging from 4% to 6% of domestic public expenditure between 1980 and 2008. However, less than ten per cent of arable land is irrigated and an additional four million hectares have been brought under irrigation in the last four decades. Ten countries have achieved agricultural growth rates of six per cent or more but the average for sub-Saharan Africa is only 3.2 per cent over the last ten years.

Most African countries might not be able to achieve first Millennium Development Goals (MDG) by 2015 and only nine might achieve the goal on the prevalence of underweight children. Out of the 36 countries, twenty-one are currently facing a food security crisis are from Africa and more than 300 million or about a third of Africans faced chronic hunger or are undernourished in 2009.[5] Climate change and food price volatility pose major new threats to food security. Since 2001, the volume of African agricultural exports has increased by 13 per cent and their value has increased by 74 per cent but Africa's share of the global agricultural export remains low at two per cent limited to a few countries. There is ample scope for India to engage with the continent to foster development in the field of agricultural green revolution, food processing and food security, and mitigate the impact of climate change.

Another focus of African governments was on creating infrastructure for economic and social growth. They agreed to strengthen national planning frameworks, reform the regulatory environment, mobilise resources and develop programmes for energy, transport, water and ICT. The targets to attain were: (a) 35 per cent of the population to have access to electricity by 2020; (b) halving the proportion of people living beyond two kilometers from an all-season road by 2015; and (c) reducing the proportion of people without access to safe water and sanitation by 75 per cent by 2015. Despite the increase in investment progress has been slow except in ICT, infrastructure weakness remains a major constraint on growth and development. In Sub-Saharan Africa only 29 per cent of the population had access to electricity (57 per cent urban and 12 per cent rural) in 2009 with a growth rate of about one per cent of the population a year.[6] High population growth has meant that per capita energy consumption has actually fallen. Thirty countries in Sub-Saharan Africa have experienced energy crises in recent years.

Only one-third of Africans living in rural areas are within two kilometers of an all-season road isolating them from urban markets, schools and hospitals. In 2008, 60 per cent of the population of Sub-

Saharan Africa had access to improved water compared to 55 per cent in 2000. For sanitation only 31 per cent of the population in Sub-Saharan Africa had access to improved sanitation facilities in 2008.[7] In sharp contrast, mobile telephony has been a success story with mobile subscribers growing from 16 million in 2000 to 370 million in 2009. This again is an area where Indians have expertise and are actively collaborating under the aegis of Pan Africa e-Network and through private sector investments.

Most African countries are shifting their attention to the sustainable development by adopting environmentally sound practices. They have ratified the Convention on Biological Diversity (CBD), the Convention to Combat Desertification (UNCCD) and the UN Framework Conference on Climate Change (UNFCCC). The NEPAD Environment Action Plan, endorsed by the AU, has set comprehensive framework in this regard.

While some initiatives have moved from planning into action but the implementation is generally weak and effectiveness limited. Inadequate institutional capacity, poor data and weak priority-setting are some of the key constraints. The proportion of land covered by forest in Africa continues to decline. Between 2000 and 2005 Africa, while holding 16 per cent of the global forests, accounted for one-third of the area deforested.[8] Degradation and loss are expected to become more severe due to pressure on land use and marine system overexploitation. The non-recognition of indigenous property rights poses serious challenges to biodiversity conservation. Two-thirds of Africa is classified as deserts or dry lands and climate change will have significant impact. It is important to note that this area presents an opportunity for cooperation and partnership.

The AU has acknowledged the primary role of education in human development. Not only have the African governments shown their intent by signing the Education for All (EFA) programme of action supported by the Fast Track Initiative (FTI); they have taken the next step also — domestic resources across Sub-Saharan Africa have been increased. Government spending on education in 2008 reached an average of 20.3 per cent. As a proportion of GDP, expenditures have also increased, from 3.7 per cent to five per cent between 2000 and 2007. As of June 2010, twenty-four African countries have had their national education plans endorsed by FTI.[9]

Net primary education enrolment has risen in African countries and in some cases quite significant.[10] In 2008, it reached 76 per cent in Sub-Saharan Africa and 94er cent in North Africa, compared to 58 per cent and 86 per cent respectively in 1999. The region as a whole is likely to attain its MDG target in this regard. There is an improvement of completion of primary-school cycles. In 2008, the primary completion rates were 64 per cent and 96 per cent in Sub-Saharan and North Africa respectively. Sub-Saharan Africa has decreased its out-of-school population by about thirteen million students since 1999. But the progress is uneven and Africa still accounts for almost half of the world's out-of-school children. Gender parity in primary education is likely to be achieved by most countries.

The picture at the secondary level is not as rosy; only 34 per cent of children in Sub-Saharan Africa were enrolled in 2007. Enrolment in tertiary education has increased slightly in Sub-Saharan Africa - six per cent in 2008. However, there is a large shortage of teachers. Building capacity and human resource development through education is another area where India can partner and provide appropriate models of intervention and support.

Similarly African governments made commitments to increase investments in health to at least 15 per cent of their annual budgets. They want to achieve universal health-care access and accelerate interventions to combat HIV/AIDS, tuberculosis and malaria.[11] Maternal and infant health was the central theme of the July 2010 AU summit.

Progress towards meeting the 15 per cent Abuja target has been limited. In 2007 average government health expenditure reached 9.6 per cent of total government expenditure. HIV/AIDS infection rates have slowly declined to 5.2 per cent in 2008. Treatment coverage has improved with 44 per cent have access to antiretroviral therapy. Tuberculosis prevalence too declined slightly, 475 per 100,000 in 2007. Under-five mortality rates declined from 184 to 144 per 1,000 live births in Sub-Saharan Africa between 1990 and 2008. Maternal mortality in Sub-Saharan Africa however remains very high at 900 per 100,000 live births with almost no improvement since 1990.

One of the reasons for this is the lack of health personnel. Sub-Saharan Africa has only three per cent of the world's health workers. It is estimated there will be a shortfall of about 800,000 health workers by 2015. This again is an area for enhancing cooperation between

India and Africa. Apart from education, Pan Africa E-network also focuses on enhancing health-care training and facilities.

Most importantly, African governments have emphasised good political governance as an essential prerequisite to development and poverty reduction. They have committed, apart from electoral reforms, to take collective action to improve democratic processes. The AU has adopted a zero-tolerance policy to unconstitutional changes of government. With the African Peer Review Mechanism (APRM), African governments have established a continental apparatus to monitor and promote good governance. A series of charters and protocols have been adopted including the African Charter on Democracy, Elections and Governance and the Declaration on Democracy, Political, Economic and Corporate Governance, as well as measures to protect and promote human rights.

AU has taken swift collective action against a number of countries (Mauritania, Guinea and Madagascar) to support constitutional change. An Electoral Assistance Fund was established in January 2009 to mobilise resources to assist the conduct of election observation, monitoring and post-conflict activities. The peer review process under the APRM has been accelerated. The total of completed reviews is fourteen and three countries are ready for a second cycle.

Progress in electoral and democratic processes has proved resilient. Positive trends have been broadly maintained with increased popular participation, competitive elections and peaceful transfers of power in a growing number of countries. Elections have become the norm rather than the exception. Winds of change are also blowing across North Africa as recent changes have shown.

African governments have intensified their security cooperation under the African Peace and Security Architecture (APSA). They have institutionalised innovative conflict prevention, management and resolution mechanisms. In particular, they have established a Peace and Security Council (PSC), an African Standby Force, a Special Peace Fund, a Panel of the Wise and an Early Warning System. The PSC is meeting regularly and has already intervened politically, and if necessary, militarily in thirteen countries. Both the Panel of the Wise and the Special Peace Fund are operational. The AU has already conducted a number of peace operations.

Armed conflicts have decreased by over a third since the early 1990s. Similarly, the number of conflict-related deaths has fallen during the period. Stability has also been maintained. However, ongoing conflicts remain complex and difficult to address and in 2010, seven African countries were experiencing major armed conflicts within their territory. Consequently, more than 200 million Africans continue to live in conflict zones. Over eleven million are internally displaced about almost half the global total. This again is an area that could be expanded for further cooperation between India and Africa.

Recent Trends in Africa Policy

India's relationship with Africa can be traced back to ancient times. In the new millennium, broadening the horizon towards Asia and Africa with policy initiatives like 'Look East', engaging West Asia has taken place. Similar engagement and initiatives have been launched with Africa also. TEAM-9 initiative is one such policy where efforts were made to reach out to West African countries especially the francophone countries with which India traditionally did not have close relations.

India is trying to leverage the ITEC programme of training facilities and project expertise with Africa. India has a developmental experience of over five decades through an incremental process of trial and error in a diverse, pluralistic democracy. This is being projected as having a special relevance for Africa due to the prevalent similarities.

The Indian president, during a visit to Africa in September 2004, announced the setting up of the Pan African e-Connectivity initiative to connect the fifty-three countries of Africa. After many rounds of extensive discussions, India and the African Union signed the MoU for the project on 27 October 2005. Similarly many other projects, like Lilongwe Water Supply System in Malawi, Ebene Cyber City Project in Mauritius, Kofi Annan IT Centre for Excellence in Ghana, Entrepreneurship Development Centre in Senegal, Nigeria Machine Tools in Nigeria, Plastic Technology Centre in Namibia, India Farmers Project in Burkina Faso, Village Electrification Projects in Soune and Touly in Senegal, Gandhi Memorial Hospital in Ethiopia, are at different stages of implementation.

In a policy outline in 2007 the prime minister outlined India's priorities. There is a need for sharing of experiences on effective strategies for sustainable development, poverty alleviation, health-care facilities and universal education and a need for greater cooperation. He also unveiled the Indian vision for a Partnership with Africa for the twenty-first century. It envisioned an Africa that is self-reliant, economically vibrant and at peace with itself and the world. India would cooperate to harness these potential of Africa and become a partner in Africa's resurgence based on the principles of equality, mutual respect and mutual benefit.

This was followed by the first ever India-Africa Forum Summit, attended by the countries representing AU and the Regional Economic Communities of Africa in 2008. Leaders of fourteen African countries and the AU Commission participated in it. It represented a turning point in enhancement of engagement with Africa. The summit adopted the Delhi Declaration and the Africa-India Framework for Cooperation to act as the blueprint for cooperation in the twenty-first century.

India also announced unilateral duty free and preferential market access for exports from all least developed countries of which thirty-four are in Africa. It will cover 94 per cent of India's total tariff lines and provide preferential market access on tariff lines that comprise 92.55 of global exports of all least developed countries. Products of immediate interest to Africa include cotton, cocoa, aluminium ores, copper ores, cashew nuts, cane sugar, ready-made garments, fish fillets and non-industrial diamonds. India would also double its quantum of credit to US$ 5.4 bn from the present US$ 2.15 bn over the next five years.

As a follow up of the summit, India is setting up four institutions, viz, the India-Africa Institute of Foreign Trade, India-Africa Institute of Information Technology, India Africa Institute of Education Planning and Administration and India Africa Diamond Institute besides ten India-Africa vocational training centres and construction of five prototype low-cost houses. The locations are being finalised by the AU Commission. The seventy-five doctoral scholarships in the field of agriculture have already been awarded and scholars have begun their academic programmes. Similarly under CV Raman International Fellowship for African Researchers has been instituted and applications have been invited from African researchers.

External Affairs Minister Pranab Mukherjee inaugurated the Pan Africa e-Connectivity project on 26 February 2009 from New Delhi. The project uses Indian expertise in information technology to bring benefits of health care and higher education in Africa especially to remote and inaccessible areas of the continent. The network will use satellite/fibre optical network for tele-medicine, tele-education and VVIP connectivity. The current projected cost of about US$ 116 million is being funded by the Indian government. The whole project consists of linking five regional universities, five regional super-specialty hospitals with a learning centre, a remote hospital and a VVIP node in every African country. Forty-seven African countries have so far signed agreements with TCIL of India. Ethiopia, under a pilot project, was the first beneficiary of the project, which was completed in 2007 at a cost of US$2.13 million. On 16 August 2010 External Affairs Minister S.M. Krishna interacted simultaneously live with ministers of twelve African countries.

The second India-Africa Forum Summit was held in Addis Ababa in May 2011. The theme of the summit was, 'Enhanced Partnership and Shared Vision'.[12] Two important documents were adopted at the summit, viz. the Addis Ababa Declaration and Framework for Enhanced Cooperation. There was an effort to give further impetus to capacity and institution building. The focus areas for this include agriculture, trade, industry especially small and medium enterprises, finance to sports and tourism. India intends to give US$ 5 bn credit for developmental purposes.

It is envisaged to set up eighty more institutions, of which five will be Pan-Africa institutions. These institutions will focus on agriculture and rural development, food processing, textiles, weather forecasting, life and earth sciences. Apart from this, regional institutions will be set up in collaboration with regional economic communities. The number of students coming to India under different schemes will be increased. These, along with short-term training programmes, complement efforts towards enhancing value addition of primary commodities within Africa.

Conclusion

The Indo-African relations are at a crossroad today. The long and close relationships have weathered the turbulence and swings of the past. The challenge is to broad-band the relations so that they can successfully navigate in the troubled waters of the contemporary international order. The current era has seen the eroding and undermining of the past assumptions and understandings. There has been a significant shift of balance especially economic balance towards the East.

The process of globalisation is providing both opportunities and challenges to different countries across the world. In this context the Indian approach towards Africa has undergone a metamorphosis.

The old assumptions have given way to more pragmatic and broad-banding of the relations. The old INTEC programme continues but the Pan-African network has become the showpiece. It is a good example of how the new opportunities of a globalised world are being leveraged to achieve more beneficial relationship. There is a growing trade relationship undertaken by a new emerging entrepreneurial class of people in India who are not averse to taking risk and seeking new frontiers and pastures. Similarly, large number of skilled and semi-skilled workers and professionals are willing to try to benefit from the growing opportunities that an assertive and emergent Africa is providing. India has also been leveraging its advantages in capacity building and human resource development. India also has allowed Africa to define some of its priorities and areas for engagement.

It is critical to enhance engagement with Africa; India will need to first understand African priorities both at the continental as well as at the level of individual countries. Thereafter provide them with meaningful alternatives and opportunities of partnership. The Africans have clearly defined their priorities but India would need to fulfil their demands and expectation for the historic goodwill to transform into long-term meaningful 'enhanced partnership and shared vision'. A resurgent Africa has become pragmatic but impatient for change and may not wait very long before shifting its attention.

References

1. African Union, 'Protocol Relating to the Establishment of the Peace and Security Council of the African Union', 10 July 2002, http://www.african-union.org
2. WTO, International Trade Statistics 2010 (Geneva, WTO, 2010), p. 10.
3. For details see http://nepad-caadp.net
4. UN ECA and OECD, Third Mutual Review of Development Effectiveness, http://www.oecd.org/apf/mrde
5. FAO, The State of Food Insecurity in the World 2010 (Rome, FAO, 2010).
6. IEA, World Energy Outlook (Paris. IEA 2009).
7. WHO/UNICEF, Progress on Drinking Water and Sanitation, 2010, update (Geneva, World Health Organization and UNICEF 2010) p. 39.
8. FAO, State of the World's Forests, 2009 (Rome, FAO, 2010).

9. For details see http://www.educationfasttrack.org
10. United Nations, 2010, Millennium Development Goals Report.
11. UN AIDS/WHO, AIDS Epidemic Update 2009 (Geneva, UN AIDS/WHO, 2009).
12. Para 1, Addis Declaration 2011, www.mea.gov.in

14

Indian Investments in African Agriculture and the Question of 'Land Grabbing'

Vyacheslav Usov

Indian achievements in agriculture and biotechnologies attracted a lot of interest in Africa. Some projects in the field of cooperation between India and African countries, which directly involve Indian expertise in agriculture and biotechnologies, have been developed since 1990s. One of the first experiments in transferring knowledge and skills gained under India's Green Revolution to some developing countries, especially in Africa, was launched in Burkina Faso in 1999 and was completed in 2002. Under the project, India supplied expert farmers to demonstrate to Burkinabe farmers the Indian technology of rice growing, including the usage of ergonomically-designed hand tools, tractors, etc. Training local farmers in this technology, related consumable inputs, such as seeds, fertilizers, pesticides, etc., farm machinery, equipments, vehicles and other necessary support was a core of the project. Farm machinery and equipment vehicles were donated to Burkina Faso government after the completion of the project. Both sides assessed the experience as a success and the request for agricultural assistance, in particular, was received from a number of African governments.

The real appraising of India-Africa agricultural cooperation was made in 2005 by Sierra Leone foreign minister and the minister for international cooperation, Momodu Karoma, who said, 'In short, technologies in India are more robust and are better suited to the African environment. On the contrary, technology in the West is very fragile and sensitive to the environment' and also outlined the 'exploitative' nature of costly Western technologies.

In April 2008, the India-Africa Forum Summit had identified agriculture as a priority economic area and prepared a framework for India-Africa cooperation. According to the Action Plan India has promised the African countries not only to train African agriculturists, but also to share best practices in the rural sector, exchange of seeds and planting materials, capacity building in the rural sector and transfer of technology.

Gurjit Singh, joint secretary in the Government of India and in-charge of east and southern Africa, told experts at the international conference on 'South-South Cooperation: India, Africa and Food Security: Between the Summits' held in Mumbai on 10-11 January 2011: 'Agriculture is without doubt at the forefront of India's engagement with Africa in the current transformation phase.' He stressed as well that agriculture and food security are also going to be high on the agenda of the second India-Africa Forum Summit that is expected to be held in one of the African countries in April-May this year. He continued: 'However despite the real achievements and expertise India has brought to Africa, recently an issue of foreign investments in African agriculture, including ones from India, got a new turn. Now it is often described in international and African mass media not in terms of assistance and South-South cooperation as it used to be only some years ago but as "neocolonialism" and "land grabbing".'

The term 'land grab' has emerged to describe the explosion of global commercial land transactions connected with the production and sale of food and bio-fuels, which over the past few years have increased globally, especially in Africa. Despite considerable media attention and demands by some farmer and civil society groups that it should be stopped, the phenomenon of 'land grab' is so recent that there are still relatively few scientific studies about the scope and consequences of the deals in Africa. The media remain the largest source of information on land deals.

A number of factors can be marked out as primary causes of unprecedented growth in the recent land investments. Except for an effect of international financial crisis in 2008 this trend has been enhanced by investment opportunities in bio-fuel production that to some extent has become a direct competitor to food production on existing cropland.

Some experts also say that a surge in land investment was partly connected with so-called global 'food crisis' generated by dramatic increases in prices of basic foods, like rice, wheat and maize in 2007 and 2008, where Russia was partly responsible. According to Devinder Sharma: 'In 2007 both Russia and Argentina, major grain exporters, put in place export bans and it sent waves of panic around the world, which have probably played a big part in fuelling land acquisition deals.' While Russia has not been really involved in land investment in Africa, it was once again blamed by David Hallam of FAO's trade and market division that export bans imposed by Russia and Ukraine in summer 2010 heightened the rise in the global price of wheat and maize and, therefore, reinforced the fears of food insecurity.

There are also some observers who attribute a real explosion in land investment in the years after 2008 to changes in food habits especially in developing economies like China and India where consumption of food since 1990s dramatically increased.

No matter what the real incentives were for recent outburst of land acquisition in Africa, the continent has become the most attractive destination for agricultural investments because of its relatively low population density and assumptions that large tracks of African land suitable for agriculture are not yet cultivated or cultivated at low levels of efficiency.

According to International Food Policy Research Institute (a Washington-based think tank), since 2006 some 15-20 million hectares of land in poor countries, most of it in Africa, have either been sold or are under negotiations for sale to foreign buyers. The World Bank report, 'Rising global interest in farmland' issued in September 2010, suggests that the main characteristic of the recent trend in land investment is a focus on countries with weak land governance and high prevalence of food insecurity. The report highlighted that total officially recorded transfers between 2004 and 2009 amount to 4.0 m hectares in Sudan, 2.7 m in Mozambique, 1.6 m in Liberia, 1.2 m in Ethiopia. While land under foreign control usually remains a relatively limited proportion of total farmland areas in host countries, such foreign acquisitions are more likely to target good land and water resources and their local impact can be significant. There might be more land deals under negotiation or already concluded that are not known because they have been made in secret and host governments are reluctant to publish the contents of the contracts.

In contrary to the past the 'new' investors are predominantly oil-rich but food-poor Gulf states, like Saudi Arabia, Qatar and the United Arab Emirates, or Asian giants like China and India. Moreover, Western and South African companies are still investing in land in Africa for bio-fuel production or investment projects. Unlike Gulf states, China and India are essentially food self-sufficient but have high population growth rates and their land and water resources are under great pressure from increasing urbanisation and industrialisation. Combined, these circumstances drive the two countries' decisions to acquire farmland in Africa in an attempt to secure food and feed supplies for the future.

The *Economist* defined this trend as an 'outsourcing's third wave' that is sweeping the poor world. Countries that export capital but import food are outsourcing farm production to countries that need capital but have land to spare. Instead of buying food on world markets, governments and politically influential companies buy or lease farmland abroad, grow the crops there and ship them back.

The first proposals for acquiring land in Africa and sending Indian farmers to East Africa to produce commercial crops were discussed between the officials of the Indian state of Andhra Pradesh and that of Uganda, Kenya and Zambia at the end of 2004. According to *Times of India* as cited by the *East African Standard,* Kenya's High Commissioner to India, Ambassador Mutuma Kathurima, told the press, 'We have large extent of vacant land and the people of Andhra have expertise in agriculture which can be shared.'

C.C. Reddy, an adviser to the government of the state said that while farmers in the state have been driven into poverty and debt, and hundreds have even committed suicide, East African countries have tens of thousands of acres of fertile land, but have not exploited its potential due to lack of expertise and investment. Spotting an opportunity, the Andhra Pradesh government decided to acquire and lease to the Indian farmers 50,000 acres of land in Uganda and Kenya for an estimated US$100 m. According to the plan almost 500 Indian farmers could be sent to grow tropical crops, such as sugar cane, tobacco, and cotton.

However, this pioneer project met severe criticism in East African mass media, among local politicians and civil groups and was put on hold. India's new land acquisition in Africa aims at attaining both food and energy security, in addition to exploiting investment opportunities in cash crops. The official line for India strategy can be described as a 'win-win' solution. The Indian government's stated goal is to limit the purchase of food grains from the international market and source it directly at much cheaper rates from poorer African countries. All the governments, including Indian government, involved in large-scale land acquisitions claim that their investments will give the agricultural sector in Africa the much-needed boost providing employment to the local people.

The government reasoning for buying or leasing agricultural land in Africa is stated to be motivated by the possibility to build more efficient and larger agricultural operations. Building huge agricultural business is almost impossible in India, but it is in Africa where there is no limit on land ownership. The Indian government supports the deal, so provides soft loans and reduced import duties to enable the shipment of agriculture produce to India.

The government documents show the details of India's official support and no less than $500 m in soft loans has been given to encourage African countries to export food to India by providing cheap lines of credit to the governments of Ethiopia, Senegal, Kenya, Madagascar and Mozambique. Under a duty-free tariff preference scheme, Ethiopian farm produce can enter the Indian market at an advantage.

Indian companies have invested more than $3 bn to buy or lease hundreds of thousands of hectares in Ethiopia, Kenya, Madagascar, Senegal and Mozambique, where they are growing rice, sugar cane and maize to feed their domestic market and also crops to produce bio-fuel. More than eighty Indian companies have invested upwards of $2.4 bn to buy up farmland in Ethiopia alone.

The list of companies that have purchased land in Africa is quite long, including companies in businesses ranging from agriculture and horticulture to engineering and metals. They include the Kolkata-based Kankaria group (manufacturing and textiles), Kommuri Agrotech (floriculture and horticulture), Surya Electricals (electrical products), Karuturi Agro Processing, AVR Engineering (construction), Nelvo International (minerals), Allied Chemicals, BP Jewellery, KSR Earthmovers, Emami Biothech, and Yes Bank. It has been reported in 'Land Grab in Africa: Emerging land system drivers in a tele-connected world' that a combined number of Indian investments in Africa's agriculture currently under negotiations can reach up to 2,400,000 hectares!

For some Indian companies Africa has become a real El Dorado. The most famous of them is a Karnataka-based company, Karuturi Global, which grows cash crops, like sugarcane and palm oil, as well as rice and vegetables. It is one of the world's largest producers of cut roses. It has signed deals for just under 350,000 hectares for a ninety-year lease to create what it claims is the world's largest agricultural land-bank. Sai Ramakrishna Karuturi, the managing director of the company, once admitted, 'I am not even a fly on the wall in India, but in Ethiopia I am the largest investor, the second-largest employer after the government....To do that in India, you have to be a Tata or an Ambani'. Not only Karuturi but many other Indian investors see Africa as a 'last frontier' or a land of opportunities. According to the secretary general of ASSOCHAM (India's apex industry body), D.S. Rawat, African governments are willing to lease land free of cost and, 'Since the lease is for 99 years, it means that a farmer is in control of the land for his life time. It means land for roughly around three generations.'

Some small farmers in India have also seen an opportunity in Africa. Gurcharan Singh, from Zirakpur in Punjab, who leased 500 acres at Diego-Suarez, 300 km from Madagascar's capital city, Antananarivo, two years ago, for example, sees himself as a huge beneficiary of this favourable deal to Indian investors. 'For me it is like a dream come true,' he says. 'I will be paying $15 per acre a year for the next 50 years. In India, I could never imagine having so much land at that price.' He has sown maize and peanuts on his farm. The rent for cultivable land in Punjab ranges between $400 and $1,000 per acre a year.

No wonder that Sharad Pawar, India's agriculture minister, rejected charges that the government has supported a new way of colonisation of African farmland. 'Some companies are interested in buying agricultural land for sugar cane and then selling it on the international markets. It's business, nothing more,' he told the *Daily Telegraph*. The same was echoed by Ambassador Gurjit Singh who dismissed all the accusations of any wrong-doing by the Indians in Africa. '"Land Grabbing" is an idea that comes largely from a reading of the internet when in reality a large portion of African arable land lies unutilised and the African nations would like to use this resource. However, since they lack the technology and the capital, this is possible only by attracting foreign investments. And India will encourage such investment but only if there are consistent rules lay down and investment is asked for by the respective governments.' Agricultural investments could be good news for Africa, bringing jobs, capital, know-how, access to markets and infrastructure - only if they are done right.

There is probably no other African country where all the problems of land acquisition by foreign investors have become more apparent than in Ethiop:.., which presently is one of the leading land markets in Africa. According to the government, Ethiopia has 74 m hectares of fertile land, of which only 15 per cent is currently used, mainly by subsistence farmers. The country's population is one of the most poverty-stricken and undernourished in the world. Meles Zenawi, the Ethiopian prime-minister, in 2000 stated that his government would discourage or prohibit attempts by Ethiopian farmers to profit from leasing their land. Some years later the Ethiopian government started developing 'open door' policy for foreign capital and investors from India and the Gulf countries which have acquired extensive farm land to grow food and bio-fuel crops for export. From the government's point of view the country needs to make use of its resource of land which is not possible without foreign investment. It has put no restrictions on the modality of participation. Investors are exempted from the payment of duties and income tax and are allowed to repatriate 100 per cent of the profits. The Indian government has also provided a soft loan of US $640 m to Ethiopia for the next five years to encourage sugar production. This is the biggest credit line New Delhi has extended to any country.

The Ethiopian government claims that only three to four per cent of its land is being offered to foreigners, and denied that the deals were causing hunger. As all land in Ethiopia is officially government-owned, it has the right to lease it out largely as it sees fit. The land deals were attracting hundreds of millions of dollars of foreign investments and tens of thousands of jobs. Abera Deressa, the government minister who helped design the latest agricultural development policy, said that foreign investors are capable to boost agricultural output by as much as 40 per cent.

Mr. Tefera Derbew, Ethiopian Minister of Agriculture once said, 'How much land will actually go to Indian investors depends entirely on the interest of the investors. If they come and take all the land, they are welcome. So far, we have transferred 307,000 hectares of land to foreign and domestic investors. Some 79 per cent of this land has been transferred to Indian companies. This land is on a 70-year lease. We are now proposing to transfer another 3.6 million hectares of land to investors from overseas. And I am confident that more than half of this 3.6 million hectares will go to Indians.' Indian investors in Ethiopia seem to be especially welcome.

It is not clear how exactly such land acquisitions will benefit the poor Ethiopians. International and African media are full of stories about local grievances against foreign land investors, especially Saudis and Indians.

Oromia and Gambella - two of Ethiopia's nine states are in the centre of this African land rush. In April 2010, Haile Hirpa, president of the Oromia studies' association, said in a letter of protest to UN secretary-general Ban Ki-moon that India had acquired 1 m hectares, Djibouti 10,000 hectares, Saudi Arabia 100,000 hectares, and that Egyptian, South Korean, Chinese, Nigerian and other Arab investors were all active in the state. 'This is the new, 21st Century colonisation,' he said.

The situation in Gambella looks even more complicated. This state for a long time was starved of investment. To reverse the situation in the region, which is populated by small minority ethnic groups, the government invited foreign companies - Indian, Saudis and Chinese, to boost its near-decaying agriculture. Now the locals say that all the deals have been done secretly and there were no consultations with the indigenous population.

Nyikaw Ochalla, director of Anywaa Survival Organisation (ASO), an indigenous Anuak from the Gambella now living in Britain, blames the government saying, 'The foreign companies are arriving in large numbers, depriving people of land they have used for centuries.... All the land round my family village of Illia has been taken over and is being cleared. People now have to work for an Indian company. Their land has been compulsorily taken and they have been given no compensation. People cannot believe what is happening.' Historically, land in Gambella was owned by local chieftains. 'Until recently, said Ochalla, 'the local chiefs virtually owned all village land rights. Now Indians and Saudis are taking over, destroying and clearing the best woodlands to grow farm products, not for local consumptions but for export.' Even if some farmers are being compensated, pastoralists are not while they claim the land to belong to their ancestors.

The *Ethiopian Review* reported: 'Hundreds of Ethiopian workers, overseen by Indian supervisors (from Karuturi Agro Products), were bent over rows of corn stalks, cutting weeds tangled around them with small blades.... Many of the workers were children. The day rate: 8 birr, about 70 cents. Ethiopians cannot own land, instead they hold "use certificates" for their tiny plots, making it difficult to get loans, or to sell or increase holdings. A worker said the company had refused to sign a wage contract and had failed to deliver promised water and power to nearby villages. Supervisors treat them cruelly, he said, and most workers were just biding time until they could go work for a Chinese construction company rumoured to pay US$ 2-4 a day.'

Certainly some of the critical reports are exaggerated or biased and come from the sources close to opposition parties of Ethiopia which, according to the minister Abera Deressa, are often based on ignorance of the government's proposals. For example, much-criticised by Ethiopian opposition media Karuturi Global in East African countries is not only involved in exploitation of African soil and labour but also in a number of social-oriented projects. In Ethiopia the Indian company distributed woolen blankets to poor and elderly people and launched 'BAN THE CAN' campaign, a social initiative by Karuturi to provide water on tap. In Kenya Karuturi provided food to drought victims and health-care services, sponsored the activities of World Wild Fund (WWF) in the country, Kenya national Cricket team and football team.

In January 2010, the President of Ethiopia, Girma Wolde-Giorgis, expressed his concern over land questions in Gambella region. In his letter to the Ministry of Agriculture, the president urged the ministry to stop giving 3,012 hectares of forest land to an Indian company Verdanata Harvest PLC. While the president warns that such a deal first of all would damage Meles Zenawi's reputation on the campaign against global warming he realised that some local officials in Gambella have played the role in silencing farmers.

Not surprisingly, the native people of Africa resent foreign investments. In September 2010, Ram Karuturi himself had to deny the charge that he grabbed local people's land depriving them of their livelihood. Saying that the land is leased from Ethiopia's Agriculture and Rural Development Ministry, he also added, 'NGOs are missing the whole point. Fears of neo-colonialism have stoked this misguided psychosis.'

The government approval of the deals, however, can't deal with the tensions that stem from acquisition of land claimed by the indigenous Ethiopian people. The Ethiopian government's open employment policy for foreign investors resulted in bringing to the country workers from India which, some say, deprives the Ethiopians from getting both managerial and menial jobs.

Some Indian journalists and activists themselves are among the fiercest critics of the deals. Suman Sahai, in *Deccan Chronicle*, 27 November 2010, writes: 'Activist groups are calling the investments a "land grab" taking away the entitlements of the African people. They say such alienation of land will deprive locals of their livelihoods. They have a point.' Devinder Sharma of India's Forum for Biotechnology and Food Security said the companies buying up land to export food from Africa were 'food pirates' and compared them with the English companies that shipped food from Ireland during the nineteenth century potato famine. 'There are 80 Indian companies trying to get land in Ethiopia, and it's all to be imported back to India. The Government of India has been encouraging them,' he said, and warned of danger if famine returned to Africa. 'If food is being shipped out and poor people are dying, what will happen? There would be riots,' he added. Indeed, members of opposition parties of Ethiopia have already made it clear that 'once this government – already highly unpopular and precarious – is no longer in power, these illegal agreements will not be considered binding.'

All in all there are two main problems for any foreign investors in African land. First, the recipient government is keeping control of the land despite its free market pretentions. This gives it the freedom to attribute long-term leases to foreign agricultural companies of its choice. Besides, many of the land contracts include infrastructure development or other technical improvements, opening up an additional bone of contention between the economic interest of the recipient country government and its poor agricultural population.

Second, land tenure systems of many recipient countries are customary and the local people rarely hold formal legal rights to their resources. Officially, all this land was listed as wasteland, but that doesn't mean that is not useful to the local population, like the Annuaks in the Gambella region. Nyikaw Ochalla, an indigenous Anuak from the Gambella region of Ethiopia, maintains: 'All of the land in the Gambella region is utilised. Each community has and looks after its own territory and the rivers and farmlands within it. It is a myth propagated by the government and investors to say that there is waste land or land that are not utilised in Gambella.'

Even if the land is formally owned by state it has been inhabited by people who have farmed it for generations. Their customary rights are recognised locally, but often not accepted in law, or in terms of foreign investment deal. FAO statistics say that only about 14 per cent of the suited land in the continent is presently cultivated. Michael Taylor, a policy specialist at the International Land Coalition, confirms, 'If land in Africa hasn't been planted, it's probably for a reason. Maybe it's used to graze livestock or deliberately left fallow to prevent nutrient depletion and erosion. Anybody who has seen these areas identified as unused understand. that there is no land in Ethiopia that has no owners and users.'

Land acquisition in Africa is obviously a complicated matter and produces losers as well as winners. International community and international organisations so far have not worked out a common approach to the problem. Sometimes they focus on the bright side, but it is not always so. In 2008, Jacques Diouf, the director-general of Food and Agriculture Organization (FAO), labelled such international land lease agreements as 'neocolonial', but a year later FAO started to talk about prospects for a 'win-win' situation.

These land leases carry with them huge risks, as some deals demonstrate. The most impressive example is Madagascar, where the announcement of a ninety-nine-year contract to lease 1.3 m hectares to South Korea's Daewoo Corporation to grow corn triggered civil unrest and then the coup d'état. 'Madagascar's land is neither for sale nor for rent,' said the new leader, Andry Rajoelina, who cancelled the deal. This case is widely known but it was not the only one. After the revolution, 465,000 hectares of land in Madagascar turned out to have been leased to an Indian company, Varun International, to grow rice for consumption in India. That deal is also being cancelled by the new government.

An in-depth study of the land-lease problem, and that identified a number of major recommendations for stakeholders was a paper published in 2009, 'Land Grab or Development Opportunity? Agricultural investment and international land deals in Africa' authored by Lorenzo Cotula, Sonja Vermeulen, Rebeca Leonard and James Keeley. Some of the important recommendations are:

- International land deals may be perceived as bringing back the 'bad old days' of colonialism, particularly in Africa. This is particularly so when rental fees are zero or close to zero. Backlashes are possible, as in the Daewoo case: this was a concern for some investors interviewed for this report. Long-term land leases - for 50 or even 99 years - are unsustainable unless there is some level of local satisfaction.
- It is possible that media hype is feeding a land rush. This means that careful and detached analysis of the factors involved in land investments in developing countries is more important than ever.
- Issues of image and reputational risk should not be underestimated. Investors can be seen as dealing with or propping up corrupt regimes and human rights violators. They may also be perceived as land grabbers in food insecure countries.
- At the local level, land rights may be hotly disputed. This means careful assessment of local contexts is critical, as well as long-term engagement with local interests (not just elites).
- Clarity is needed about the costs and benefits of the business transaction from the start. This includes realistic estimates and honest communication of what the project will bring.

In 2010 international 'code of conduct' was suggested to prevent some of the most negative consequences of the land deals. The principles advocated by the World Bank and sponsored by Japan assert that the existing rights to land should be respected, investment should not imperil food security and livelihood of local population, and all those affected should be consulted. The meeting of the UN Committee on Food Security (CFS) that took place in Rome on 15 October 2010, failed to endorse those principles, while expressed support for the process of developing the draft, Voluntary Guidelines on the Responsible Governance of Tenure of Land and Other Natural Resources. The committee also requested its High Level Panel of Experts on Food Security and Nutrition (HLPE) to conduct a study on land tenure and international investments in agriculture and to present its findings at its next session in October 2011.

Some NGOs and experts have already criticised the Voluntary Guidelines for being too weak. However, even if they are endorsed they can hardly tackle all the differences.

Some years ago, Elizabeth Sidiropoulos, National Director, South African Institute of International Affairs, said that 'India comes to Africa in the shadow of China'. While China-Africa relations are well known and attract a lot of attention, India prefers to cultivate a much quieter but more sophisticated and capacity-building approach. At the India-Africa 2008 Forum Summit the Indian minister of state for commerce, Jairam Ramesh, noted: 'The first principle of India's involvement in Africa is unlike that of China. China says go out and exploit the natural resources, our strategy is to add value.'

Nevertheless, active involvement of Indian companies in dubious land acquisitions in Africa seems often perceived in terms of much-criticised Chinese approach and contains potential risks for the investors themselves. In case the African countries that are leasing their land fall into difficulties in feeding their own populations, as they are likely to do if world grain prices rise sharply, the first resource they will turn to are the foreign plantations on their territory. Governments that cannot feed their populations face overthrow, and will break contracts without the slightest hesitation.

References

1. Basic Facts About Burkina Faso, http://meaindia.nic.in/foreignrelation/burkina.pdf
2. Basic Facts About Burkina Faso, http://meaindia.nic.in/foreignrelation/burkina.pdf
3. *Africa Quarterly*, Vol. 45, No. 1, November 2005, New Delhi: Indian Council for Cultural Relations, p. 18.
4. India puts food security at heart of Africa agenda, 10 January 2011, IANS, http://farmlandgrab.org/post/view/17977
5. Sharma, Devinder, 'With farmlands being grabbed, Africa too awaits march of the millions in Ground Reality', 4 February 2011, http://www.countercurrents.org/dsharma050211A.htm
6. Aloisi, Silvia, Reuters Africa, 15 October 2010. http://af.reuters.com/article/topNews/idAFJOE69E0CM20101015
7. Cherian, John, 'Grabbing Africa, The global rush to acquire agricultural land in bountiful Africa evokes concern and protests', *Frontline*, Vol. 27, Issue 09, 24 April - 07 May 2010, http://www.frontlineonnet.com/fl2709/stories/20100507270906100.htm

8. Committee on World Food Security, thirty-sixth session, Rome, 11-14 and 16 October 2010, Policy Roundtable, 'Land Tenure and International Investment in Agriculture', http://www.fao.org/docrep/meeting/019/k8929e.pdf

9. 'Outsourcing's Third Wave', *The Economist*, 21 May 2009, http://www.economist.com/node/13692889

10. Kamau, John, 'Indian Farmers to Receive 99-Year Arid Land Lease', *The East African Standard*, Nairobi, 13 November 2004; posted on the web, 15 November 2004, www.allAfrica.com

11. Pasricha, Anjana, 'Drought-Hit Indians Head for Africa in Farming Program', 21 November 2004, www.voanews.com

12. Muwanga, David, *Indian Farmers Seek 40,000 Hectares*, New Vision, Kampala, 19 November 2004, www.allAfrica.com

13. Anjana Pasricha. Drought-Hit Indians Head for Africa in Farming Program. 21 November 2004. www.voanews.com.

14. Wengraf, Lee, 'The new African land grab', SocialistWorker.org, 7 September 2010, http://socialistworker.org/2010/09/07/new-african-land-grab

15. Sahai, Suman, 'The new colonisers', *Deccan Chronicle*, 27 November 2010, http://www.deccanchronicle.com/op-ed/new-colonisers-857

16. Cherian, John. Grabbing Africa. The global rush to acquire agricultural land in bountiful Africa evokes concern and protests. Frontline. Volume 27. Issue 09. 24 April - 07 May 2010. http://www.frontlineonnet.com/fl2709/stories/20100507270906100.htm; Nelson, Dean. India joins 'neocolonial' rush for Africa's land and labour. 28 Jun 2009. http://www.telegraph.co.uk/news/worldnews/asia/india/5673437/India-joins-neocolon..

17. Sahai, Suman. The new colonisers. Deccan Chronicle November 27th, 2010. http://www.deccanchronicle.com/op-ed/new-colonisers-857; Nelson, Dean. India joins 'neocolonial' rush for Africa's land and labour. 28 Jun 2009. http://www.telegraph.co.uk/news/worldnews/asia/india/5673437/India-joins-neocolon.

18. Ramsurya, M.V., 'Indian companies buy land abroad for agriculture', *Economic Times*, 4 January 2011, http://farmlandgrab.org/post/view/10070; Friis, Cecilie and Anette Reenberg, 'Land Grab in Africa: Emerging land system drivers in a teleconnected world', GLP Report No. 1, http://www.globallandproject.org/Documents/GLP_report_01.pdf

19. Friis, Cecilie and Reenberg, Anette. Land Grab in Africa: Emerging land system drivers in a teleconnected world. GLP Report No. 1. http://www.globallandproject.org/Documents/GLP_report_01.pdf
20. Sahai, Suman. The new colonisers. Deccan Chronicle November 27th, 2010. http://www.deccanchronicle.com/op-ed/new-colonisers-857
21. Nelson, Dean, 'India joins 'neocolonial' rush for Africa's land and labour', 28 Jun 2009, http://www.telegraph.co.uk/news/worldnews/asia/india/5673437/India-joins-neocolon.
22. Srivastava, Mehul and Sharma, Subramaniam, 'India Billionaires Go On Buying Spree in "Last Frontier" Africa', *Bloomberg*, 25 October 2010, http://www.bloomberg.com/news/2010-10-24/ethiopian-rose-fields-give-india-billionaires-tips-on-african-buying-spree.html
23. This time for Africa: Africa calling Indian farmers. Trust of India. 11 August 2010. http://farmlandgrab.org/14776
24. Sharma, Viney, 'Indian farmers look to reap rich gains in Madagascar', *Economic Times*, 5 January 2011, http://article.wn.com/view/2011/01/14/Indian_farmers_look_to_reap_rich_gains_in_Madagascar
25. Nelson, Dean. India joins 'neocolonial' rush for Africa's land and labour. 28 Jun 2009. http://www.telegraph.co.uk/news/worldnews/asia/india/5673437/India-joins-neocolon.
26. Singh, Gurjit. India's role in capacity building in Africa with a special focus on the agricultural sector. Speech delivered at the International Conference 'South-South Cooperation: India, Africa and Food Security: Between the Summits'. Mumbai. 10-11 January 2011.
27. Vidal, John. 'Land-grabbing' in Africa. April 29, 2010. Anyuak Media. http://www.anyuakmedia.com/Ethionews_temp_10_4_29.html
28. Meles Zenawi, from: 'The Reporter'-Addis Ababa, 3 May 2000 http://www.hartford-hwp.com/archives/33/053.html
29. Tehshome, Genet. Indian investments in agriculture sector in Ethiopia. International Conference 'South-South Cooperation: India, Africa and Food Security: Between the Summits'. Mumbai. 10-11 January 2011.
30. Cherian, John. Grabbing Africa. The global rush to acquire agricultural land in bountiful Africa evokes concern and protests. Frontline. Volume 27. Issue 09. 24 April - 07 May 2010. http://www.frontlineonnet.com/fl2709/stories/20100507270906100.htm
31. Bagchi, S., 'Punjab suicides cast shadow on polls', BBC News, 12 April 2009, http://news.bbc.co.uk/2/hi/south_asia/7992327.stm
32. Vidal, John. 'Land-grabbing' in Africa. April 29, 2010. Anyuak Media. http://www.anyuakmedia.com/Ethionews_temp_10_4_29.html

33. Butler, Ed. Land grab fear for Ethiopia rural communities. BBC World Service, Ethiopia. 16 December 2010. http://www.bbc.co.uk/news/business-11991926

34. Tolossa, Fikre. Land Grab in Africa: The case of Ethiopia. 3 March, 2011. http://addisvoice.com/2011/03/land-grab-in-africa-the-case-of-ethiopia/

35. Vidal, John. 'Land-grabbing' in Africa. April 29, 2010. Anyuak Media. http://www.anyuakmedia.com/Ethionews_temp_10_4_29.html

36. Goswami, Rahul. African landrush. Infochange and Features. April 2010. http://farmlandgrab.org/post/ptint/11985

37. Ray, Shantanu Guha and Vilasini, Roy. Ethiopians say Indians grabbing land, Indian farmers claim it is official. Tehelka. 17 September, 2010. http://www.tehelka.com/story_main46.asp? filename= Bu250910 Ethiopians.asp

38. International Conference 'South-South Cooperation: India, Africa and Food Security: Between the Summits'. Mumbai. 10-11 January 2011.

39. Goswami, Rahul. African landrush. Infochange and Features. April 2010. http://farmlandgrab.org/post/ptint/11985

40. Karuturi presentation at the International Seminar 'India-Africa Enduring Partnership: Emerging Areas of Cooperation'. 4 March, 2011. Mumbai, India.

41. Ethiopia: President Girma Speaks out Against Land Grab in Gambella. 31 January 2011. http://gadaa.com/oduu/7931/2011/01/31/ethiopia-president-girma-speaks-out-against-land-grab-in-gambella/

42. Ray, Shantanu Guha and Vilasini, Roy. Ethiopians say Indians grabbing land, Indian farmers claim it is official. Tehelka. 17 September, 2010. http://www.tehelka.com/story_main46.asp? filename=Bu250910 Ethiopians.asp

43. Ray, Shantanu Guha and Vilasini, Roy. Ethiopians say Indians grabbing land, Indian farmers claim it is official. Tehelka. 17 September, 2010. http://www.tehelka.com/story_main46.asp? filename=Bu250910 Ethiopians.asp

44. Sahai, Suman. The new colonisers. Deccan Chronicle November 27th, 2010. http://www.deccanchronicle.com/op-ed/new-colonisers-857

45. Nelson, Dean. India joins 'neocolonial' rush for Africa's land and labour. 28 Jun 2009. http://www.telegraph.co.uk/news/worldnews/asia/india/5673437/India-joins-neocolon..

46. An Open Letter to Gennet Zewide, Ethiopian Ambassador to India. Solidarity Movement for a New Ethiopia.http://www.anyuakmedia.com/Obang_SMNE_10_9_30.html

47. Indian Ocean Newsletter N° 1294 | 10/09/2010. http://farmlandgrab.vps444.speedyrails.ca/post/view/16180

48. Vidal, John. How food and water are driving a 21st-century African land grab. 7 March 2010. The Observer. http://www.guardian.co.uk/environment/2010/mar/07/food-water-africa-land-grab

49. Friis, Cecilie and Reenberg, Anette. Land Grab in Africa: Emerging land system drivers in a teleconnected world. GLP Report No. 1. http://www.globallandproject.org/Documents/GLP_report_01.pdf

50. Vidal, John. How food and water are driving a 21st-century African land grab. 7 March 2010. The Observer. http://www.guardian.co.uk/environment/2010/mar/07/food-water-africa-land-grab

51. Cherian, John. Grabbing Africa. The global rush to acquire agricultural land in bountiful Africa evokes concern and protests. Frontline. Volume 27. Issue 09. 24 April - 07 May 2010. http://www.frontlineonnet.com/fl2709/stories/20100507270906100.htm; Vadala, Alexander. International Land Acquisitions and Food Security: India in Ethiopia. International Conference 'South-South Cooperation: India, Africa and Food Security: Between the Summits'. Mumbai. 10-11 January 2011.

52. Dyer, Gwynne. The Zimbabwe Independent. 26 May 2009. African Land Grab. YaleGlobal Online. http://yaleglobal.yale.edu/content/african-land

53. Cotula L., Vermeulen S., Leonard R, Keeley J. Land grab or development opportunity? Agricultural investment and international land deals in Africa. IIED/FAO/IFAD, London/Rome. 2009. http://reliefweb.int/sites/reliefweb.int/files/resources/9CF7A03B203294A0492575C2000CC265-Full_Report.pdf

54. UN Fails To Back 'Land Grabs' Code Of Conduct. 15 October 2010. http://www.radiovop.com/world-breaking-news/4687-un-fails-to-back-land-grabs-code-of-conduct.html

55. Committee on World Food Security. Thirty-sixth Session. Rome, 11-14 and 16 October 2010. Policy Roundtable 'Land Tenure and International Investment in Agriculture http://www.fao.org/docrep/meeting/019/k8929e.pdf

56. Forum on Food Security and Nutrition: Land Tenure. HLPE Consultation on Land Tenure and International Investments in Agriculture. Discussion No. 66. http://km.fao.org/fsn/discussions/land-tenure/en/

57. Vines. Alex. India's Africa Engagement: Prospects for the 2011. Chatam House. Programme Paper: AFP 2010/01. December 2010. http://www.chathamhouse.org.uk/files/18076_1210vines.pdf

15

Agro-Industry as an Emerging Sector: Mutual Interests of India and Africa

Suresh Kumar

Introduction

Agriculture accounts for more than 25 per cent of the GDP in most African countries and employs more than 70 per cent of the workforce.[1] Africa has approximately 783 million hectares of arable land (27 per cent of the world total), which is adequate to effectively feed its population. The output is highly concentrated in Egypt and Nigeria, accounting for approximately one-third of total agricultural output of the continent; they are in the top ten countries of Africa, producing nearly 75 per cent. Africa is the only region in the world where agricultural productivity has not grown noticeably. In fact, the Green Revolution, which enhanced agricultural growth in many Asian countries, is yet to take place in Africa.[2] The African agro-industry as a sector has substantial potential to improve the economies and hence the livelihood of its large populace. Increased agricultural output and agro-industry income also has a multiplier effect because of its links with markets for the output of the manufacturing and services sector. Agriculture and agro-industry sector has been at the forefront of the recent transition in India-Africa relations. Various African nations perceive the success of the Green Revolution in India as a role model. Moreover, India remains focused on capacity building, human resource development, micro-, small- and medium-enterprises and the transfer of technology and skills as a key ingredient of its policy.

The agro-industry in Africa needs farm mechanisation that will facilitate increase in productivity. The production boost in agriculture is likely to initiate the agro-industry in Africa. With surplus production of food in Africa, the agro-industry will get the input of raw materials to produce different food products and cater to the needs of urban as well as rural areas.

Approximately eighty Indian companies have collectively invested US$2.3 bn in Ethiopia, Kenya, Madagascar, Senegal and Mozambique.[3] A leading integrated tea company based in India acquired Uganda-based Rwenzori Tea Investments for US$25 mn in December 2009. In recent times, Indian companies have also started investing in agro value-added products. An Indian business house leased a 50-acre model dairy farm in Uganda in 2006.[4] Another Indian company, specialising in textiles, recently opened a spinning mill in Burkina Faso.[5] Such investments are expected not only to generate local employment but also create opportunities for local skill development. Agro-industry sector of India-Africa traction is welcome by both countries. 'Today, national development issues incorporate agriculture sector as prerequisite to country's progress and prosperity in Africa. Indo-Africa is pursuing mutual cooperation under the theme of "Today's Investment-Tomorrow's Prosperity". The development and mutual partnership covers self-reliance schemes avoiding huge debt as a result of this brotherhood.'

India and Africa – Opportunities in Agro-Industry

The regional organisations of Africa (SADC, EAC, COMESA, ECOWAS and AU) and India should participate in a regional market and get to enjoy the economies of scale and enhance their own global competitiveness. Regional market integration leading to regional market access is particularly relevant in the context of trade and investment in the agro-industry sector and physical infrastructure development. Indian economic engagement invites private-sector investors, which sets an additional strength working with African partners.

Africa's agro-industry needs to initiate an environment for intra-regional trade in different products and services as well as imports from outside the region with regional agreement. Reduced import duties, uniform standards for agro-industry products, and creation of a common market and services can bring about price reductions and improved services benefitting the consumers across the region. India has played a key role in Africa's physical infrastructure development ranging from construction, watershed management, telecommunication, energy development, road and railway construction. But, for the benefits of the engagements to reach a larger number of countries, and also for Indian engagement to upscale, there is a need for a higher level of regional coordination in Africa. It has been said that projects like laying fibre-optic cables, building roads and power transmission lines could then be taken up across countries, and the economies of scale would benefit the entire region.

India can play a catalytic role in furthering the regional economic integrative forces. Government of India's Line of Credit (LOC) has provided significant benefits to this region. The LOCs have helped the African government in its endeavour to facilitate easy financing to agro-industry, transfer of technology, value addition of primary commodities, employment generation, greater international trade and bilateral cooperation with India. The LOCs also helped India to increase its exports to this region. The objective will be not just a quantitative increase in trade and investment, but aim at a qualitative enhancement (through transfer of technology) of Africa's economic competitiveness and technological capabilities. It is one of the cutting-edge differences between India's relationship as an emergent power with Africa as compared to traditional partners.

Development of Agro-Industry

The agriculture system in Africa is based on the traditional methods of farming that feeds only one square meal to the family. The production boost in agriculture needs farm mechanisation, which will facilitate increase in productivity. This in turn is likely to initiate the agro-industry in Africa. Once there is surplus production of food in Africa, the agro-industry will get the input of raw materials to produce different food products and cater to the needs of urban as well as rural areas. The increased agro-industrial production will be an additional source of income for the agriculturalist in Africa.

This initiative of production improvement needs tractors and machinery for the use of more arable land. Indian investors provide agriculture tools and implements, such as seed-cum-fertilizer drill that facilitates seed saving, saving in fertilizer, enhancement in cropping intensity and increase in gross income and returns to farmer in Africa. India manufactures agricultural tractors, mould board plough, disc plough, sub-soiler as primary tillage; spring-loaded tillers, harrows, levellers, bund former, scraper, rotary tiller as secondary tillage; and also back hoe with tractor, laser grader, graders, scrapers with tractors as earth-moving equipments. Escorts, Sonalika, Eicher, HMT, International Tractors, Mahendra & Mahendra, are some of the largest producers of agricultural equipments in India. The land in Africa is naturally highly fertile so agricultural mechanisation will greatly enhance the production.

There are different agro-industries that may be promoted in Africa like, fish and fish-farming industry, organic farming, floriculture, sericulture, food and beverages sector, etc.

1. Agro-Industry of Fish and Fish Farming

India and Africa need an effective approach to eradicate poverty and subsistence agriculture, ensure food security and improve people's livelihood, develop fisheries and other animal resources and thereby become self-reliant. Both may work for sustainable development of fisheries and animal resources with necessary support of scientific research for conservation of land and environment. Fish cultivation on ground as an alternate source of food may increase many folds depending upon its natural feeding (such as Carp Larvae). One reinvigorates pond- and river-fish cultivation using these larvae, which will add nutrient in food production and avoid the use of chemical and other chemical food nutrients on the one hand and safeguard environment biodiversity on the other hand.

India plays vital role in international as well as regional cooperation developing fisheries and other sea resources as an alternate source of food and maintains sea-diversity as part of environment conservation. For example, India as a regional partner is assisting Myanmar in the exercise of their delineation of their continental shelf. India and Africa jointly need to work for sustainable development of fisheries and animal resources with necessary support of scientific research for conservation of land and environment.

2. Agro-Industry of Organic Farming

Africa has ample land that needs to be developed for agriculture. The private sector of India[6] has started investing in Africa's agriculture sector and developing organic farming as part of agro-industry. The organic farming deals with the different sub-sectors such as:

(a) Agro-Industry of Fruits and Vegetables. The investment opportunities (as per the physical condition of the region) in this sector are:

- There is huge investment opportunity on cracking, grinding, roasting and packaging nuts, like cashews and others.
- There is also considerable potential for processing of cocoa and producing chocolate and confectionery products for regional market, as well as exports.
- Use of Indian technology to start production of edible and other oils by using corn seed, rapeseed, cottonseed, sunflower, sesame, coconut, etc. West Africa is known for production of palm oil and use of scientific technology will help to lower its cost of production.
- There is already a large production of oil seeds in Eastern Africa and yet there is a potential to increase it further. Investors have the opportunity to set up edible-oil industries to cater to local, as well as regional, needs.
- There is potential to increase production of various fruits, such as mangoes, pineapples, oranges, passion fruits, bananas, avocados, to cater to the supply at regional level as well as export market. It opens the opportunity for processing of fruits at local level and hence an investment opportunity for production of juices, jelly, jams, etc.
- Production and export of dehydrated fruits.
- Investment in cold storage facilities at collection points.
- Organic farming of fruits and vegetables.
- Packaging of vegetables and fruits for exports.
- Opportunity for local manufacturing of attractive packaging for fruits and vegetable.
- Irrigation schemes for commercial farms to ensure harvests throughout the year.

(b) Agro-Industry of Floriculture. This agro-industry is a big source of export income in Africa. Indian investors are investing in

this sector and are getting good responses from the local people in Africa. It persuades the Indian investors to produce the cereals using scientific technology for local consumption along with floriculture. The opportunities exist in this sector such as:

- North-Eastern Africa (Kenya, Ethiopia, Uganda and Tanzania) has seen phenomenal growth in the production and export of cut flowers. The export market focuses on European Union countries, such as Germany, Netherlands, United Kingdom, Sweden, Italy, Switzerland and France.
- Investment in pre-cooling and cold storage will facilitate exporters in maintaining high standards of their produce for exports, as is required by the market.
- Packaging of flowers for exports.

(c) Agro-Industry of Sericulture. There is a huge export market too for silk cloth and garments. Sericulture and silk production have an enormous potential in Africa provided it is made available to rural people, especially women, and its marketing is organised independently. It can serve as an excellent mode for employment generation and augmentation of income. Indian investors can provide latest technological inputs to primary producers by evolving and establishing new systems of organising production and marketing. Silkworms feed on mulberry leaves, hence the rearing of silkworms involves cultivation of mulberry trees, which provide a regular supply of leaves. Worms are introduced through DFLs (Disease Free Laying eggs) procured from a quality centre called grainage.

African farmers can promote mulberry cultivation alongside their agriculture field. Even small farmers with less than four acres of land can work in clusters of three to four hundred to initiate production of sericulture. Investment in mechanisation in silkworm-rearing operations is needed to cut down production costs. Small machines for such operations, such as leaf chopping, harvesting and def-loosing of cocoons, are necessary. Knowledge of silkworm-rearing technology could help producers in Africa. Indian investors can promote training to the local people in this field. Investment opportunities that would also trigger increased production are mainly in:

- Cocoon post-harvesting and processing equipment.
- Multi-end silk-reeling machine.
- Spindle-spinning machine.

- Cocoon-boiling machine.
- Warping machine.
- Power- and hand-looms.
- Cocoon dryers.
- Cocoon and raw-silk testing equipment.
- The product development will initiate development of beauty products, powder and natural dyes technology, and processing and packaging of mulberry green tea.

(*d*) *Agro-Industry of Food and Beverage Sector.* Because of subsistence farming in Africa, the rural population is migrating to urban centres in search of employment and survival. The food and beverage sector provides opportunities in:

- Value addition to a variety of agricultural produce locally available.
- Planting and processing of coffee, production in instant coffee particularly in Uganda, Kenya and Ethiopia.
- Breweries and distilleries of alcoholic beverages.
- Soft drink and packed fruit drinks manufacture.
- Commercial farming and processing of sugar, corn flakes, gram flakes, etc.
- Establishment of fast food restaurants of international chains/ brands.
- Different pickles produced for European, American and Middle East market.
- Local and regional cold distribution chain to minimise the deterioration of products.

(*e*) *Agriculture Engineering.* As mentioned earlier, India produces a variety of agricultural equipment, such as tractors, mould board ploughs, disc ploughs, sub-soilers, spring loaded tillers, harrows, levellers, bund formers, scrapers, rotary tillers, back hoe with tractor, laser graders, scrapers with tractors as earth moving equipments. Escorts, Sonalika, Eicher, HMT, International Tractors, Mahendra & Mahendra are some of the large producers of such tools in India. India also produces sowing machinery, such as post hole digger, paddy planter, seed drill for cotton seeds, seed-cum-fertilizer drill, potato planter and multi-row vegetables planters, irrigation systems (sprinkler and drip), irrigation pumps (centrifugal pumps), stationary diesel-engine-driven centrifugal pumps, engine set, electric pumps and submersible pumps, sowing and harvesting machinery (maize combine, sugarcane combine, mowers, paddy combine, reaper, wheat combine, fruits harvester, onion harvester, potato digger, cotton picker) and post-harvest machinery (bailer, tipping trailer, sugar-cane grabber, trailer, thresher and maize sheller.[7] This agricultural mechanisation will enhance the production as the land in Africa is naturally highly fertile. There are different agro-industries that may be promoted in Africa, which will give value addition for their products such as:

- Mechanisation of rice production by use of rotivators, transplanters and cultivation equipment.
- Farmer associations and private entrepreneurs will be encouraged to install pass and mobile rice mills.
- Investment opportunities exist in seed production, manufacture of sprayers and pesticides, veterinary services, construction of cold storage facilities and refrigerated transport for horticultural and other perishable products.
- Industrial units for manufacturing tractors.
- Industrial units for manufacturing pump-sets for irrigation.
- Industrial units for the manufacturing of agro-food products.
- Small Industrial units for agro-chemicals (fertilizers and pesticides).
- Industrial units for manufacture of textile (cotton fabrics, garment manufacturing, yarn).

To promote India–Africa relations, India has launched special scholarships for African students in the field of agriculture to provide support to the Nyerere Programme of the AU. Under this programme, twenty-five seats are offered to students for pursuing a doctoral programme, the Government of India provides each student with a stipend of INR15,000 per month; it also offers fifty students the opportunity to pursue Masters' degree programmes in India, with a stipend of INR12,000 per month.[8]

Endnotes

1. CII India-Africa Project Partnership, 2005. Background paper. Delhi.
2. 'Challenges to Agricultural Development in Africa', 2011, UN Economic Commission for Africa. www.uneca.org/era2009/chap4.pdf: accessed 28 January 2011.

3. 'Indian farming companies buying in Africa', *The Economic Times*. http://economictimes.indiatimes.com/Corporate-Trends/Indian-farmingcompanies- buying-land-in-Africa/articleshow/4713183.cms, accessed on 28 January 2011.
4. RJ Corp charts mega plans to venture into virgin Africa. *The Economic Times*, http://economictimes.indiatimes.com/news/news-by-industry/cons-products/food/rj-corp-charts-mega-plans-to-venture-into-virgin-africa/articleshow/5414639.cms, accessed 28 January 2011.
5. Indian business groups are investing heavily in Africa. Cote d'Ivoire – Diaspora website, www.ivoirediaspo.net/?s=Indian+ business+ groups+ are+investing+heavily+in+Africa&x=5&y=11, accessed 27 January 2011.
6. Karuturi and other companies.
7. Improving Farm Productivity through Agro Machinery (2008), Escorts Limited, Faridabad.
8. Exim Bank, 2011, India-Africa Partnership Potential, Ernst & Young. Delhi.

References

1. African Oil, http://www.iimcal.ac.in/research/download/OFDI_Partha-pal.pdf: accessed on 9 March 2011.
2. 'African nations offering land for free to Indian farmers', *The Economic Times*. http://economictimes.indiatimes.com/news/economy/agriculture/African-nations-offering-land-for-free-to-Indian-farmers/articleshow/6293149.cms, accessed 28 January 2011.
3. Annual Report (2007-08), Ministry of Earth Sciences, Government of India.
4. Botswana Today, 2010, Embassy of Botswana, Delhi.
5. CII Conclave, April 2009, Hotel Taj, New Delhi.
6. CII: www.ciionline.org: accessed 20 June, 2008.
7. CII India-Africa Project Partnership, 2005. Background paper. Delhi.
8. *Development or Exploitation? Foreign Investment in Ethiopia's Agriculture*, Ethiopian Embassy Publication, 14 March 2011, Delhi.
9. Food Processing Plant Launched, *All Africa*, 26 August 2009 via Dow Jones Factiva. © 2009 All Africa.
10. *Hindu, The,* 15 October 2005, Delhi.
11. Institute of Export Promotion, Maputo, Mozambique, 2011.
12. IPEM, 2011, 2nd Mozambique International Packaging and Packaging Equipment Trade Fair, Setembro.

13. Joining Hands, MEIPL.
14. Kenya in the Front Line, 2010, Kenya Tourist Board.
15. Kenya, 2011, A Hub for Investment, Ministry of State for Planning, National Development and Vision, 2030, Nairobi.
16. Mauritius, 2011, Your Investment and Business Hub, Board of Investment.
17. Mohan Breaking Boundaries, 2005.
18. Oil and Gas, 2005, IBEF, (CII).
19. 'Programme on Food Processing, Storage, Marketing Out', *All Africa*, 16 March 2009, via Dow Jones Factiva, © 2009 *All Africa*, Raising Agricultural Productivity in Africa. 2011. Africa Progress Panel. www.africa progresspanel.org/files/3812/8352/7667/Raising%20 agricultural%20 productivity%20in%20Africa—FORWEB.pdf: accessed 28 January 2011.
20. Resolution, 2006. Resolution of the Abuja Food Security Summit (FS/Res (1)). Summit on Food Security in Africa. December 4-7, 2006, Abuja, Nigeria. http://www.africanunion.org/root/au/ conferences/past/2006December/REA/summit/doc/Abuja Res Final tracked.doc
21. Sonalika Profile, 2011, Faridabad, Delhi.
22. *Sudan Tribune*, 6 November 2007, Khartoum.
23. *Times of India*, 7 July 2006, Delhi.
24. Your Partner in Progress, Overseas Infrastructure Alliance, March 2008.
25. Zimbabwe Investment Authority, Ministry of Power and Energy Development, Ministry of Finance - The Medium Term Plan 2010-2015 Document, Banks and Banking Survey 2009 - Zimbabwe Independent Newspaper, CZI July 2008 Manufacturing Sector Survey, Financial Gazette (7 January).

Index

B

E

J

R